Women, Crime and Prison Life

WOMEN, CRIME AND PRISON LIFE

Sudhir Rai

CENTRUM PRESS
NEW DELHI-110002 (INDIA)

CENTRUM PRESS
H.O.: 4360/4, Ansari Road, Daryaganj,
New Delhi-110002 (India)
Tel: 23278000, 23261597, 23255577, 23286875
B.O.: No. 1015, Ist Main Road, BSK IIIrd Stage,
IIIrd Phase, IIIrd Block, Bangalore-560085 (INDIA)
Tel: 080-41723429
Email: centrumpress@gmail.com
Visit us at: www.centrumpress.com

Women, Crime and Prison Life

First Edition, 2011
ISBN 978-93-80921-64-8

PRINTED IN INDIA

Printed at Tarun Offset Printers, Delhi-110053

Contents

	Preface	*vii*
1.	Status of Women in India	1
2.	Crime and Deviance	15
3.	Women Trafficking for Sexual Exploitation	74
4.	Stranger Danger: Explaining Women's Fear of Crime	133
5.	Women, Crime and Informal Economy	150
6.	Violence against Girl Child in India	162
7.	Crime against Women in India	208
8.	Crime against Old Women	224
9.	Prison Visiting System in India	229
10.	Women Prisoners	245
	Bibliography	293
	Index	295

Preface

The women in India have been subject to many great changes over the past few millennia. From equal status with men in ancient times through the low points of the medieval period, to the promotion of equal rights by many reformers, the history of women in India has been eventful. In modern India, women have adorned high offices in India including that of the President, Prime minister, Speaker of the Lok Sabha, Leader of Opposition, etc. The current President of India is a woman.

The book makes a comprehensive study of the lives of women in prisons in India and the offences committed by them. For the purpose, it examines their socio-economic background and highlights the importance of this as a factor determining perpetration of crime.

It examines the characteristics of women prisoners, the types of crime committed by them, their life as inmates in prisons, relations of the inmates with one another and others, and the problems faced by them during incarceration. Based on profiles of jail inmates in the Indian states of Punjab, Haryana and Chandigarh, it scrutinizes that there is a big gap between the legal system and social reality especially where inequalities in treatment of women prisoners and other facets are concerned.

Author

1

Status of Women in India

The status of women in India has been subject to many great changes over the past few millennia. From equal status with men in ancient times through the low points of the medieval period, to the promotion of equal rights by many reformers, the history of women in India has been eventful. In modern India, women have adorned high offices in India including that of the President, Prime minister, Speaker of the Lok Sabha, Leader of Opposition, etc. The current President of India is a woman.

HISTORY OF WOMEN

There are very few texts specifically dealing with the role of women; an important exception is the strIdharmapaddhati of Tryambakayajvan, an official at Thanjavur around c.1730. The text compiles strictures on womanly behaviour dating back to the Apastamba sutra (c. 4th c. BCE).where the term "desire to hear" covers a range of meanings from the devotee's homage to god, or the obsequious service of a slave.

ANCIENT INDIA

Scholars believe that in ancient India, the women enjoyed equal status with men in all fields of life. However, some others hold contrasting views. Works by ancient Indian grammarians such as Patanjali and Katyayana suggest that women were educated in the early Vedic period Rigvedic verses suggest that the women married at a mature age and were probably free to select their husband. Scriptures such as Rig Veda and Upanishads mention several women sages and seers, notably

Gargi and Maitreyi. Some kingdoms in the ancient India had traditions such as "bride of the city". Women competed to win the coveted title of the nagarvadhu. Amrapali is the most famous example of a nagarvadhu. Women enjoyed equal status and rights during the early Vedic period. However, later (approximately 500 B.C.), the status of women began to decline with the Smritis and with the Islamic invasion of Babur and the Mughal empire and later Christianity curtailing women's freedom and rights.

Although reformatory movements such as Jainism allowed women to be admitted to the religious order, by and large, the women in India faced confinement and restrictions. The practice of child marriages is believed to have started from around sixth century.

MEDIEVAL PERIOD

The Indian woman's position in the society further deteriorated during the medieval period when Sati among some communities, child marriages and a ban on widow remarriages became part of social life among some communities in India. The Muslim conquest in the Indian subcontinent brought the purdah practice in the Indian society. Among the Rajputs of Rajasthan, the Jauhar was practised. In some parts of India, the Devadasis or the temple women were sexually exploited.

Polygamy was widely practised especially among Hindu Kshatriya rulers. In many Muslim families, women were restricted to Zenana areas. In spite of these conditions, some women excelled in the fields of politics, literature, education and religion. Razia Sultana became the only woman monarch to have ever ruled Delhi. The Gond queen Durgavati ruled for fifteen years, before she lost her life in a battle with Mughal emperor Akbar's general Asaf Khan in 1564. Chand Bibi defended Ahmednagar against the mighty Mughal forces of Akbar in 1590s. Jehangir's wife Nur Jehan effectively wielded imperial power and was recognized as the real force behind the Mughal throne. The Mughal princesses Jahanara and Zebunnissa were well-known poets, and also influenced the ruling administration Shivaji's mother, Jijabai was deputed as queen regent, because of her ability as a warrior and an administrator. In South India, many women administered villages, towns, divisions and heralded social and religious institutions.

The Bhakti movements tried to restore women's status and questioned some of the forms of oppression. Mirabai, a female saint-poet, was one of the most important Bhakti movement figures. Some other female saint-poets from this period include Akka Mahadevi, Rami Janabai and Lal Ded. Bhakti sects within Hinduism such as the Mahanubhav, Varkari and many others were principle movements within the Hindu fold to openly advocate social justice and equality between men and women.

Shortly after the Bhakti movement, Guru Nanak, the first Guru of Sikhs also preached the message of equality between men and women. He advocated that women be allowed to lead religious assemblies; to perform and lead congregational hymn singing called Kirtan or Bhajan; become members of religious management committees; to lead armies on the battlefield; have equality in marriage, and equality in Amrit (Baptism). Other Sikh Gurus also preached against the discrimination against women.

HISTORICAL PRACTICES

Traditions among some communities such as sati, jauhar, and devadasi have been banned and are largely defunct in modern India. However, some cases of these practices are still found in remote parts of India. The purdah is still practised by Indian women among some communities, and child marriage remains prevalent despite it being an illegal practice, especially under current Indian laws.

Sati

Sati is an old, largely defunct custom, among some communities in which the widow was immolated alive on her husband's funeral pyre. Although the act was supposed to be a voluntary on the widow's part, it is believed to have been sometimes forced on the widow. It was abolished by the British in 1829. There have been around forty reported cases of sati since independence. In 1987, the Roop Kanwar case of Rajasthan led to The Commission of Sati (Prevention) Act.

Jauhar

Jauhar refers to the practice of the voluntary immolation of all the wives and daughters of defeated warriors, in order to avoid capture and consequent molestation by the enemy. The practice was followed by the wives of defeated Rajput rulers, who are known to place a high premium on honour.

Purdah

Purdah is the practice among some communities of requiring women to cover their bodies so as to cover their skin and conceal their form. It imposes restrictions on the mobility of women, it curtails their right to interact freely and it is a symbol of the subordination of women. It does not reflect the religious teachings of either Hinduism or Islam, contrary to common belief, although misconception has occurred due to the ignorance and prejudices of religious leaders of both faiths.

Devadasis

Devadasi is a religious practice in some parts of southern India, in which women are "married" to a deity or temple. The ritual was well established by the 10th century A.D. In the later period, the illegitimate sexual exploitation of the devadasi's became a norm in some parts of India.

Women in British Rule

European scholars observed in the 19th century that Hindu women are "naturally chaste" and "more virtuous" than other women. During the British Raj, many reformers such as Ram Mohan Roy, Ishwar Chandra Vidyasagar, Jyotirao Phule etc. fought for the upliftment of women. Peary Charan Sarkar, a former student of Hindu College, Calutta and a member of "Young Bengal" set up the first free school for girls in India in 1847 in Barasat, a suburb of Calcutta (later the school was named Kalikrishna Girls' High School). While this list might suggest that there was no positive British contribution during the Raj era, that is not entirely so, since missionaries' wives like Martha Mault née Mead and her daughter Eliza Caldwell née Mault are rightly remembered for pioneering the education and training of girls in south India - a practise that initially met with local resistance, as it flew in the face of tradition. Raja Rammohan Roy's efforts led to the abolition of the Sati practice under Governor-General William Cavendish-Bentinck in 1829. Ishwar Chandra Vidyasagar's crusade for the improvement in condition of widows led to the Widow Remarriage Act of 1856. Many women reformers such as Pandita Ramabai also helped the cause of women upliftment. Kittur Chennamma, the queen of the princely state Kittur in Karnataka, led an armed rebellion against the British in response to the Doctrine of lapse. Abbakka Rani the queen of coastal Karnataka led the defence against invading European armies notably the Portuguese in 16th century. Rani Lakshmi Bai, the Queen of Jhansi, led the Indian Rebellion of 1857 against the British.

She is now widely considered as a nationalist hero. Begum Hazrat Mahal, the co-ruler of Awadh, was another ruler who led the revolt of 1857. She refused the deals with the British and later retreated to Nepal. The Begums of Bhopal were also few of the notable female rulers during this period. They did not observe purdah and were trained in martial arts. Chandramukhi Basu, Kadambini Ganguly and Anandi Gopal Joshi were few of the earliest Indian women to obtain educational degrees.

In 1917, the first women's delegation met the Secretary of State to demand women's political rights, supported by the Indian National Congress. The All India Women's Education Conference was held in Pune in 1927. In 1929, the Child Marriage Restraint Act was passed, stipulating fourteen as the minimum age of marriage for a girl through the efforts of Mahomed Ali Jinnah. Though Mahatma Gandhi himself married at the age of thirteen, he later urged people to boycott child marriages and called upon the young men to marry the child widows. Women played an important part in India's independence struggle. Some of the famous freedom fighters include Bhikaji Cama, Dr. Annie Besant, Pritilata Waddedar, Vijayalakshmi Pandit, Rajkumari Amrit Kaur, Aruna Asaf Ali, Sucheta Kriplani and Kasturba Gandhi. Other notable names include Muthulakshmi Reddy, Durgabai Deshmukh etc. The Rani of Jhansi Regiment of Subhash Chandra Bose's Indian National Army consisted entirely of women including Captain Lakshmi Sahgal. Sarojini Naidu, a poet and a freedom fighter, was the first Indian woman to become the President of the Indian National Congress and the first woman to become the governor of a state in India.

WOMEN IN INDEPENDENT INDIA

Women in India now participate in all activities such as education,sports, politics, media, art and culture, service sectors, science and technology, etc. Indira Gandhi, who served as Prime Minister of India for an aggregate period of fifteen years is the world's longest serving woman Prime Minister. The Constitution of India guarantees to all Indian women equality (Article 14), no discrimination by the State (Article 15(1)), equality of opportunity (Article 16), equal pay for equal work (Article 39(d)). In addition, it allows special provisions to be made by the State in favour of women and children (Article 15(3)), renounces practices derogatory to the dignity of women (Article 51(A) (e)), and also allows for provisions to be made by the State for securing just and humane conditions of work and for maternity relief. (Article 42).

The feminist activism in India picked up momentum during later 1970s. One of the first national level issues that brought the women's groups together was the Mathura rape case. The acquittal of policemen accused of raping a young girl Mathura in a police station, led to a wide-scale protests in 1979–1980. The protests were widely covered in the national media, and forced the Government to amend the Evidence Act, the Criminal Procedure Code and the Indian Penal Code and introduce the category of custodial rape. Female activists united over issues such as female infanticide, gender bias, women health, and female literacy. Since alcoholism is often associated with violence against women in India, many women groups launched anti-liquor campaigns in Andhra Pradesh, Himachal Pradesh, Haryana, Orissa, Madhya Pradesh and other states. Many Indian Muslim women have questioned the fundamental leaders' interpretation of women's rights under the Shariat law and have criticized the triple talaq system.

In 1990s, grants from foreign donor agencies enabled the formation of new women-oriented NGOs. Self-help groups and NGOs such as Self Employed Women's Association (SEWA) have played a major role in women's rights in India. Many women have emerged as leaders of local movements. For example, Medha Patkar of the Narmada Bachao Andolan. The Government of India declared 2001 as the Year of Women's Empowerment (Swashakti). The National Policy For The Empowerment Of Women came was passed in 2001. In 2006, the case of a Muslim rape victim called Imrana was highlighted in the media. Imrana was raped by her father-in-law. The pronouncement of some Muslim clerics that Imrana should marry her father-in-law led to widespread protests and finally Imrana's father-in-law was given a prison term of 10 years, The verdict was welcomed by many women's groups and the All India Muslim Personal Law Board. In 2010 March 9, one day after International Women's day, Rajyasabha passed Women's Reservation Bill, ensuring 33% reservation to women in Parliament and state legislative bodies.

WOMEN CULTURE

Sari (a single piece of a long cloth wound around the body) and salwar kameez are worn by women all over India. Bindi is part of the women's make-up. Unlike common belief, the bindi on the forehead does not signify marital status, however the Sindoor does. Rangoli (or Kolam) is a traditional art very popular among Indian women.

EDUCATION AND ECONOMIC DEVELOPMENT

In 1992-93, only 9.2% of the households in India were female-headed. However, approximately 35% of the households below the poverty line were found to be female-headed.

EDUCATION

Though it is gradually rising, the female literacy rate in India is lower than the male literacy rate. Compared to boys, far fewer girls are enrolled in the schools, and many of them drop out. The National Sample Survey Data of 1997, only the states of Kerala and Mizoram have approached universal female literacy rates.

The majority of the scholars, the major factor behind the improved social and economic status of women in Kerala is literacy. Under Non-Formal Education programme (NFE), about 40% of the centres in states and 10% of the centres in UTs are exclusively reserved for females. As of 2000, about 0.3 million NFE centres were catering to about 7.42 million children, out of which about 0.12 million were exclusively for girls. In urban India, girls are nearly at par with the boys in terms of education.

However, in rural India girls continue to be less educated than the boys. In 1998 report by U.S. Department of Commerce, the chief barrier to female education in India are inadequate school facilities (such as sanitary facilities), shortage of female teachers and gender bias in curriculum (majority of the female characters being depicted as weak and helpless).

WORKFORCE PARTICIPATION

Contrary to the common perception, a large per cent of women in India work. The National data collection agencies accept the fact that there is a serious under-estimation of women's contribution as workers. However, there are far fewer women in the paid workforce than there are men. In urban India Women have impressive number in the workforce. As an example at software industry 30% of the workforce is female. They are at par with their male counter parts in terms of wages, position at the work place. In rural India, agriculture and allied industrial sectors employ as much as 89.5% of the total female labour. In overall farm production, women's average contribution is estimated at 55% to 66% of the total labour. In 1991 World Bank report, women accounted for 94% of total employment in dairy production in India. Women constitute 51% of the total employed in forest-based small-scale enterprises.

One of the most famous female business success stories is the Shri Mahila Griha Udyog Lijjat Papad. In 2006, Kiran Mazumdar-Shaw, who started Biocon - one of India's first biotech companies, was rated India's richest woman. Lalita Gupte and Kalpana Morparia (both were the only businesswomen in India who made the list of the Forbes World's Most Powerful Women), run India's second-largest bank, ICICI Bank.

LAND AND PROPERTY RIGHTS

In most Indian families , women do not own any property in their own names, and do not get a share of parental property. Due to weak enforcement of laws protecting them, women continue to have little access to land and property. In fact, some of the laws discriminate against women, when it comes to land and property rights. The Hindu personal laws of mid-1956s (applied to Hindus, Buddhists, Sikhs and Jains) gave women rights to inheritance.

However, the sons had an independent share in the ancestral property, while the daughters' shares were based on the share received by their father. Hence, a father could effectively disinherit a daughter by renouncing his share of the ancestral property, but the son will continue to have a share in his own right. Additionally, married daughters, even those facing marital harassment, had no residential rights in the ancestral home. After amendment of Hindu laws in 2005, now women in have been provided the same status as that of men. In 1986, the Supreme Court of India ruled that Shah Bano, an old divorced Muslim woman was eligible for maintenance money. However, the decision was vociferously opposed by fundamentalist Muslim leaders, who alleged that the court was interfering in their personal law. The Union Government subsequently passed the Muslim Women's (Protection of

Rights Upon Divorce) Act. Similarly, the Christian women have struggled over years for equal rights of divorce and succession. In 1994, all the churches, jointly with women's organisations, drew up a draft law called the Christian Marriage and Matrimonial Causes Bill. However, the government has still not amended the relevant laws.

CRIMES AGAINST WOMEN

Police records show high incidence of crimes against women in India. The National Crime Records Bureau reported in 1998 that the growth rate of crimes against women would be higher than the population growth rate by 2010. Earlier, many cases were not registered with the police due to the social stigma attached to rape and molestation cases. Official statistics show that there has been a dramatic increase in the number of reported crimes against women.

SEXUAL HARASSMENT

Half of the total number of crimes against women reported in 1990 related to molestation and harassment at the workplace. Eve teasing is a euphemism used for sexual harassment or molestation of women by men. Many activists blame the rising incidents of sexual harassment against women on the influence of "Western culture".

In 1987, The Indecent Representation of Women (Prohibition) Act was passed to prohibit indecent representation of women through advertisements or in publications, writings, paintings, figures or in any other manner. In 1997, in a landmark judgement, the Supreme Court of India took a strong stand against sexual harassment of women in the workplace. The Court also laid down detailed guidelines for prevention and redressal of grievances. The National Commission for Women subsequently elaborated these guidelines into a Code of Conduct for employers.

DOWRY

In 1961, the Government of India passed the Dowry Prohibition Act, making the dowry demands in wedding arrangements illegal. However, many cases of dowry-related domestic violence, suicides and murders have been reported. In the 1980s, numerous such cases were reported. In 1985, the Dowry Prohibition (maintenance of lists of presents to the bride and bridegroom) rules were framed.

These rules, a signed list of presents given at the time of the marriage to the bride and the bridegroom should be maintained. The list should contain a brief description of each present, its approximate value, the name of whoever has given the present and his/her relationship to the person. However, such rules are hardly enforced.

A 1997 report claimed that at least 5,000 women die each year because of dowry deaths, and at least a dozen die each day in 'kitchen fires' thought to be intentional. The term for this is "bride burning" and is criticized within India itself. Amongst the urban educated, such dowry abuse has reduced considerably.

CHILD MARRIAGE

Child marriage has been traditionally prevalent in India and continues to this day. Historically, young girls would live with their parents till they reached puberty. In the past, the child widows were condemned to a life of great agony, shaving heads, living in isolation, and shunned by the society. Although child marriage was outlawed in 1860, it is still a common practice.

The UNICEF's "State of the World's Children-2009" report, 47% of India's women aged 20–24 were married before the legal age of 18, with 56% in rural areas. The report also showed that 40% of the world's child marriages occur in India.

FEMALE INFANTICIDES AND SEX SELECTIVE ABORTIONS

India has a highly masculine sex ratio, the chief reason being that many women die before reaching adulthood. Tribal societies in India have a less masculine sex ratio than all other caste groups. This, in spite of the fact that tribal communities have far lower levels of income, literacy and health facilities.

It is therefore suggested by many experts, that the highly masculine sex ratio in India can be attributed to female infanticides and sex-selective abortions.

All medical tests that can be used to determine the sex of the child have been banned in India, due to incidents of these tests being used to get rid of unwanted female children before birth. Female infanticide (killing of girl infants) is still prevalent in some rural areas. The abuse of the dowry tradition has been one of the main reasons for sex-selective abortions and female infanticides in India.

DOMESTIC VIOLENCE

The incidents of domestic violence are higher among the lower Socio-Economic Classes (SECs). The Protection of Women from Domestic Violence Act, 2005 came into force on October 26, 2006.

TRAFFICKING

The Immoral Traffic (Prevention) Act was passed in 1956. However many cases of trafficking of young girls and women have been reported. These women are either forced into prostitution, domestic work or child labour.

OTHER CONCERNS

HEALTH

The average female life expectancy today in India is low compared to many countries, but it has shown gradual improvement over the years. In many families, especially rural ones, the girls and women face nutritional discrimination within the family, and are anaemic and malnourished. The maternal mortality in India is the second highest in the world. Only 42% of births in the country are supervised by health professionals. Most women deliver with help from women in the family who often lack the skills and resources to save the mother's life if it is in danger. The UNDP Human Development Report (1997), 88% of pregnant women (age 15-49) were found to be suffering from anaemia.

FAMILY PLANNING

The average woman in rural areas of India has little or no control over her reproductivity. Women, particularly women in rural areas, do not have access to safe and self-controlled methods of contraception.

The public health system emphasises permanent methods like sterilisation, or long-term methods like IUDs that do not need follow-up. Sterilization accounts for more than 75% of total contraception, with female sterilisation accounting for almost 95% of all sterilisations.

NOTABLE INDIAN WOMEN

ARTS AND ENTERTAINMENT

Singers and vocalists such as M.S. Subbulakshmi, Gangubai Hangal, Lata Mangeshkar and Asha Bhosle, and actresses such as Aishwarya Rai, are widely revered in India. Anjolie Ela Menon is one of the famous painters.

SPORTS

Although the general sports scenario in India is not very good, some Indian women have made notable achievements in the field.

Some of the famous female sportspersons in Indian include P. T. Usha, J. J. Shobha (athletics), Kunjarani Devi (weight lifting), Diana Edulji (cricket), Saina Nehwal (badminton), Koneru Hampi (chess) and Sania Mirza (tennis). Karnam Malleswari (weightlifter), is the only Indian woman to have won an Olympic medal (Bronze medal in 2000).

POLITICS

Through the Panchayat Raj institutions, over a million women have actively entered political life in India. As per the 73rd and 74th Constitutional Amendment Acts, all local elected bodies reserve one-third of their seats for women.

Although the percentages of women in various levels of political activity has risen considerably, women are still under-represented in governance and decisionmaking positions.

LITERATURE

Many well known women writers are in Indian literature as poets and story writers. Sarojini Naidu, Kamala surayya, Shobha De, Arundhati roy, Anita Desai are some of them. Sarojini Naidu is called the nightingale of India. Arundhati Roy was awarded the Booker Prize (Man Booker Prize) for her novel The God of Small things.

2

Crime and Deviance

UNDERSTANDING DEVIANCE AND CONTROL

Deviance is nonconformity to social norms or expectations. For many people, the word 'deviance' is used only in relation to moral, religious, or political norms. The 'deviant' is seen as someone whose behaviour departs from normal moral standards or who deviates from a political or religious orthodoxy. The sociological concept of deviance, however, takes a broader point of view and recognizes that there can be deviation from social norms of all kinds.

Along with sexual deviants, political deviants, and religious deviants must be counted those whose behaviour runs counter to legal or customary norms more generally — criminals, the mentally ill, alcoholics, and many others. What makes these people deviant is the fact that their behaviour seems to run counter to the norms of a social group. It is this that the homosexual, the prostitute, the child molester, the schizophrenic, the suicide, the radical, the heretic, the Ecstasy user, and the burglar all have in common.

All of them seem to engage in behaviour that is not seen as normal in their society. No form of behaviour is deviant in and of itself. To judge behaviour as deviant is to judge it from the standpoint of the norms of a particular social group. The defining statement for the sociological study of deviance is Becker's justly famous claim that:

- Social groups create deviance by making the rules whose infraction constitutes deviance, and by applying these rules to particular people and

> labelling them as outsiders. From this point of view, deviance is not a quality of the act the person commits, but rather a consequence of the application by others of rules and sanctions to an 'offender'. The deviant is one to whom that label has successfully been applied; deviant behaviour is behaviour that people so label.

Even where there is a consensus over standards of behaviour within a society, these standards may change over time. What was formerly considered as normal, conformist behaviour may come to be seen as deviant. High levels of consensus are uncommon, and it is more typical for there to be rival definitions of normality and deviance within a society. In these circumstances, conformity to the expectations of one group may mean deviating from the expectations of another. Revolutionary terrorists, for example, may be regarded as deviants from the standpoint of established social groups, but they are seen very differently by members of their own political movement.

In all these contested situations, it is the views of the powerful that prevail, as they have the ability to make their views count. This insight is particularly associated with a so-called labelling theory of deviance that is closely linked to symbolic interactionism. This point of view, it is the fact of being labelled as a deviant by the members of a powerful or dominant social group that makes an action deviant. This is why ethnic minorities are in many societies treated as deviant groups if they are seen as violating the normal customs and practices of the majority ethnic group.

Similarly, those women who depart from what is seen as normal female behaviour by, say, entering what are regarded as male occupations, might be regarded as deviant by many men and by some other women. Whether the behaviour of a person is deviant depends upon whose values are taken as being the basis for determining what is to count as normal or conformist behaviour. In this part as suggested, look at a number of forms of deviance. As suggested, look at the formation of deviant identities through interaction between deviants and the agents of social control. As suggested, show that what is deviant in one context may be conformist in another, and that the critical element is the social reaction that labels behaviour one way or another. Having discussed some of the features that are common to all forms of deviance, as suggested, look in more detail at criminality, drug use and abuse, and sexual difference.

BIOLOGY AND DEVIANCE

In the past, but also in some more recent discussions, the social dimension of deviance has often been ignored. Deviant behaviour has been seen in purely individual terms and as something to be explained by biology. From this point of view, all 'normal' individuals conform to social expectations, and so those who differ must have something wrong with them. A deviant body is seen as explaining a deviant mind and deviant behaviour.

Such a claim ignores the fact that no behaviour—except, perhaps, purely automatic reflexes such as blinking in bright sunlight—can be seen independently of the meanings that it carries and the social contexts in which it occurs.

EVOLUTION, RACE, AND DEVIANCE

For many writers on difference and deviance in the nineteenth century, and still for some today, biology provides the key to explaining human behaviour. Nineteenthcentury evolutionary theory led to the widespread acceptance of the idea that there was a 'great chain of being', an evolutionary hierarchy of species that connected humans to apes and to the lower animals.

The supposed racial divisions of the human species that we discuss in were all accorded their place in this evolutionary hierarchy. It was widely believed that individuals 'recapitulate' the evolution of their species in their own biological development. They go through various animal-like stages in their foetal development and during their later development outside the womb. Particular races, it was held, had developed only to the particular level that was allowed by their biology: the white races had developed the furthest, while the black races showed an inferior development. White children, for example, were seen as having reached the same stage of evolution as black adults, who had not developed beyond these more 'childlike' characteristics and forms of behaviour.

These assumptions underpinned contemporary views of deviance. The nineteenth-century English doctor John Down, for example, classified various forms of mental disability in terms of the 'lower' races to which their characteristics corresponded. He argued that some 'idiots' were of the 'Ethiopian' variety, some of the 'Malay' or 'American' type, and others of the 'Mongolian' type. His special study of the genetics of the latter group meant that those with Down's syndrome were, for many years, known as 'Mongols'—a derogatory label that continued to be very widely used until the 1970s. Each society tends to see its own members as being the highest, most-evolved exemplar of the human species. The Japanese, for example, saw themselves as being at the pinnacle of evolution and civilization, and their term for Down's syndrome was 'Englishism'.

The most notorious of these evolutionary approaches to deviant behaviour was the theory of crime set out by Cesare Lombroso, who held that many criminals had been born with 'atavistic' features. Criminals had definite biological failings that prevented them from developing to a fully human level. They showed, perhaps, certain apelike characteristics, or sometimes merely 'savage' features that gave them the distinct anatomical characteristics from which they could easily be identified: large jaws, long arms, thick skulls, and so on. These atavistic features, Lombroso argued, also led them to prefer forms of behaviour that are normal among apes and savages, but are criminal in human societies.

These criminal tendencies were apparent, Lombroso claimed, in their other 'degenerate' personal characteristics: the criminal, he believed, is idle, has a love of tattooing, and engages in orgies. Lombroso claimed that about 40 per cent of all criminals were 'born criminals' of this kind. They were driven into criminality by their biology. Other law-breakers were simply occasional, circumstantial offenders and did not have the 'atavistic' characteristics of the born criminal. The excesses of Lombroso's theory and the racial assumptions that underpinned it have long been discarded. However, many people still see criminality as resulting from innate characteristics.

Violence and aggression, for example, are often seen not only as specifically male characteristics, but in their extreme forms as being due to genetic peculiarities. It has been proposed, for example, that many violent criminals have an extra Y chromosome in their cells. Some have suggested that rape can be explained as a consequence of normal, genetically determined male behaviour. In the 1990s, the success of the Human Genome Project led to many strong claims about the genetic basis of crime.

The idea of the born criminal was supported in a report that 'Pimping and petty theft appear to be genetically conditioned but a person's genes have little influence on their propensity for committing crimes of violence'. Violence was reported to be due to a 'mild brain dysfunction in early life', and it was claimed that improved standards of health care for pregnant women could reduce violent crime by over 20 per cent. The link between biology and social behaviour is not this straightforward.

While there may, indeed, be a biological basis to violent behaviour—and the matter is still hotly debated— the ways in which this is expressed and the consequences that flow from it depend upon the meanings that are attached to it and the particular social situations in which it occurs. The behaviour of a soldier in time of war involves violence that is channelled into disciplined action against a national enemy. This violence is condoned and encouraged, and it may even be rewarded as heroism or bravery.

The behaviour of someone at a football match who attacks a member of the opposing team's supporters involves far less violence, but it is likely to be condemned and denounced as hooliganism that must be stamped out. No biological explanation of violence can explain why one act is that of a hero and the other is that of a villain. Of course, this is not to make the absurd claim that it is only the social reaction that differs between the two cases.

The point is that, while some people may have a disposition towards violent behaviour, a biological explanation can, at best, explain the disposition. It cannot explain when and how that disposition is expressed in social action, or is inhibited from expression. Nor can it explain the reactions of others to violence.

An explanation of deviance must refer to the processes of socialization through which people learn to give meaning to their behaviour and to the processes of discipline and regulation through which some people come to be identified as deviants and to be processed in particular ways by a system of social control.

SOCIAL REACTION AND DEVIANCE

There are three levels of explanation in the study of deviant behaviour. A first level of explanation is concerned with the existence of the many different forms of human behaviour that occur in any society. Biology may contribute towards an explanation of this diversity, but it can never provide the whole explanation.

It is always necessary to take account of processes of socialization. A second level of explanation is concerned with the variation in norms between social groups, as manifested particularly in cultural and subcultural differences. Socialization takes place within particular social groups, and it is the norms of these groups that provide the standards for the identification of particular kinds of behaviour as deviant. The third, and final, level of explanation is concerned with the ways in which particular individuals are identified as deviants by others and so come to develop a deviant identity.

This is a matter of social reaction and control. In the rest of this part as suggested, outline some of the general processes that are involved in deviance and control and the processes that are common to a range of deviant and conformist identities. You may like to read this through fairly quickly, not worrying about all the details, and then go on to the discussion of specific forms of deviance. When you have read one or two of these parts, return to this general discussion of deviance and control and try to work through its details.

PRIMARY AND SECONDARY DEVIATION

Two key concepts in the study of deviance are primary deviation and secondary deviation, which were first systematized by Lemert. Primary deviation is the object of the first two levels of explanation. It is behaviour that runs counter to the normative expectations of a group, and is recognized as deviant behaviour by its members, but which is 'normalized' by them.

That is to say, it is tolerated or indulged as an allowable or permissible departure from what is normally expected. It is ignored or treated in a low-key way that defines it as an exceptional, atypical, or insignificant aberration on the part of an otherwise normal person. The normalization of the deviant behaviour defines it as something that is marginal to the identity of the deviator.

Many justifications for the normalization of deviant behaviour are employed: a man is seen as aggressive because he is 'under stress' at work, a woman behaves oddly because it is 'that time of the month', a child is being naughty because he or she is 'overtired', an elderly woman steals from a supermarket because she is 'confused', a middleaged man exposes himself in public because he has a 'blackout' and 'did not know what came over him', and so on.

What Lemert calls secondary deviation, or deviance proper, is the object of our third level of explanation. It arises when the perceived deviation is no longer normalized and is, instead, stigmatized or punished in some way. The social reaction and its consequences become central elements in the deviator's day-to-day experiences and it shapes future actions. When public opinion, lawenforcement agencies or administrative controls exercised by the welfare and other official agencies react in an overt and punitive way, their reaction labels the person as a deviant of some kind. This labelling stigmatizes the behaviour and the person, who must now try to cope with the consequences of the stigma. Stigmatization may involve the rejection, degradation, exclusion, incarceration, or coercion of the deviant, who becomes the object of treatment, punishment, or conversion.

Those who are stigmatized find that their lives and identities come to be organized around their deviance. They may even come to see themselves as a deviant—as a 'thief ', as 'mentally ill', and so on—taking on many of the stigmatizing attributes of the popular and official images. Even if the deviator rejects this identity, the fact that he or she is identified in this way by others becomes an important factor in determining future behaviour.

The development of secondary deviation may, initially, involve an acceptance of the negative, stigmatizing stereotypes that others hold of the deviant. Deviants may often, however, be able to construct a more positive image of their deviance and build an identity around a rejection of the stigma. They accept the label, but, instead of merely reflecting back the public stereotype, they construct an alternative view that reflects their own experiences and those of people like them. They construct accounts—narratives — of their coming to be the kind of people that they are, and these narratives become central features of the construction and reconstruction of their identity.

In much the same way that the Black Power movement constructed more positive images of black identity, so such movements as Gay Pride have led to the construction of positive images of homosexuality. Not all deviance results from the conversion of primary deviation into secondary deviation through an external social reaction. Deviators may, for example, escape the attention of those who would label them, remaining 'secret deviants'. Such people may, nevertheless, move into secondary deviation precisely because of their attempts to keep their deviant behaviour secret. By anticipating the reactions of others, they begin to act towards themselves in terms of the stigmatized deviant identity, even if they do not embrace this identity themselves. The man who engages in homosexual acts in private, for example, may become drawn into association with other gay people because the risks of his inadvertent exposure as gay in other social situations are too great.

There is also the possibility of false accusation. Someone who has not violated expectations may, nevertheless, be labelled as a deviant and processed accordingly. Such people will experience many of the same consequences as those who have been correctly labelled. Although they may feel a sense of injustice about their wrongful accusation, they may, as a result of their experience of stigmatization, come to act in ways that are quite indistinguishable from other deviants.

Such highly publicized cases of wrongful imprisonment for terrorist bombings as those of the Birmingham Six and the Guildford Four highlight the more general situation of false accusation that is apparent in, for example, the child who is wrongly punished by a teacher for cheating or the political dissidents in the Soviet Union who were officially designated as mentally ill. Primary deviation that is not normalized does not always result in secondary deviation or commitment to a deviant identity.

Many people drift in and out of deviant behaviour without being committed to it at all. Because they are not committed to their deviant acts—they do not see them as a fundamental expression of their identity—they are able to abandon them whenever they choose, or when the circumstances are not right. Conversely, of course, they may feel able—though not required—to deviate whenever the opportunity and the inclination are present.

Drift, then, is an important aspect of the structuring of deviant behaviour. Matza suggests, for example, that juvenile delinquency rarely becomes a matter of secondary deviation, precisely because juveniles drift back and forth between deviant and conformist behaviour without ever becoming committed to delinquency as a way of life. Many of those who become involved in crime do not embrace a deviant identity—they do not see themselves as criminals, burglars, or housebreakers. Rather, they see their involvement in criminal activities as an aspect of the larger social situation in which they find themselves. They may, for example, be long-term unemployed, in serious financial hardship, and faced with the opportunity of illegal gain. Such people drift into crime for situational reasons, and become secondary deviants only if they are unable to drift out again.

Certain opportunities may be denied to them, while other courses of action become easier. They become secondary deviants if the whole structure of interests within which they act—the advantages and disadvantages, rewards and punishments—tend to force them into continued deviance. Those who have been imprisoned for theft or burglary, for example, may experience restricted employment and promotion opportunities in the outside world that make it difficult for them to abandon their criminal life and to enter or re-enter conventional occupations.

Where people do take on a deviant identity, however, their behaviour will be shaped by commitment as well as constraint. Those who have become committed to a deviant identity will be committed to a whole range of behaviours that are associated with that identity. These ways of behaving will seem more 'natural' to them than any others, and they will identify with the behaviours as much as with the label itself. Commitment and constraint generally operate together: a firmly committed deviant is more likely to face disadvantaged opportunities, and a tightly constrained deviant is more likely to feel a sense of difference from others. If their circumstances change, and these constraints alter, they may find it possible to drift out of crime once more.

DEVIANT ROLES AND CAREERS

Where deviance has become a central feature of a person's identity and way of life, it can take the form of role deviance. In this situation, a person's activities become organized into a distinct and recognizable social role to which particular normative expectations are attached. The deviant is expected to act in deviant ways: conformity to these particular role expectations confirms the person's deviant identity! Until recently, male homosexuals, for example, were widely expected to exhibit their deviance by behaving in 'effeminate' ways, and one who conformed to these expectations had adopted the public, stereotyped homosexual role. Deviant roles, like conformist roles, often have a career structure. This is particularly likely where the role is defined within a group of deviants, rather than by public stereotypes alone.

Where the deviant role involves a particular sequence of events and experiences that are common for all its occupants, role deviance becomes what has been called career deviance. This may be highly formalized, paralleling the kinds of career structures that are found in conventional occupations. Full-time thieves, for example, may be members of teams who make their living from their deviance and that have their own internal structures of leadership, reward, and 'promotion'. When organized as career deviance, the deviant role is likely also to involve what Goffman has called a moral career. This term describes the internal or personal aspects of a career, the specific sequence of learning experiences and changes in conceptions of self and identity that occur as people follow their deviant career.

It is a process through which people come to terms with their stigma and their commitment to a deviant identity. With each phase of the public career associated with the role, its occupants must reconsider their past in an attempt to make sense of their new experiences.

They single out and elaborate, with the benefit of hindsight, those experiences that they believe can account for and legitimate their present situation. This is a continuous process in which their personal biography—their life story—is constantly constructed and reconstructed in the light of their changing circumstances.

DEVIANT GROUPS AND COMMUNITIES

Career deviants are especially likely to become involved with groups that support and sustain their identities and that help them to come to terms with the constrained opportunities that they face. Gangs and cliques are formed, clubs and pubs are colonized as meeting places, and organizations and agencies are set up to promote shared interests or political goals. With advances in technology, new forms of support and communication become possible. The spread of the telephone allowed people to maintain distant communication far more effectively than was possible through writing letters, and computer technology now allows global communication through the Internet and e-mail.

Those who are involved in two or more of these groups will tie them into larger social networks that bond the groups into cohesive and solidaristic communities with a shared sense of identity. Criminal gangs, for example, may be involved in localized networks of recruitment and mutual support, to which individual criminals and juvenile gangs may also be attached. These networks form those subcultures of crime that comprise an underworld.

The subcultures are means through which skills and techniques can be learned and in which criminals can obtain a degree of acceptance and recognition that is denied to them by conventional groups. Goffman has argued that the groups of 'sympathetic others' that form the supportive subcultures of deviance comprise two distinct types of people: the own and the wise. The own are those who share the deviant identity.

They have a common understanding of stigmatization from their personal experiences, and they may be able to help in acquiring the tricks of the trade that allow a deviant to operate more effectively, as well as by providing emotional support and company in which a deviant can feel at home. The own help people to organize a life around their deviance and to cope with many of the disadvantages that they experience.

The wise, on the other hand, are 'normals' who have a particular reason for being in the know about the secret life of the deviants and for being sympathetic towards it. They are accepted by the deviants and are allowed a kind of associate membership in their activities. They are those for whom the deviants do not feel the need to put on a show of normality or deviance disavowal: they can safely engage in back-region activities with them. The wise can include family members and friends, employees, and even some control agents who have day-to-day contact with them.

The own and the wise together form a network of contacts and connections that support deviants in the construction of their narratives of identity. Some of the wise may actively support deviants in sustaining their deviance, though there are limits to the willingness of people to become too closely involved in activities where the stigma of deviance is likely to 'rub off ' on to them. Active support, then, is most likely to come from the own, and this is particularly true where there is a need for representatives to speak or act for their interests and concerns in public.

Such representatives may sometimes become very active and make a living—and a new identity—out of their role as spokespersons for particular deviant groups. They make a 'profession' of their deviance in quite a novel way, perhaps appearing in the press and on radio and television whenever issues of concern are discussed. There are, of course, limits to this. Only certain forms of deviance are allowed to have the legitimacy of their stigmatization debated in public.

Gays and the mentally ill, for example, have active and important organizations that can lobby for their interests, while thieves and burglars do not. Pressure groups on behalf of those involved in serious crime are, for the most part, limited to campaigns for prison reform and are led by the wise and by reformed offenders.

The general account of deviance and control that we have presented must be treated with caution, as all of its elements will not apply equally to every case of deviance and stigmatized identity. It is a general framework that provides the concepts that can sensitize researchers to the specific issues that occur in particular cases. As suggested, show this by considering a number of forms of criminal behaviour. As suggested, show that certain aspects of illness can also be understood as forms of deviance.

CRIME AND LEGAL CONTROL

Crime is that form of deviance that involves an infraction of the criminal law. Not all laws are 'criminal'. Lawyers recognize civil law, constitutional law, and various other categories of legal norm. Civil law, for example, concerns relations among private individuals, such as the contractual relations involved in such areas as employment relations and consumer purchasing.

A person who breaks a contract by, say, unfairly dismissing someone from her or his job or failing to supply goods that are 'fit for their purpose' has infringed the civil law, and action can be taken only by the particular individual affected. The police have no right to become involved, and a completely separate system of courts is involved in hearing any civil case. The outcome of a successful civil case is some kind of 'restitution', such as financial compensation or 'damages'.

The criminal law, by contrast, consists of those legal norms that have been established by the state as a public responsibility, and which the police and the criminal courts have been designated to enforce. Someone who infringes the criminal law can be arrested, charged, and tried at public expense and, if found guilty, will be subject to repressive or punitive penalties such as a fine or imprisonment. The criminal law of a society can cover a wide range of actions.

In Britain, for example, it covers such acts as driving above the legal speed limit, stealing a car, breaking into a house, possessing certain drugs, forging a signature on a cheque, murdering someone, and arson. Penalties attached to these offences range from small fines for speeding to life imprisonment for murder, and, until 1998, execution for treason.

The crimes that are most visible or that are perceived to be the most threatening are not necessarily those that have the greatest impact in real terms. In practice, many minor crimes are normalized: few people report cases of speeding or dropping litter, and the police may often choose to disregard such offences. The main types of serious offence recorded in the criminal statistics for England and Wales. The statistics show a large increase in the level of crime. A different picture emerges, however, from the British Crime Survey, which draws its evidence from a sample survey of the general public. This survey of victims and potential victims showed a fall in the amount of crime between 1995 and 2005. The reached a peak in 1995, but crime had fallen by 44 per cent by 2005.

Both vehicle crime and burglary fell by over a half, while violent crime fell by 43 per cent. The chances of being a victim of crime fell from 40 per cent in 1995 to 24 per cent in 2005. This is the lowest level since 1981. Young men, however, are far more likely to be a victim of crime, while relatively few of those aged over 65 have been victims. People's attitudes, however, reflected the official statistics and their reporting in the media, with 61 per cent of people believing that crime had risen in the country as a whole.

Government policy on minor crime and delinquency in Britain has recently centred around the issue of 'anti-social behaviour' and the 'respect' agenda that emerged during the 2005 general election campaign. The 'respect' agenda is based on the idea that the low-level criminality and nuisance behaviour that upsets people on a day-to-day basis—petty vandalism, rudeness, drunkenness—should be dealt with through local communities themselves, by inculcating a climate of respect towards other people's property. Improving discipline in schools, for example, is seen as a way of establishing such control.

This is seem as an extension of an earlier policy of controlling more serious petty criminality through the issuing of Anti-social Behaviour Orders. These are orders issued by a civil court, rather than a criminal court, prohibiting a person from specific acts of concern to complainants. Although these are civil court orders, a breach of an ASBO is a criminal offence and can bring the offender under legal control. Public concern over crime relates mainly to theft and violence, which are regarded as being serious enough to warrant sustained attention from the police. This concern, reflected in periodic moral panics, tends to ensure that many of those who are involved in theft and criminal violence do so as a form of secondary deviation. As a result, many of them develop a criminal identity. In this part as suggested, look at forms of professional and career crime and at those normalized forms of crime commonly called white-collar crime. As suggested, also look at the gendered nature of criminal activity, in relation both to the undertaking of criminal acts and to becoming the victim of crime.

PROFESSIONAL AND CAREER CRIME

Theft—stealing property belonging to another person—is one of the few forms of crime to have a highly organized character and to offer the chance of a career or profession to those engaged in it. Theft includes burglary, robbery, forgery, confidence tricks, pickpocketing, and numerous other fraudulent activities. Not all of these are organized as career crime, of course, and not all of those who drift into theft even make the transition from primary deviation to secondary deviation.

School children who steal from shops, for example, rarely continue into a career of thieving. Nevertheless, theft is, indeed, one of the most organized forms of crime. Career crime is nothing new. Mary McIntosh traces it back to the actions of pirates, bandits, brigands, and moral outlaws who often combined criminal with political aims. If the Robin Hood image of the rural outlaw is a rather idealized fiction, it nevertheless grasps an important element in pre-modern theft. With the growth of towns in the early modern period, opportunities for street and house crime became much greater, and there was a growth in the amount of what McIntosh calls craft crime.

This is the small-scale, skilled theft engaged in by pickpockets, cutpurses, and confidence tricksters. These forms of career crime proliferated through the eighteenth and nineteenth centuries and remain an important part of everyday crime. McIntosh traces the origins of what she calls project crime to a later period. This is large-scale robbery and fraud, and became fully established only in the early years of the twentieth century. It has become the predominant form of theft only since the 1950s.

CRIME AND THE UNDERWORLD

Where rural bandits and outlaws were enmeshed in the surrounding social life of the rural communities from which they were drawn, urban craft crime tended to be based in a distinct criminal underworld. The growth of such criminal areas was first reported in the sixteenth century, but it was in the eighteenth and nineteenth centuries that they achieved their fullest development.

The criminal underworld of a city such as London comprised various 'rookeries' that formed the dwelling places and meeting places of craft criminals of all kinds. Segregated from the rest of society, the underworlds provided for the security, safety, shared interests, and concerns of the craft thieves. The underworlds were rooted in the surrounding slum districts of the poor working class. Poverty, unemployment, overcrowding in poor physical conditions, and a lack of leisure opportunities other than the pub, were the conditions under which many people drifted into crime and some became confirmed in a criminal career.

An urban underworld formed an occupational community with a subculture that established norms of criminal behaviour, a slang and argot, and an esprit de corps that sustained the shared identity of the thieves. Central to the underworld code was the injunction not to 'squeal', 'squawk', 'grass', or inform on others. Association with other thieves, and a lack of association with the targets of their theft, inhibited any concern for the feelings of the victims of crime. It also meant that thieves could learn from other thieves the techniques and skills that would help them in their own crimes. In addition, their leisuretime associates formed a pool of partners in crime.

They were able to find markets for their stolen goods, and they could attain a degree of protection and insulation from detection and law enforcement. Underworld life, however, has been fundamentally altered by the urban redevelopment of the inner-city areas and the dispersal of population to the suburbs. One of the principal roots of the London underworld had been in the Spitalfields and Cable Street districts of the East End, where there has been much redevelopment. While certain central pubs and clubs remain important venues for career criminals, much activity is now more dispersed through the city, and the underworld forms an extended social network rather than being confined to a particular physical locale.

Even in the 1960s, however, a tradition of craft crime still survived in Spitalfields, and the surrounding district had high levels of crime: there were especially high levels of burglary, violence against the person, gambling, and prostitution. Much crime, however, was 'petty, unsophisticated, unorganized and largely unprofitable—if often squalid and brutal'. A subculture of crime continues to sustain career crime, which has, however, changed its character.

Alongside older forms of craft crime, project crime has become more significant, and this has also helped to transform the structure of the underworld. Where craft theft involved the stealing of small amounts of money from large numbers of people, project crime involves a much smaller number of large thefts. Growing affluence and, in particular, the increasing scale of business activity have meant that the potential targets of theft have become much bigger. As a result, criminals have had to organize themselves more effectively and on a larger scale if they are to be successful against these targets.

Improved safes, alarm systems, and security vans can be handled only by organized teams of specialists: safe-breakers, drivers, gunmen, and so on. Such crimes, organized as one-off projects, require advanced planning and a much higher level of cooperation than is typical for craft crime. Teams for particular projects are recruited through the cliques and connections that comprise the underworld, and these may sometimes be organized on a semi-permanent basis. The criminal underworld that existed in the East End of London from the Second World War until the 1960s, for example, contained numerous competing gangs that were held together largely by the violent hegemony of the Kray twins and their associates. The east London gangs engaged in violent feuds with their counterparts from the south London underworld, and the leading members of the East End and south London gangs occasionally met on the neutral ground of the West End. It is through the subculture of crime that people can be socialized into criminal identities, whether as a craft thief or a project thief.

The professional thief, like the professional doctor, lawyer, or bricklayer, must develop many technical abilities and skills. He must know how to plan and execute crimes, how to dispose of stolen goods, how to 'fix' the police and the courts, and so on. These skills must be acquired through long education and training, and it is through his involvement in the underworld that the thief can acquire them most effectively. Based on his detailed study of a professional thief, Sutherland has shown how the person who successfully learns and applies these techniques earns high status within the underworld. The beginning thief, if successful, is gradually admitted into closer and closer contact with other thieves.

It is they who can offer him 'better' work and from whom he can learn more advanced skills. Once successful, the thief dresses and behaves in distinct ways and proudly adopts the label 'thief ' in order to distinguish himself from a mere 'amateur', small-time criminal. As well as gaining respect within the underworld, he may also gain a degree of recognition and respect from police, lawyers, and newspaper crime writers. These people are aware of his activities and have often accommodated themselves to professional crime: apart from the corruption that sometimes occurs, there may also be shared interests in not reacting immediately and punitively towards all crime.

BURGLARY AS A WAY OF LIFE

One of the few contemporary investigations of career theft in Britain is an investigation of domestic burglaries. Burglary is illegal entry into a building with the intent to steal. Domestic burglary was, for a long time, subject to the death penalty, and from 1861 to 1968 it carried a maximum sentence of life imprisonment. Following the Theft Act of 1968, the maximum penalty has been fourteen years' imprisonment. In practice, only just under a half of convicted burglars have been given custodial sentences. Recognizing the problems involved in assessing rates of crime, Maguire and Bennett concluded that about 60 per cent of all burglaries were committed by a relatively small number of persistent, career criminals.

The remaining 40 per cent were committed by juveniles who had drifted into delinquency and would, for the most part, drift out of it again. Maguire and Bennett interviewed a number of persistent burglars, most of whom were committed to their criminal careers. They had, typically, carried out between 100 and 500 break-ins during their careers. They combined this with involvement in car theft, burglary from commercial premises, and cheque forgery.

They were mainly young, single, and with no dependants. The men described themselves as 'thieves', or simply as 'villains', and they described their crimes as 'work' from which they could earn a living and from which they would eventually retire. Maguire and Bennett are, however, more critical of this self-image than Sutherland had been. In particular, they highlight a number of ways in which the thieves sought to neutralize the moral implications of their actions through self-serving rationalizations.

Thieves claimed, for example, that any distress suffered by the victims was no concern of theirs. They were simply doing a job, carrying on their trade, and this distress was an unavoidable consequence of their routine, professional activities. This claim was further bolstered by the claim that, in any case, they stole only from the well-to-do, who could easily afford it and who were well insured.

In fact, many of their victims were relatively poor council house residents who could ill afford to be burgled. Similarly, the thieves sought to boost their own status by disparaging the amateurism of the majority of 'losers', 'wankers', 'idiots', and 'cowboys' who carried out unsuccessful thefts. However, Maguire and Bennett argue, it is more accurate to see the persistent career thieves as divided into low-level, middle-level, and high-level categories on the basis of the scale of their crimes. Thieves move up and down this hierarchy a great deal over the course of their careers. High-level burglaries are undertaken by thieves who are members of small networks of committed criminals who keep themselves separate from other, small-time criminals.

Sometimes they work alone, and sometimes in pairs, but always they keep their principal criminal contacts within their network. Middle-level burglaries are carried out by those who are involved in larger and less exclusive networks of thieves with varying abilities and degrees of commitment. There is less consistent adherence to the code of mutual support, and less effective contacts with receivers of stolen goods and with other specialist criminals.

Finally, low-level burglaries are undertaken by individual thieves with only loose connections to one another and who are indiscriminate in both their criminal connections and their choice of crimes. It is at the lower level that people first enter burglary, as the loose social networks are closely embedded in the surrounding structure of the local community. In most cases, this is a process of drift by some of those who have previously been involved in juvenile delinquencies. When describing their careers, however, the thieves minimized the element of drift and presented a self-image of themselves as people who had chosen to enter careers of crime.

Those who drift into lower-level burglary and become at all successful may graduate, in due course, to middle-level or high-level burglary through the contacts and connections that they make. Those in the networks carrying out the high-level burglaries were, in a sense, at the pinnacle of the career hierarchy, though Maguire and Bennett show that they are unlikely to be at all involved in large-scale project crimes undertaken by the London gangs. Their activities are confined to housebreaking, shop-breaking, car theft, shoplifting, and cheque forgery. They have little or no involvement in such specialist crimes as hijacking lorries, bank raids, or embezzlement. Very few burglars—even those at the high level—make a major financial success of their chosen careers, and most spent at least one period in prison. Imprisonment is not, however, a purely negative experience, as it gives the burglar an opportunity to 'widen his circle of criminal acquaintances, learn new techniques and be encouraged to try his hand at more lucrative offences'. Nevertheless, few burglars continued with burglary beyond their thirties or forties. Most drifted into what they hoped would be safer forms of work.

Entry into legal employment is difficult for someone with a criminal record, and few make the transition successfully. Walsh has shown that some burglars are able to combine career crime with a continuing involvement in legitimate employment—typically short-term jobs in the building and construction industry or in other casual work such as catering and cleaning. It seems likely that some who retire from burglary may be able to continue or to re-enter such casual and temporary work.

Career crime has probably never been a completely self-contained, full-time activity. Even in the heyday of the Victorian underworld of the East End, criminal activities were combined with casual labour and street trading, one type of work supplementing the earnings from the other. Hobbs has shown how the East End has long been organized around an entrepreneurial culture of wheeling and dealing, trading and fixing, that makes no sharp distinction between legal and illegal activities.

Theft may, indeed, be career crime, a way of life, but it does not take up all of a thief's time and cannot usually provide him with a regular or substantial income. Those involved in thieving, then, must combine it with other ways of gaining an income. Casual labour is combined with their own thieving and the performance of the occasional criminal task for other, more successful thieves. Those who are themselves more successful may be involved as much in trading and dealing as in thieving, and their entrepreneurial activities are likely to range from the legitimate, through various 'shady' deals, to the criminal. The fulltime criminal is not a full-time thief, even if he stresses this aspect of his life in constructing his own identity. Much thieving is undertaken by those who are in lowpaid or semi-legitimate work or who are unemployed. There is considerable evidence that the growth of the drugs market in the 1980s has sharpened a distinction between the full-time criminal and the mass of ordinary thieves.

The establishment of a large and extensive market in drugs has connected together the criminal networks of London, Manchester, Birmingham, Glasgow, and other large cities. This has allowed a greater degree of organization to be achieved in the project crimes that sustain drugtrafficking. Those who are involved in this organized crime, however, have highly specialized skills—for example, in relation to VAT fraud—and are very different from those who steal hi-fis and videos from domestic premises.

The significance of the drug market for ordinary thieves is that it offers possibilities for casual and occasional trading in small quantities of drugs that supplement their more established sources of income.

GENDER, ETHNICITY, CLASS, AND CRIME

The public perception of crime concentrates on robbery, burglary, theft, mugging, rape, and other crimes of theft and violence. The popular view sees this crime as male, working-class activity. Professional crime is seen as the work of certain adult males and as expressing conventional notions of masculinity. This point of view does get some support from the criminal statistics, which seem to show the very small number of women who are convicted of criminal offences; 5.9 per cent of all men in 2000 were found guilty or were cautioned for a notifiable offence, compared with 1.2 per cent of women. It also appears that the kinds of crimes committed by women are less 'serious' than those committed by men.

All parts of Britain show that women have very little involvement as offenders in domestic or commercial theft, vehicle theft, or street violence, though they are often, of course, involved in these as victims. They are, however, more heavily involved in shoplifting than are men, prostitution is an almost exclusively female crime, and only women can be convicted of infanticide. There is some evidence, however, that the number and types of crime committed by women may have altered since the 1960s.

In a similar way to the crimes of women, many middleclass crimes are not generally regarded as 'real' crimes. While there is a great public fear of street violence and domestic burglary, there is relatively little concern about fraudulent business practices, violations of safety legislation, or tax evasion. While such offences, arguably, have much greater impact on people's lives than does the relatively small risk of theft or violence, they are either invisible to public opinion or are not seen as proper 'crimes'. In this part as suggested, assess the adequacy of these views of crime, exploring aspects of the crimes of women, ethnic minorities, and the affluent.

DISTRIBUTION BY GENDER, ETHNICITY, AND CLASS

The kinds of crimes that are committed by women, like those committed by men, reflect the gender-defined social roles that are available to them. Both men and women are involved in shoplifting, for example, but women are more likely to steal clothes, food, or low-value items. Men are more likely to steal books, electrical goods, or high-value items. This reflects the conventional domestic expectations that tie women to shopping for basic household goods in supermarkets, while men are able to shop for luxuries and extras.

Put simply, both men and women tend to steal the same kinds of items that they buy. Similarly, men are heavily involved in vehicle crimes, including car theft, while women are heavily involved in prostitution. This involvement in prostitution can be seen as an extension of a normal feminine role that allows implicit or explicit bargaining over sex. This connection between crime and conventional genderroles is particularly clear in the patterns of involvement that women have in offences related to children. Those who are most responsible for childcare are, other things being equal, more likely to be involved in cruelty to children, abandoning children, kidnapping, procuring illegal abortions, and social-security frauds. Theft by women generally involves theft from an employer by those involved in domestic work or shop work. Even when involved in large-scale theft, women are likely to be acting in association with male family members and to be involved as receivers of stolen goods rather than as thieves. There are, of course, problems in estimating the actual number of offences from the official statistics but the overall pattern is clear.

Because women are less likely to be arrested and convicted for certain offences—something that we look at below— the difference between male and female involvement in crime is exaggerated by the official figures. The differing patterns of offence do, however, exist. Only in the case of sexual offences is the pattern for male and female involvement more equal, the apparent predominance of women resulting from the fact that their sexual behaviour is more likely to be treated in ways that result in conviction. The sexual double standard means that the authorities normalize much male sexual delinquency, but express moral outrage at female sexual delinquency. As Smart argues:

- None of these types of offences requires particularly 'masculine' attributes. Strength and force are unnecessary and there is only a low level of skill or expertise required. The women involved have not required training in violence, weapons or tools, or in specialised tasks like safe breaking. On the contrary the skills required can be learnt in everyday experience, and socialization into a delinquent subculture or a sophisticated criminal organisation is entirely unnecessary.

There is growing evidence that members of ethnic minorities in Britain have become more heavily involved with the legal system since the 1960s. They are now especially likely to appear as offenders and, more particularly, as victims of crime and as police suspects. Housebreakings and other household offences show little variation among the various ethnic groups, about one-third of all households being victims of such crime. African Caribbeans, however, are almost twice as likely as whites to be the victims of personal attacks. This is, in part, a consequence of the fact that African Caribbeans live, disproportionately, in inner-city areas where such crimes are particularly likely to take place.

However, their experiences also have a racially motivated character. The growing victimization of black and Asian people reflects a real growth in racial violence and racist attacks by members of the white population. While criminal acts carried out during the urban riots of the 1980s often had a racial aspect to them, blacks and Asians are far more likely to be the targets of racial crimes than they are to commit them. There has, nevertheless, been a growing involvement of young African Caribbeans in many kinds of street crime.

The police hold to a widely shared prejudice that African Caribbeans, in particular, are heavily involved in crime and that special efforts need to be taken to control them. Many studies have shown the racism inherent in police actions that stop black people in the street and subject them to closer scrutiny than other members of the population. African Caribbeans are more likely than whites, and members of other ethnic minorities, to be approached by the police on suspicion, to be prosecuted, and to be sentenced.

This is reflected in a growing hostility of ethnic minorities towards the police, who are often seen as racists rather than as neutral defenders of law and order. Offences carried out by men from the middle classes are generally described as white-collar crime. This term originally referred to crimes and civil-law infractions committed by those in non-manual employment as part of their work.

It is now used a little more broadly to refer to three categories of offence:

- *Occupational crimes of the affluent*: offences committed by the relatively affluent and prosperous in the course of their legitimate business or profession. Examples are theft from an employer, financial frauds, and insider dealing in investment companies.
- *Organizational crimes*: offences committed by

organizations and businesses themselves—that is, by employees acting in their official capacities on behalf of the organization. Examples are non-payment or under-payment of VAT or Corporation Tax, and infringements of health and safety legislation leading to accidents or pollution.

- Any other crimes committed by the relatively affluent that tend to be treated differently from those of the less affluent. An example is tax evasion, which is treated differently from social-security fraud.

The concept of white-collar crime, then, is far from clear-cut. It does, however, help to highlight the class basis of much crime. The number of people involved in whitecollar crimes is barely apparent from the official statistics, as many go unrecorded. Its status as hidden crime, however, is paradoxical in view of its financial significance. It was estimated that the total cost of reported fraud alone in 1985 was £2,113 million, twice the amount accounted for by reported theft, burglary, and robbery.

Official estimates suggest that the actual cost of all fraud in Britain in 2003 was £13,800 million. The relatively low representation of women in recorded crime is the main reason why female criminality has been so little researched. Lombroso and Ferrero set out a deterministic theory, based on the claimed peculiarities of female biology, which still has some influence in the late 1990s. They held that women were less highly evolved than men and so were relatively 'primitive' in character.

They were less involved in crime, however, because their biology predisposed them to a passive and more conservative way of life. They were, however, weak willed, and Lombroso and Ferrero saw the involvement of many women in crime as resulting from their having been led on by others. The female drift into crime was a consequence of their weak and fickle character. The extreme position set out by Lombroso and Ferrero has long been abandoned, but many criminologists do still resort to biological assumptions when trying to explain female criminality. Pollak, for example, held that women are naturally manipulative and deceitful, instigating crimes that men undertake. What such theories fail to consider is that, if women do indeed have lower rates of criminality, this may more usefully and accurately be explained in terms of the cultural influences that shape sex–gender roles and the differing opportunities available to men and to women.

Like the crimes of women, the crimes of the affluent have been little researched. Early discussions of white-collar crime were intended as criticisms of the orthodox assumption that criminality was caused by poverty or deprivation. Those who carried out thefts as part of a successful business career, Sutherland argued, could not be seen as acting out of economic necessity. Sutherland's own account stressed that white-collar crime was learned behaviour and that, in this respect, it was no different from other forms of criminality. All crime, he held, resulted from the effects of 'differential association' on learning: those who interact more frequently with others whose attitudes are favourable to criminal actions are themselves more likely to engage in criminal acts.

This implies that patterns of conformity among the affluent and the deprived, among men and among women, are to be understood in the context of their wider role commitments and the interactions in which they are involved with their role partners. Those who are predisposed to see criminal actions as appropriate will, if the structure of opportunities allows it, drift into crime. There is no need to assume that women are fundamentally different from men, or that the working classes are fundamentally different from the middle classes.

WOMEN AND CRIME

It appears, then, that women, like men, drift into criminal actions whenever the structure of opportunities is such that it seems a reasonable response to their situation. The particular situations in which they find themselves are determined by the ways in which sex–gender identities are institutionalized in their society, and so their patterns of criminality are gendered. Cultural stereotypes about men and women, as as suggested, show, are also a major influence on the nature of the social reaction to female criminality. The absence of strong punitive responses to most forms of female crime means that the progression from primary to secondary deviation is less likely to occur.

Women may drift into crime, but they only rarely pursue criminal careers. A form of female crime that seems to be the principal exception to this rule is prostitution. In law, a prostitute is someone who sells sex, and this is almost invariably seen as a female offence. Men involved in prostitution, other than as clients, tend to be seen as engaged in acts of 'indecency' rather than of 'soliciting' for prostitution. Under British law, a woman who has been arrested and convicted for soliciting is officially termed a 'common prostitute' and is liable to re-arrest simply for loitering in a public place.

As most prostitution is arranged in public, on the streets, it is difficult for women so labelled to avoid the occasional spell in custody. They may also find it difficult to live a normal life off the streets:

- It is virtually impossible for them to live with a man or even another woman as it is immediately assumed that such people are living off immoral earnings, thereby making themselves vulnerable to a criminal charge. Also, the legal definition of a brothel, as a dwelling containing two or more prostitutes, has made it difficult for two women to live together even where only one is a prostitute.

In 2006 the government in Britain announced its intention to change the law to allow up to three prostitutes to work together without their place of work being defined as a brothel. The reaction of the police is critical in determining whether a woman who breaks the law is defined as a criminal. Police work is structured around the cop culture, a culture that strongly emphasizes masculinity and that underpins the harassment and abuse of female police officers and the derogation of many female offenders. Prostitutes, for example, are seen as flouting the domesticity of the conventional female role and have been subject to harassment and entrapment. Nevertheless, prostitutes are often able to establish a mutual accommodation with the police, an arrangement in which each can get on with their job with the minimum of interference from the other. When there is pressure on the police to take action, however, such arrangements break down.

In these circumstances, prostitutes are highly vulnerable and can be quite susceptible to police persuasion and suggestion. On the other hand, women who conform to conventional role expectations are seen as in need of protection, and cautioning is more widely used for female offenders than it is for males. There is some evidence that this differential treatment of male and female offenders also occurs in the courts. Sexist assumptions in court practices have led some to suggest that women experience greater leniency than men. Others, however, have suggested that greater harshness is more likely. Heidensohn correctly points out that this may simply reflect the well-known lack of consistency in sentencing, though she reports evidence that supports the view that women are treated more harshly.

Indeed, Edwards has suggested that women are subjected to much closer scrutiny in courts precisely because the female offender is seen as unusual or unnatural. Women are on trial not only for their offence but for their deviation from conventional femininity. Their punishment or treatment is intended to ensure that they adjust themselves back to what is seen as a natural feminine role. Very few convicted women are given custodial sentences.

Men are two or three times more likely to be imprisoned for an offence than are women, and their sentences tend to be longer. The women who are imprisoned are mainly those who have been convicted of such things as theft, fraud, forgery, or violence. Prisons do make some attempt to recognize that women's domestic commitments are different from those of men, and a number of motherand- baby units have been set up. Some well-publicized cases have been reported, however, of pregnant prison inmates who have been forced to give birth while manacled to a prison officer. Studies of female prisons in the United States have shown how these prisons are important sources of emotional and practical support for their inmates, often involving the establishment of lesbian family relationships. This appears to be less marked in Britain.

CRIMES OF THE AFFLUENT

The crimes of the affluent, the prosperous, and the powerful can be explained in terms of the same motives as any other criminal act. They differ from 'ordinary' theft and burglary only in terms of their social organization and the social reaction to them. The character and motivation of those involved are no more, and no less, pathological than those of any others who drift into crime.

White-collar crimes, however, are much less likely to result in full-time criminal careers. The nature of the social reaction makes the development into secondary deviation much less likely. Much corporate and occupational crime takes place in the financial services industry, where changing patterns of regulation have created greater opportunities for illicit activities. The British financial system was, for much of the nineteenth and twentieth centuries, regulated in a highly informal way. Recruitment to banks, insurance companies, and other financial enterprises took place through an old-boy network centred on the public schools and the Oxford and Cambridge colleges.

The Stock Exchange, as the central institution in the financial system, was at the heart of this system of informal regulation. The system rested on trust and loyalty: those who had been to school together and shared a similar social background felt that they could trust one another in their business dealings. The motto of the Stock Exchange was 'My word is my bond', and many deals were sealed on the shake of hands rather than with a written contract. During the 1970s the government introduced a number of changes to this system of regulation in response to the growing internationalization of the money markets. This culminated in the so-called Big Bang of October 1986, when the Stock Exchange was finally opened up to foreign competition. New codes of practice were introduced to reflect the more diverse social backgrounds of those involved in the buying and selling of currency, shares, and commodities.

The old system of trust could no longer be relied on, and more formal mechanisms were required. The Bank of England was given greater powers of control and supervision, and in 1997 the Labour government created a new Securities and Investment Board to regulate the whole system. The offences with which the new system of regulation has had to deal are those that have been made possible by the changing structure of the financial system. The investment management firm of Barlow Clowes, for example, set up new offshore investment funds to provide high returns to its wealthy clients who wanted to minimize their tax bills.

The head of the company was found to have financed an extravagant lifestyle at the expense of the investors in the funds. The growth of domestic takeover business made possible massive fraud by some directors and managers associated with Guinness and its financial advisers in 1986. These directors and managers manipulated share dealings to keep up the price of Guinness shares on the stock market and to help its takeover of another company. Their actions were the subject of an official inquiry and, later, a criminal trial that resulted in some of them being imprisoned. Much white-collar crime is low in visibility.

It tends to occur in the context of normal business routines, and it is less likely to be noticed, even by its victims. Fiddling business expenses, for example, is almost undetectable, and many employers treat it as a source of tax-free perks for their employees. Large-scale fraud, when discovered, is more likely to result in an official reaction, though it will often be hushed up if it might suggest a failure of supervision or control by senior managers. Crimes of the affluent are far more likely to be regulated by specialized enforcement agencies than by the police, and this has important consequences for the nature of the social reaction. These agencies—the Health and Safety Executive, the Factory Inspectorate, the Inland Revenue, and so on— generally have a remit to maintain and promote high standards of business and trading, and the enforcement of the criminal law is only one part of this remit. Their officials, therefore, develop 'compliance strategies' that stress persuasion and administrative sanctions aimed at crime prevention, rather than the detection and punishment of offences. The level of prosecutions is, therefore, very low. Few cases go to court, and very few result in imprisonment. In these ways, the transition to secondary deviation is avoided.

DRUGS AND DRUG ABUSE

The use of drugs is now one of the most widely discussed forms of deviance. In its most general meaning, a drug is any chemical that can have an effect on the human body and, perhaps, a physical effect on the mind. Some drugs occur quite naturally in many widely used drinks and foods. Caffeine, for example, is found in both coffee and tea, alcohol is the basis of beer, wine, and spirits, and vitamins are found in fresh fruit and vegetables.

Many drugs are used as medicines, usually under the control of doctors. Morphine, penicillin, and steroids, for example, are used very widely and under a variety of commercial trade names in hospitals, clinics, and surgeries. Many other medical drugs are freely available for purchase without prescription: aspirin, codeine, ibuprofen, and numerous other analgesic drugs can be bought in any highstreet pharmacy and in many supermarkets.

This broad, dictionary definition of 'drugs', however, is not what newspaper columnists, politicians, and social commentators mean when they use the word. These people generally use the word in a much narrower sense to refer to the non-medical use of drugs. This is the deliberate use of chemical substances to achieve particular physiological changes, simply for the pleasure or the other non-medical effects that they produce.

It is in this sense, for example, that many parents and teachers rail against the use of drugs by children and young people. The nonmedical use of drugs in the twentieth century has, indeed, been largely an activity of the young. Drug use, then, is seen as a deviant activity, as non-medical drug abuse. It becomes, therefore, a matter for social control. For this reason, the non-medical use or possession of many drugs has been made illegal. There is a great deal of ambiguity over how widely this meaning of the word 'drug' is to be taken, and whether all non-medical drug use is to be regarded as a deviant activity. Many freely available products have the same characteristics as illicit drugs.

Tobacco, for example, can be freely bought in shops and it is a major source of tax revenue for the government. At the same time, however, it contains nicotine, an addictive stimulant to the nervous system that is a major health hazard both to those who smoke and to those around them. Similarly, alcoholic drinks, which can have serious physiological and psychological effects if taken in large quantities, are an accepted and even encouraged part of a normal social life for most people. Like tobacco, alcohol is available in shops and supermarkets, it is a multi-million pound industry, in which many people find legitimate employment, and— unlike cigarettes—it can be advertised freely on television.

Some chemicals with domestic or industrial uses, but which can also be used to produce 'high' feelings, can be purchased quite legitimately and with even fewer restrictions. Recent research has suggested that chocolate may operate in the same way as heroin, nicotine, and cannabis, by its effect on the limbic system in the brain. Eating chocolate can produce a 'rush' or high feeling because it affects the brain in the same way as the active ingredient in cannabis.

Glues and solvents, which are used as stimulants and hallucinogenics by many young people, can be purchased in hardware and do-it-yourself shops. The use of heroin, cocaine, or Ecstasy, on the other hand, is widely disapproved of and their use is surrounded by numerous legal restrictions over their acquisition and sale. Many such drugs are the objects of advertising campaigns that are aimed at discouraging their use by encouraging people to 'say no' if offered them. They can usually be obtained only from illegal sources. Medical trials have been set up in Britain, however, to investigate the part that might be played by cannabis, on prescription, in the treatment of multiple sclerosis and as a pain-killer. Morphine has long been available in pharmacies in Codeine and similar analgesic tablets, and both cocaine and morphine could be bought over the counter in British high streets until 1916. In 2002 it was announced that heroin would be made available to addicts on prescription.

The different social reaction to alcohol, chocolate, glue, and heroin cannot be explained simply in terms of the medical dangers involved in using any specific stimulant. If the potential danger was the principal determinant of the social reaction, alcohol and tobacco would have been criminalized many years ago.

LEARNING DRUG USE

The idea of addiction to drugs is central to discussions of their non-medical uses. Addiction is seen as occurring where people have become physiologically dependent on the use of a particular drug and suffer serious and persistent withdrawal symptoms when its use is stopped. However, dependence is as much a psychological as a physiological fact and, as such, it is shaped by social factors.

People must learn how to use particular drugs, and they become committed to their use only through complex social processes from which physiological dependence cannot be isolated. 'Addiction' is a medically constructed label and a social role that combines elements of the sick role and, in some cases, the criminal role. Drugs do, of course, have specific physiological effects: alcohol and barbiturates depress mental activity, cocaine and caffeine stimulate it, and LSD distorts experiences and perception.

Their full effects, however, depend upon the social context in which they are used. Individuals who use drugs learn from one another not only the techniques that are necessary for their use, but also how to shape and to experience the kinds of effects that they produce. The nonmedical use of drugs, then, is a deviant activity that, like all forms of deviance, is surrounded by normative frameworks that structure the lives of users and lead them to experience particular deviant careers and associated moral careers. 'Drug addiction' is a deviant identity that reflects a specific deviant career.

Becoming a Cannabis User

In an influential study of deviant activity, Becker documented the career stages that are involved in becoming a marijuana user. He showed that people drift into cannabis use for a variety of reasons. Once they begin its use, however, they will—if they persist—follow a particular sequence of stages. Becker called these stages the 'beginner', the 'occasional user', and the 'regular user'. As users follow this career sequence, cannabis-smoking becomes an ever more important part of their identity.

Becker shows, however, that cannabis use rarely involves full-blown secondary deviation, despite the fact that its use is illegal. Cannabis use is a low-visibility activity that rarely comes to the attention of those who might publicly stigmatize users, and so these users are less likely to progress to secondary deviation. Becker's research was undertaken in the early 1950s, and public attitudes have altered somewhat since then. There was an increase in cannabis use in both the United States and in Britain during the 1960s.

It has, since then, become accepted or tolerated in many situations. In California in 1996, for example, legal restrictions were relaxed in order to allow for its medical use in the treatment of certain cancer patients. Indeed, it has been suggested that cannabis use has become normalized for many people. Research shows that about a quarter of 16 –24 year olds in Britain in 2000 had tried cannabis during the previous year. Most of these users regard their use in the same way that most adults regard alcohol and tobacco use. In 2004, legislation came into effect in Britain that partly decriminalizes the possession of cannabis by altering its classification to that of a 'Class C' drug. This meant that possession of cannabis will no longer result in automatic prosecution but could be dealt with through an official warning. It was anticipated that the police would, in most situations, pay little attention to those who merely possess cannabis for their own use. When Becker undertook his research, cannabis use was both illegal and surrounded by social meanings that associated it with irresponsibility, immorality, and addiction. Becker showed that, while the drug is not physically addictive, its image and its illegality led to specific patterns in its use.

Unlike cigarettes, cannabis cannot be bought at the local newsagent or the supermarket—though it can be obtained in this way in the Netherlands. Most people, therefore, had neither the opportunity nor the inclination to smoke it. Those who were most likely to begin to use the drug, Becker argued, were those who were involved in social groups where there was already a degree of cannabis use.

It was here that there were likely to be opportunities for new users. Becker saw the typical locales for exploratory drug use as organized around values and activities that oppose or run counter to the mainstream values of the larger society. When he undertook his research, these had their focus in social groups around jazz and popular music, students, and 'bohemians'. These groups tended to have a more critical and oppositional stance towards conventional social standards. Participants were likely to see many other people using the drug, and their own first use was likely to become a real possibility if an opportunity presented itself.

Today, when marijuana use has become more generalized among young people, exposure to its use in peer groups is likely to be the initial introduction for many young people. Someone enters the beginner stage in the use of cannabis when he or she is offered the opportunity to smoke it in a social situation where others are smoking, where there is a degree of social pressure to conform to group norms, and where the group itself provides a relatively safe and secluded locale away from the immediate possibility of public censure. Becker shows that people who move from the stage of the beginner to that of the occasional user must learn a number of skills and abilities associated with the use of the drug. Someone willing to use the drug may know that it causes a 'high' feeling, but they are unlikely to know exactly how to produce this. The principal skill that must be learned, then, is the actual technique for smoking cannabis. This is different from that used in tobacco smoking. Only if the smoke is inhaled in the correct way, with an appropriate amount of air, can cannabis have any significant effect on a person's body and mind. Group membership is essential for the easy learning of this skill, as the new user is surrounded by those who can demonstrate it in their own smoking. Those who fail to learn the proper technique will never experience the physical effects of cannabis and so are unlikely to persist in using the drug.

A user must also acquire the ability to perceive the effects of the drug and, therefore, must learn what it is to be high or stoned. This is not as strange as it may seem. Users may have experiences that they fail to recognize as effects of the drug, but that others recognize as central features of their high state. Through interaction with others, new users begin to learn what signs and symptoms to look out for and what, therefore, can be taken as indicating that they have successfully learned the smoking technique.

Last, but not least, they must learn to enjoy the effects of cannabis. They must learn to treat dizziness, tingling, and distortions of time and space as pleasurable experiences, rather than as unpleasant and undesirable disturbances to their normal physical and mental state. Only those who successfully acquire these skills and abilities—the smoking technique, the ability to perceive the effects, and enjoyment of the effects—will persist as cannabis users.

As occasional users, cannabis smokers acquire further justifications and rationalizations for its use, and these reinforce their continued use of the drug. The subculture of the group provides ready-made answers to many of the conventional objections to cannabis use that may be raised in their minds. Users may claim, for example, that cannabis is less dangerous than the alcohol that is tolerated and encouraged by conventional opinion. They are also likely to hold that cannabis smokers are in complete control of when and where they choose to use the drug; that the drug is not in control of them. The regular user of cannabis can neutralize any conventional or official labels that may be applied to them by non-users. People who lack the support of other users are less likely to become regular users if they accept the stereotype of addiction or the idea that they are likely to escalate towards the use of hard drugs.

If ideas of addiction, escalation, and mental weakness cannot be neutralized, smokers may revert to occasional use, rather than becoming committed, regular users. To protect themselves from stigmatization, regular users try to learn how to control the effects of the drug, inhibiting its effects at will, so that they are able to pass as normal in front of non-users or the police.

They must, nevertheless, run certain risks of detection, as regular use requires access to illegal dealers whose criminal activities may bring the user to the attention of the police. In order to minimize their chances of discovery as users, they are likely to spend more and more of their time in the company of their own, the other regular users who can provide a supportive and relatively safe environment in which to smoke.

PATTERNS OF DRUG USE

People learn how to use drugs in particular social contexts. Becker's work explored cannabis use in the specific context of post-war America, though his conclusions have a much wider application. In this part as suggested, look at the changing context of drug use in Britain. We look first at an account of deviant drug use in the 1970s, and then we turn to the contemporary, normalized use of drugs by young people.

Deviant Drug Use

Although it was developed in the 1950s, Becker's argument retains much of its relevance for contemporary patterns of cannabis use, and it has much to say about the use of other drugs. This was first confirmed in a study undertaken by Jock Young in London. Young's primary concern, however, is the origins of the negative social reaction to cannabis use. Why is it, he asks, that there is no similar social reaction to the use of tobacco? He holds that the reason is to be found not in the drug, but in the motivation that people are seen as having for using it. Drugs that are seen as being used to aid productivity are likely to be tolerated, while those that have a purely hedonistic purpose are seen as 'drug abuse'. European and North American societies tolerate or even encourage the drinking of coffee and tea, and the smoking of tobacco when working under pressure or as a 'release' from the pressure of a heavy work schedule. The worker 'earns' the right to 'relax with a smoke and a drink' after work, and people may be allowed to smoke at work if it 'helps them to concentrate'. Alcohol is widely used, and it is tolerated as a way in which people may, periodically, ease the transition from work to leisure. It is culturally normalized.

It is only when alcohol is used to excess and interferes with normal, everyday activities that its use is defined as deviant. No such tolerance is allowed for the user of cannabis, which is not seen as linked in any way to work productivity. Young also points out that there can be cultural variations in response to the same drug. Andean peasants use cocaine as an aid to work, and it is a normalized feature of their society. In Britain and the United States, however, cocaine is regarded very differently.

Young has shown that these variations in response to drugs can be explained in terms of the relationship between a dominant set of social values and a secondary subterranean set of values. The dominant values of contemporary societies stress work and everyday routines, but they coexist with other values that stress the need for excitement, leisure, and pleasure. These hedonistic, or pleasure-oriented, values are subterranean because they concern experiences that can be pursued only when the demands of employment and family life have been met. It is through their work—paid employment and unpaid work in the household—that people acquire the 'right' to freely enjoy their leisure activities and to pursue the subterranean values. Young sees this as involving a socialized conflict between the desire for pleasure and the repression of this desire as people engage in their everyday activities. Through their socialization, he argues, adults acquire a feeling of guilt about any expression of these hedonistic values that has not been earned through hard work. Subterranean values can be exercised only with restraint and only so long as they do not undermine the normal everyday realities of work and family life. The drugs that have come to be seen as problematic in contemporary societies are those that are used to induce an escape from everyday realities into an alternative world where hedonistic values alone prevail.

They are seen to be associated with subcultures that disdain the work ethic and enjoy pleasures that have not been earned through work: 'It is drug use of this kind that is most actively repressed by the forces of social order. For it is not drugtaking per se but the culture of drugtakers which is reacted against: not the notion of changing consciousness but the type of consciousness that is socially generated'. In contemporary societies, Young argues, this kind of drug use is to be found in the inner-city subcultures and many youth subcultures. Young found an overwhelming emphasis on drug use in the 'Bohemian youth culture' of the hippies of the 1960s. The use of mind-altering drugs was raised to a paramount position as one of the fundamental organizing principles for the identities of its members. This subculture— primarily a subculture of middle-class, student youth— was organized around spontaneity and expressivity and a rejection of work. It was in hippie culture that the main structural supports for cannabis use were found, and in the late 1960s Young documented its increasing emphasis also on the strong hallucinogenic drug LSD. What he called the delinquent youth culture, on the other hand, was more characteristic of some working-class areas.

Young saw this as generating an ambivalent attitude towards drug use. While the delinquent subculture was organized around its strong emphasis on subterranean values, drug use was merely tolerated or allowed—it was not required.

Normalized Drug Use

Young's work was undertaken in a period of full employment and relative affluence. The period since he wrote has seen the emergence of mass unemployment and economic insecurity, exacerbated by a global recession. Despite some improvement, employment remains insecure or uncertain for many young people. Illegal drug use today is not so much focused on hippie youth who reject the work ethic. It is now more strongly emphasized by the inner-city unemployed who have little experience of or prospect for secure and regular paid employment. Some glimpses of this were apparent in Young's references to the subculture of inner-city black Americans, as it had developed from the 1920s.

He saw this as strongly supportive of cannabis use and as a principal source of heroin use. Their poverty and inferior status forced them into a rejection of conventional values and an embrace of subterranean values. Indeed, this was one of the principal contexts of drug use studied by Becker. This group has recently been identified as the core of a so-called underclass.

In the 1970s, 'conformist youth culture' could still be seen as fully embracing conventional culture and its conditional commitment to hedonistic values. Its members were committed to work and to family, and their leisuretime activities posed no challenge to the dominance of the conventional values. Young saw this culture as having little significance for deviant drug-taking, holding that conformist youth simply made illicit use of alcohol for the same purposes as their parents.

It is clear today, however, that cannabis use has become common within this culture since the 1980s and that there was a growth in the use of Ecstasy in the 1990s. Declining employment opportunities in a period of recession broke the link between conventional work values and hedonistic values for many young people. Where there was little or no employment, the question of 'earning' pleasure simply did not arise. As a result, drug use has increased among all parts of youth. Almost half of 16 year olds in Manchester in 1992 were reported to have used an illegal drug, generally cannabis, and just under three-quarters had been in situations where drugs were available and on offer. In a national survey of 15–16 year olds in 1996, 42 per cent had used an illegal drug. The British Crime Survey for 2000 found that a quarter of those aged 16–19 and over a quarter of those aged 20–24 had used cannabis during the previous twelve months. A survey in 2004 of 16–24 year olds found that 39 per cent reported that they had used illegal drugs.

Cannabis was the most commonly used drug, with 30 per cent of the young adults having used it. Use of Ecstasy, cocaine, or amphetamines was much lower, at about 4–7 per cent of 16–24 year olds. Heroin use, however, has been increasing in Britain, and the average age at which heroin users had first begun to experiment with the drug is 15. Three-quarters of the young people in inner-city areas are reported to have tried crack cocaine. Class and gender show little association with drug availability and take-up, but ethnicity does. Black youths are rather more likely to come into contact with drugs than are white youths, as suggested in an earlier study by Pryce and Asians are far less likely to do so: only 32 per cent of young Asians in Manchester in 1992 reported having been offered drugs.

The ease of access to drugs such as cannabis—44 per cent of boys and 38 per cent of girls in 1996 had used it— shows that Becker's view of the importance of subcultures to occasional users must now be qualified. Changes in the urban and class conditions that sustained 'delinquent' subcultures in the past, combined with a more commercialized structure of illegal drug-trading, have resulted in a wider availability of drugs.

Drug use is now an integral, normalized part of a generalized youth culture, and not of specific class-based or deviant subcultures. Even the police are tolerant towards its use and generally caution those cannabis users who come their way. Along with music, clothes, magazines, and a love of fast cars, drugs and alcohol are a part of the everyday, pleasure-seeking experience of virtually all young people. The counter-cultural Bohemian and hippie orientations that Young identified in the 1960s are no longer an important part of this youth subculture, which is now a consumerist and leisure-oriented subculture organized around the pursuit of pleasure that is disconnected from the requirement to 'earn' it through productive work. Despite its high profile in the news media, Ecstasy is far less widely used than cannabis. In a national survey in 1996, 9 per cent of boys and 7 per cent of girls reported having taken Ecstasy.

Amphetamines, LSD and solvents are all more widely used than Ecstasy: 20 per cent of boys and 21 per cent of girls had used solvents. Ecstasy, amphetamines, and LSD were all associated with regular involvement in dance clubs and raves, but in these venues, cannabis remains the most widely used illegal drug. Indeed, alcohol —consumed under age—was even more widespread: 94 per cent of 15–16 year olds in a national survey reported that they had consumed alcohol, generally on a regular basis. Over one-third were tobacco smokers, the rate of use and the rate of growth in use being higher among girls than among boys. These findings support the claim that there is now a 'poly-drug' culture in which users are not confined to the use of any one drug.

Cannabis remains the drug of preference, but it is taken alongside other drugs. Not all drugs used by young people are normalized features of the conformist youth culture. Heroin use, for example, is found among less than 2 per cent of young people, and these generally have little involvement in consumerism and conventional family life. Indeed, 'conformist' drug users tend to regard heroin as a drug that would undermine their lifestyle.

It is something to be avoided in favour of the more 'pleasure-oriented' drugs. Auld show that there is a characteristic episodic user of heroin: neither the occasional nor the regular user, but someone who has periods of sustained heroin use, followed by periods 'coming off'. Retreatism and withdrawal from what is perceived as a hostile world are principal motives for those who have experienced a lifetime of emotional and physical abuse in broken families and poor districts. Such users find it difficult to band together for mutual support in the deprived city areas where the homeless congregate, and their lifestyle forces them into close association with a vast criminal underworld of dealers and organized crime. In these circumstances, heroin users are very likely to make the transition from primary to secondary deviation. In the inner-city areas, the growth of an informal economy has been associated with the expansion of an extensive fringe of irregular activities—street-level thieving, dealing and exchange of stolen and illicit goods of all kinds. The unemployed residents of these areas seek to make more than the bare public assistance level of income through involvement in these activities.

Cannabis has, since the 1960s, become more closely tied to professional drug-dealing and, along with hard drugs such as heroin and cocaine, is traded on the streets. It has been estimated that, by 1997, the number of drug deals in London alone had reached an annual total of 30 million, with a total value of £600 million. Only around one in 4,000 street deals results in an arrest.

Through their involvement in this irregular economy, the unemployed can easily become involved in drugdealing, and the opportunities for use are great. Small-scale users and others become drawn into large networks of organized drug crime. There is a hierarchical division of labour in the supply of drugs, and the largest rewards tend to go to those who are furthest removed from street-level dealing.

ORGANIZED CRIME, INTERNATIONAL CRIME, AND TERRORISM

Crime is often seen in highly individual and informal terms, though we have tried to emphasize the ways in which it is generated in and through cultural and subcultural forms of social organization related to class, gender, and ethnic differences. It is important, however, to recognize that much criminality is professionally organized, and we have, again, tried to indicate some of the ways in which this is socially organized. In the next part, we turn to an examination of these issues of the formal social organization of crime in much greater detail. We look, in particular, at crime as a business, organized nationally and internationally in ways that challenge conventional businesses in the scale of their activities. We trace how processes of globalization have produced extensive transnational criminal organizations. We look also at the growing significance of international terrorism—the use of criminal acts for political purposes—and trace some of the parallels and connections between terrorism and organized crime.

ORGANIZED CRIME

We have looked at certain forms of professional, career crime in earlier parts of this stage but we have not discussed what is commonly referred to as 'organized crime'. This can be defined as that form of criminal activity that is organized as a business enterprise through the systematic use of administrative mechanisms, formal coordination, alliances, and joint ventures, and do so in relation to a range of markets for goods and services.

Organized crime is criminal activity that goes beyond the relatively smallscale professional and gang activity considered so far. Like these, it has its roots in the specific subcultures of criminality that comprise the underworld, but it also has quite distinctive causes and conditions. Where organized crime exists, it affects the whole pattern of crime within a society. In this part as suggested, look at the common characteristics of organized crime in the United States, Russia, Japan, and Hong Kong, commonly seen as the foci of 'Mafia' style criminality in the world today.

Mafia and Cosa Nostra

Public recognition of something called the Mafia or Cosa Nostra in the United States dates largely from the 1950s and 1960s, when a series of Senate hearings brought the activities of a number of leading Italian-American criminals to public attention. The most influential model of 'Mafia' organization is that depicted by Donald Cressey, originally produced in association with a Presidential Task Force on organized crime. Cressey presented a picture of a huge national confederation involved in fraud, drugs, prostitution, corruption, gambling, and violence, but also using its funds in conventional business operations such as property, finance, clubs, and restaurants. Its methods had come to parallel those of other business enterprises and it was impossible to disentangle illegal from legal activities and profits. This type of organized crime may never have been quite as tight and centralized as they seemed to the public and as they were portrayed in such films as The Godfather, but it was, in many ways, a distinctive form of criminal activity.

Such organized crime became a prominent feature of major American cities in the 1920s and 1930s. It is often seen as a direct outgrowth of the rural networks of support and control that proliferated in Sicily and other isolated parts of Italian society in the nineteenth century and that were transplanted to the United States by migrants from these areas. These were loose networks of friends and relations, rather than secret societies, and were organized around the 'honour' of family and locality and were involved in a wide range of neighbourhood and regional activities. The true origins of organized crime are more recent and more complex.

It arose in its contemporary form after the great waves of European migration to New York, Chicago, and other American cities and was an outgrowth of the very specific conditions of the 1920s and 1930s. The urban slums gave rise to many loosely organized groups that were rooted in their distinctive subcultures. We have already shown how similar gangs also emerged in districts of London. The emergence of such gangs can be explained by the distinctive subcultures found in lowerclass areas of large cities and the corresponding differential association in which this results.

It depends also, however, on the attractiveness of an 'innovative' response to the anomie found in such areas. The gangs of the major US cities became especially involved in the production and sale of 'bootleg' alcohol, made profitable by the 'Prohibition' legislation of the American state. The central participants in the bootlegging of whiskey were European immigrants and the descendents of immigrants, and both Italians and Sicilians were prominent.

They were actively involved in a range of criminal activities within their neighbourhoods and became drawn into intensive conflict for customers. An alliance of Sicilian and Italian gangs was forged in 1930–31 and came to be known by outsiders as the Mafia. Far from being a direct descendent of the rural neighbourhoods, then, the gang grouping of the 1930s was a new phenomenon and a distinctive product of American society. It is true, nevertheless, that many of the leading figures in the emerging criminal gangs were recent migrants who had fled the clampdown on the Italian mafia by Mussolini's Fascist regime in the late 1920s.

For all these reasons, Cressey rejected the 'mafia' label, holding that it is inaccurate and was not used by the participants themselves. Participants themselves preferred such impersonal terms as the 'organization', 'business', or 'firm', and sometimes 'Cosa Nostra'. The organization existed, Cressey argued, as a federation of separate and autonomous family-based gangs, each of which defended its particular territory and held that it had a legitimate claim on the support of its local population.

In acting 'honourably' towards 'their' people, providing them with the political influence and personal welfare they were denied by the city and national authorities, they earned the respect of people living in their neighbourhoods. This was reinforced by a structure of coercion that ensured that no one in the locality would challenge the right of the gang to monopolize its profitable ventures. Typical of such territorial groups was the Capone Mob of 1930s Chicago. By the 1960s, Cressey argued, there were over thirty such family mobs.

Each family boss—or 'Don'—had absolute authority in his territory. Through a series of cross-cutting alliances designed to protect the territorial claims of each of the gangs, a vast national organization had been built. The Organization itself had no single leader, but was run by a committee of major mobsters known as the 'Commission'. Cressey held that, by the late 1960s, the Organization was dominated by nine powerful families: three from New York, three in the surrounding cities of Buffalo, Newark, and Boston, and one each in Philadelphia, Detroit, and Chicago. The various families recognized the role of the Commission in resolving disputes and coordinating activities at a national level. The criminal activities of a family were typically organized through a hierarchy of executive positions, running from the Don through his deputy and advisers to the 'Buffer', who acts as the interface or intermediary between the senior family members and the lower-level operatives. The Buffer had various 'Lieutenants' responsible for particular operating units, each of which had its to liaise with the 'Soldiers' who actually operate particular activities—money lending, lotteries, vending machine rackets, protection, and so on.

Beyond the level of the Soldiers, numerous non-Italians were employed or contracted for specific purposes at street level to take bets, answer telephones, sell narcotics, collect protection money, and so on. Cressey further claimed that the Organization and its families operated just as to a strict code of behaviour that governs all their activities.

This code comprises five principles:

- *Loyalty*: This is the basic injunction to respect the interests of other families and to keep silent about family activities.
- *Rationality*: This is the requirement to act coolly and calmly in pursuit of the family's business: not to take drugs, not to get into fights, and to follow orders as a good team player.
- *Honour*: This is tied to ideas of masculinity and patriarchalism, involving respect for women and for the senior members of the family.
- *Courage*: Family members are to withstand pressure and punishment without complaint. This is, again, tied to a strong ethos of masculinity.
- *Commitment:* Family members are to uphold their way of life without being drawn into the conventions of regular employment or social conformism.

Joseph Albini has warned that the Organization must be regarded not as a bureaucratic enterprise but as a looseknit system of patron–client or network relationships. As such, its structure is constantly in flux and no rigid model can describe its shape at any particular time. It is clear, nevertheless, that Cressey highlighted the ways in which such a loose-knit structure can coordinate and control the actions of its constituent gangs through both formal and informal mechanisms.

Other Organized Crime

Much discussion of organized crime in the United States has been concerned with that of Italian Americans, but a number of sociologists have pointed to the existence of many other forms of organized crime. Robert Davidson has documented the rise of Asian-American gangs in Chicago and other cities. Those from China, the Philippines, India, Korea, and other parts of Asia now form a significant part of the US population. In a number of areas of Asian settlement, there has been a growth of criminal involvement in drug trafficking, especially the trade in heroin from South East Asia. Organized gangs in American cities use their connections with Chinese triads operating from Hong Kong to obtain heroin for re-sale in the United States.

Actual sales to users are handled by street gangs, but the bulk trade itself is a highly organized business. Outside the United States, evidence for strong organized criminal gangs has been found in Japan, Russia, and other parts of Eastern Europe. Organized crime had begun to develop in the final twenty years of Communism in Russia, when corrupt and self-serving politicians used illegal means to further their own interests, but it was the collapse of Communism that really stimulated its growth.

The disappearance of the strong, totalitarian state in Russia and the consequent privatization of state economic assets allowed many private individuals to amass considerable wealth through dealing in state assts. Many former Communist politicians were able to use their knowledge and connections to build up personal fortunes themselves and to join this emerging Russian 'mafia'. Organized crime has proliferated because of the economic dislocations that followed the ending of Communism, as this allowed the criminal syndicates to obtain and monopolize scarce resources from which they could benefit. Russian organized crime, like its American counterpart, is organized through loose 'syndicates' that operate on the basis of patron–client relationships.

In these relationships, a person of power or wealth helps or protects specific others, who, in return, perform services for their patron. The relationship is not a contractual, employment relationship but rests on informal patterns of trust and obligation. Hierarchies of patron–client relationships form networks of reciprocity and obligation centred on the most powerful individuals.

Those involved in these networks are engaged in a range of illegal activities. Although Russia has virtually no bank robberies, bank fraud is rife and banks pay high levels of protection money to avoid becoming the targets of robberies. Forging of documents is widespread, as is illegal arms trading, including dealing in nuclear materials, prostitution, drug smuggling, money laundering, and illegal imports. Crime is so closely integrated with conventional business that it has been argued that there is a 'shadow economy' of marginal and unregulated business with its 'black market' for distributing goods.

There are high levels of political corruption, giving the criminal syndicates considerable influence over the state. Organized crime in Hong Kong and mainland China originated in the 'triad' secret societies, though it now reaches beyond them. Triads are a long-standing feature of traditional Chinese society and prospered in Hong Kong during its separation from the rest of China. A triad is a family- and neighbourhood-based grouping that provides support and services for its members and organizes its activities on the basis of secrecy and elaborate rituals of membership.

Acting outside, and often against, the central state, triads became involved in a range of legal and illegal activities. Triad activity in Hong Kong grew after the Communist revolution in China, when many prominent leaders were expelled from the mainland. The economic success of Hong Kong since the

1960s provided many opportunities for triads to expand their involvement in prostitution, gambling, and drugs. Thus, while there is continuity between the traditional triads and those of today, systematic involvement in organized crime is a recent and more specific phenomenon. Triads tend to be organized as loose networks of independent gangs that regard themselves as part of a larger 'family' or clan in which there is a decentralized structure of command. The various gangs are loosely ranked as 'Red Pole', 'Blue Lantern', and ordinary. Although they cooperate for common purposes, they are also involved in recurrent and intense conflict over the pursuit of their interests. Organized crime in Japan originated in gambling groups and itinerant dealers who banded together for mutual protection and were given official encouragement to organize markets at shrines and temples and to regulate the supply of labour for public works constriction.

By the early twentieth century, they were a strongly entrenched feature of Japanese society and had come to be known as Yakuza. They were used as government tools for strikebreaking and for fighting left-wing political groups and they had strong links with right-wing political leaders. The Yakuza took their present form, however, after the Second World War. Industrial reconstruction and slow political liberalization created opportunities for profitable enterprise in the black markets and in the supply of labour for construction and dock work.

They moved into the growing entertainment industry of bars, prostitution, and pachinko, and they extended their protection and extortion activities. Intense conflict among Yakuza led to the emergence of a small number of major syndicates, paralleling the structure of business groups that had developed in the conventional economy. Despite a police clamp down in the 1960s, organized crime in Japan remains highly concentrated. Hill has established that there are currently about 90,000 men involved in organized crime in Japan and that about 40 per cent are involved in gangs affiliated to one of the three big syndicates: Yamaguchi-gumi, Iwagawa-kai, and Sumiyoshi-kai. The syndicates have great similarities to Cressey's model of the Cosa Nostra and are organized in ways that draw on the idea of the traditional family household, with its paternalistic and authoritarian patterns of control by the 'father' over junior members. Formal administrative mechanisms are also used, however, and the syndicates are organized into series of ranks such as 'boss', executive, soldier, and trainee.

A Yakuza syndicate and its affiliated groupings are organized in relation to a tight discipline and obedience, embodied in a strict code of behaviour that is enforced, when necessary, through violence. Yakuza are currently involved in protection rackets, the supply of drugs, gambling, the sale of festival trinkets, prostitution, debt collection, loan sharking, rent collection, and the supply of labour through sub-contractors. In many of these areas they act under commission from conventional businesses and public authorities, which rely on the ability of the Yakuza to manage and manipulate their employees, shareholders, and voters through blackmail and coercion.

INTERNATIONAL CRIME

Organized crime, we have suggested, has certain similarities with conventional business activity. Like many businesses, those involved in organized crime have expanded their activities to an international level. Organized criminal gangs in the United States, China, Russia, and elsewhere have been involved in extensive international transactions and have increasingly begun to organize their activities on a global scale. State borders have always provided opportunities for, as well as barriers to, criminal activity.

Within the United States, organized crime has been able to operate under different state jurisdictions, as laws vary from one part of the country to another, and it has been only a small step further to operate across international state borders. Providing goods and services that are legal in one state but illegal in another provides great opportunities for such operations. The smuggling of alcohol and tobacco, because of variations in tax levels, is one example of such international crime that has existed for a very long time. The growing complexity of legal regulations and of the economic and political interdependence of nation states has created the immense opportunities that organized crime groups have been able to exploit. It has been argued that the globalization of the political economy has resulted in a globalization of crime.

Causes and Consequences

The most obvious and important criminal activity is smuggling, and this has always existed alongside and interdependently of legal international trade. The liberalization of international trade, creating global markets and encouraging business enterprises to operate freely and without regard for national borders has created a situation in which smuggling operations come to be seen, almost, as forms of 'free trade' activity. International smugglers can present themselves as providing commodities that market restrictions prevent from flowing freely across the world.

Although smuggling is often thought of in terms of a tourist carrying a few hundred cigarettes or a bottle of whiskey, the scale of smuggling is immense and it is highly organized. It has been estimated that smuggling is a major global business, valued at more than $600 billion a year, especially through money-laundering operations that are closely tied to established banking and financial activities. The transformation of the transport industry with the rise of large container ships and juggernaut lorries, has transformed the methods of smuggling. Previously, drugs such as marijuana and cocaine were smuggled into the United States in small planes and speedboats, but organized criminal groups are now transporting larger consignments in sealed containers alongside conventional cargos.

Containers and sealed lorries are also used to smuggle migrants across national borders. These mechanisms are anonymous and impersonal, making it more difficult for states to trace those responsible. The flow of goods from Mexico to the United States, for example, combines both legal and illegal commodities. Drug traffickers have established factories and distribution centres in northern Mexico and have taken advantage of the deregulated trucking industry to transport their drugs into the United States alongside legitimate trade in fruit and vegetables. Within the European Union, the opening-up of national borders has made it easier for lorries to transport economic migrants, asylum seekers, and drugs into Germany, France, and Britain.

The liberalization of financial markets was intended to promote the transnational flow of capital, but it has also promoted a huge growth in money laundering. This is the process through which the proceeds from illegal activities can be converted into legal—and untraceable—financial assets through the use of multiple international bank accounts and investments in tax havens and other financial centres. This has been particularly important for organized criminal groups from Russia and Colombia. The transformation of the international financial system has also created opportunities for new forms of crime.

The almost exclusive reliance on credit cards for consumer purchases has made the copying of credit cards and the 'skimming' of credit details from them into a major criminal activity. Information from cards skimmed in a London restaurant can be used to produce cards that can, within hours, be used to make purchases in New York, Athens, or Rome. The technology required makes this an obvious area for the involvement of organized criminal groups, which have increased their level of investment in technologies for fraud in the face of the growth on international credit card trading.

Criminal Organizations

The actors involved in international crime are many and diverse. Organized crime groups vary from one country to another, and even within countries. They are not organized in precisely the same way as large-scale business enterprises engaged in conventional activities, but they do have certain common characteristics as international actors and they use many of the same mechanisms as those conventional businesses. Criminal groups from numerous countries extend their international scope and combine with other criminal groups in a number of ways. At its loosest, there may be a recognition of the respective spheres of influence and territories of each group, but these easily give way to mutual supplier relationships that may persist over time. Colombian drug producers, for example, have established stable supply linkages with Italian organized criminal groups, and the latter are given exclusive rights to redistribute the drugs across western Europe. The Russian organized crime groups have established links with organized criminal groups in the Netherlands and Japan for supplying women from Eastern Europe for prostitution.

Such supply relations may involve barter rather than money transactions: guns may be exchanged for drugs, for example. Stronger forms of transnational organization occur when groups form what Williams has called tactical and strategic alliances. Short-term tactical cooperation may lead to longer-term strategic alliances that allow systematic and extensive cooperation. Drug trafficking into the United States, for example, has involved the establishment of strong strategic linkages between Colombian producers and dealers in the Dominican Republic, these links being built as their earlier reliance on Mexican intermediaries became less profitable. Most recently, the Colombian dealers have built strategic alliances with Russian groups to handle distribution through eastern and central Europe.

If there are no transnational bureaucratic criminal organizations, the loose networks do, nevertheless, have certain formal mechanisms of cooperation. It has been reported that summit meetings of major criminal groups have been used to regulate spheres of influence and to plan joint ventures. Although the participants are not, in any sense, representatives or leaders of whole national criminal gangs, the meetings do bring together many of the important criminal groups and bring some stability to international criminal activity. These meetings are complemented by bilateral meetings and by continued contacts through intermediaries. Some criminal groups, it has been suggested, have made such mediation and courier business their main activity. Much discussion has focused on the idea that the Chinese triads of Hong Kong have expanded through the overseas Chinese communities to establish transnational triad organizations.

Hong Kong has been seen as the directing centre for such global criminal activities, and the drive to globalization has been strengthened since the 1997 return of Hong Kong to rule—and strong political control—from Beijing. While Chinese organized criminal groups have certainly established strong links across national borders, there is no global triad structure. Chinese communities are diverse in their ethnicity and there is little basis for dominance by Hong Kong migrants. Chinese criminal gangs have become very active in drug smuggling and people smuggling, but they do so as parts of the larger growth in global criminal activity that has been described.

TERRORISM

Terrorism is political action against a state and its citizens that pursues its goals through extreme violence, often on a spectacular or mass scale, and that is generally criminalized through legislation, proscription, and exclusion. It has become, since the 1960s, one of the most important targets for police and security service operations and it has entered the public consciousness as a major—and perhaps permanent—source of concern at work, in travel, and during leisure.

X-ray and security checks at airports and other public places have become an accepted, if unwelcome, weapon in what many politicians describe as 'the war against terrorism'. Violent political conflict has a history as long as the human species. Its organized form as the internal opposition of political groups to state authorities has a history almost as long. Eric Hobsbawm has termed this 'social banditry' when it takes the form of redistributive political action pursued through violent acts that are criminalized by the state. Social bandits engage in a range of criminal activities in support of their political aims, and their overall political strategy and tactics are labelled as criminal by the state that they attack. In rural societies, social banditry is generated by a sense of grievance and wrong-doing and a desire to secure vengeance and justice. Examples of such social banditry include the idealistic robber of the Robin Hood myth, the guerrilla or resistance fighter, and the violent avengers who terrorize their opponents. Pacification of their societies by industrializing states, especially those that established liberal and democratic structures, greatly reduced the level of social banditry and institutionalized the legitimate and non-violent opposition of political parties.

Even in these societies, however, criminalized forms of political violence could still erupt. Many European governments of the nineteenth century were concerned about the activities of 'anarchists', who were widely seen as motivated by the French revolution. Anarchists were seen as forming secret societies and organizations through which they could plot acts of violence, and a number of bombings and assassinations did take place in this period. The most protracted forms of political violence, however, have been linked with separatist and nationalist claims, as in the Irish Republican Army in the United Kingdom from the late nineteenth century until the establishment of the Republic of Ireland in 1922.

The IRA attacked political or military targets and saw itself as engaged in a war against an imposed state. From the 1960s, these forms of political violence were renewed, but they also began to be transformed as dispossessed groups generated by international conflicts began to take their struggles to the metropolitan and colonial states that they saw as responsible for their oppression.

This was the beginning of that form of violent political conflict described as terrorism. The violent political organizations of the late 1960s and 1970s—groups such as the IRA, the Red Army Faction, the Red Brigade, and ETA—were formed, like the IRA of fifty years earlier, as highly centralized and tightly coordinated organizations with a structure of command modelled on that of conventional armies. Indeed, many used militaristic terminology in their names and in their tactics. They emerged in the political upheavals of the 1960s and saw themselves pursuing radical, leftist policies through violent means because they were unable to pursue their goals through conventional political means.

They often saw themselves as part of an international struggle, though their international links were limited and each group tended to operate on a national basis. Their targets were politicians and businessmen, embassies and banks, and national airlines.

3

Women Trafficking for Sexual Exploitation

CLARIFYING CONCEPTS

This Chapter tries to demystify certain concepts about trafficking which have often been misunderstood and distorted. The clarity of these concepts is essential for proper understanding of the trafficking situations and for taking appropriate response.

TRAFFICKING VS. PROSTITUTION

Trafficking does not mean prostitution. They are not synonymous. In understanding trafficking, one should delink it from prostitution. As per the existing law, Immoral Traffic Act 1956 prostitution becomes an offence when there is commercial exploitation of a person. If a woman or child is sexually exploited and any person gains out of the same, it amounts to commercial sexual exploitation, which is a legally punishable offence wherein the culpability lies against all exploiters.

Trafficking is the process of recruiting, contracting, procuring or hiring a person for CSE. Therefore, trafficking is a process and CSE is the result. The 'demand' in CSE generates, promotes and perpetuates trafficking. This is a vicious cycle. Trafficking could also be a means for other types of violations such as for developing pornographic material, for promoting sex tourism, for sexual exploitation under the facade of bar tending, massage parlours etc, or even for exploitative labour where sexual abuse may or may not coexist. ITPA envisages only trafficking for CSE.

Commercial activity need not be in a brothel, but could also occur in places including a residential dwelling, a vehicle, etc.

Therefore a police officer who is acting under ITPA has powers to take steps in all such situations where trafficking leads to or is likely to lead to CSE in any form, including those under the facade of massage parlours, bar tending, 'tourist circuit', 'escort services', 'friendship clubs', etc.

DEFINING 'TRAFFICKING'

The definition of trafficking can be found in the various sections of ITPA. Section 5 speaks about procuring, taking and even inducing a person for the sake of prostitution. Even attempt to procure and attempt to take or cause a person to carry on prostitution amounts to trafficking. Therefore 'trafficking' has been given a broad scope. A detailed definition of trafficking is available in the Goa Children's Act 2003.

Though it is focused on child trafficking, the definition is comprehensive. Under section 2, "child trafficking" means "the procurement, recruitment, transportation, transfer, harbouring or receipt of persons, legally or illegally, within or across borders, by means of threat or use of force or other forms of coercion, of abduction, of fraud, of deception, of the abuse of power or of a position of vulnerability or of giving or receiving payments or benefits to achieve the consent of a person having control over another person, for monetary gain or otherwise".

The Offence of Trafficking, Essentially, has the Following Ingredients

Displacement of a Person from One Community to Another

The displacement could be from one house to another, one village to another, one district to another, one state to another or from one country to another. Displacement is also possible within the same building. An example will clarify the point.

Presume that the brothel keeper controls several young women who are inmates and that one of the women has a teenage daughter staying with her. If the brothel keeper, by duress or bribe, manages to get the mother to agree to allow the teenager to be used for CSE, the teenager has been moved out of the 'mother's community' and into the 'brothel community'. This displacement is adequate to constitute trafficking.

Exploitation of the Trafficked Person

The ITPA and related laws envisage sexual exploitation of the trafficked person. The process of exploitation may be manifest, as in a brothel, or latent, as in certain massage parlours, dance bars, etc, where it takes place under the facade of a legitimate commercial activity.

Commercialization of Exploitation and Commodification of the Victim

The trafficked victim is exploited as if she is a commodity. The exploiters generate revenue out of the exploitation. They may share a part of the revenue with the victim too. The victim who is getting a share of the money generated is often 'branded' as an accomplice and arrested/charge-sheeted and even convicted.

The trafficked victim, whose freedom even to think, let alone move out, is dictated by the exploiters, should never be treated as an accomplice. Even if she gets a share of the 'earnings', the fact that she has been trafficked to CSE does not alter her status as a victim.

THE ORGANIZED CRIME OF TRAFFICKING

Human trafficking is a crime of crimes. It is a basket of crimes. In this basket one can dig out the elements of abduction, kidnapping, illegal detainment, illegal confinement, criminal intimidation, hurt, grievous hurt, sexual assault, outraging modesty, rape, unnatural offences, selling and buying of human beings, servitude, criminal conspiracy, abetment etc. Therefore, multiple abuse and abusers located at different points of time and place together constitute the organized crime of trafficking. A host of human rights violations like denial of privacy, denial of justice, denial of access to justice, deprivation of basis rights and dignity etc constitute other part of the exploitation. Therefore, there is no doubt that trafficking is an organized crime.

THE TRAFFICKED PERSON

In the context of ITPA and related laws, a trafficked person could be a male or a female of any age who has been trafficked for CSE in a brothel or any place where CSE takes place. ITPA provides punishment even for attempt to traffic a person. Therefore, even before the person is physically trafficked, the law comes into operation.

CHILD

Child is a person who has not attained the age of 18 years. Any child who is vulnerable to trafficking is considered a "person in need of care and protection" under the Juvenile Justice Act, 2000.

Law enforcement agencies are duty bound to rescue such children, produce them before the Child Welfare Committee and extend all care and attention.

TRAFFICKED ADULT

Regarding adults, the mere consent of the person does not exclude the possibility of trafficking. If the consent was obtained under duress, coercion, fear or any pressure, then the consent has no meaning and, therefore, all such instances amount to trafficking. Thus, even when an adult woman is 'picked up' from a brothel on the charge of 'soliciting', it cannot be presumed that she is guilty of soliciting unless and until the 'mens rea' is investigated. A woman trafficked for CSE is a victim of CSE and not an accused.

TRAFFICKERS AND OTHER EXPLOITERS

Trafficking is an organized crime. There are several persons involved at several places, starting with place of recruitment, places of transit and places of exploitation.

Therefore, the list of exploiters includes the following:

- The brothel in charge and other exploiters in the brothel, or the final place of exploitation, which would also include:
  - The brothel "madam" or the person in charge of the 'dance bar' or 'massage parlour' or such other place where exploitation takes place.
  - The 'managers' and all other dramatis personae in such places.
  - The hoteliers or persons in charge of hotels, etc where exploitation takes place. This includes keepers of places/vehicles used as a brothel, persons who allow premises to be used as a brothel, persons who detain victims in brothels and other places of exploitation, and those who allow public places to be used for prostitution.
- The "customer" or "clientele", who is the abuser of the trafficked woman, is undoubtedly, an exploiter. He is the one who perpetuates 'demand' and CSE and is, therefore liable under ITPA and other laws..
- *The financiers*: All those who finance the various processes involved in trafficking are part of the nexus. This may include those who finance recruitment, transportation, stay, accommodation, and even those who indulge in money lending and borrowing at the brothels.
- *The abettors*: All those who abet or support the exploitation or any process involved in trafficking are triable under ITPA.
- *Those who are living on the earnings of CSE*: Any person who knowingly lives, wholly or partly, on the earnings of prostitution is liable. This includes all those who have a share in the illegal benefits derived from the exploitation. The financiers who lend or collect money from the brothels and do business out of such transaction are also liable under this part. The hotelier who profits from the exploitation of girls is undoubtedly an accused u/s 4 ITPA.

- The spotter, the recruiter, the seller, the purchaser, the contractor, the agent or anybody acting on their behalf.
- The transporters, the harbourers and those who provide shelter are also part of the racket.

- *All conspirators*: In nearly all trafficking situations, several persons conspire at the various stages involved in the process of exploitation, thereby constituting a case of conspiracy. If there is a meeting of minds, followed by an overt act in pursuance thereof, the law of conspiracy is attracted. The ITPA, those who conspire to allow any premises to be used as a brothel or those who live on the earnings of exploitation, even partly, or those who procure or induce or take the person for prostitution are all considered conspirators.

Therefore, the list of exploiters and abusers is inevitably long, undulated and not always apparent at first glance. Only professional investigation can expose the linkages involved and bring all such persons to book.

CRIMINAL ACTS AND RIGHTS VIOLATIONS ON THE TRAFFICKED PERSONS

In the existing scenario, trafficking is usually confused with prostitution and therefore, there is no proper understanding of the seriousness of trafficking. It would be appropriate here to list out the wrongs, violations, harms and crimes that are committed by various persons on a trafficked victim.

These violations can be realised only during a careful interview of a trafficked person. Once the victim is allowed, facilitated and promoted to speak, the unheard story will reveal a long list of violating acts perpetrated on her. As a typical example, under the Indian Penal Code, a trafficked girl child has been subjected to a multitude of violations.

She has been:

- Displaced from her community, which tantamounts to kidnapping/abduction

- Procured illegally.
- Sold by somebody
- Bought by somebody
- Imported from a foreign country
- Wrongfully restrained
- Wrongfully confined
- Physically tortured/injured
- Subjected to criminal force
- Mentally tortured/harassed/assaulted
- Criminally intimidated
- Outraged of her modesty
- Raped/gang raped/repeatedly raped
- Subjected to perverse sexual exploitation
- Defamed
- Subjected to unlawful compulsory labour
- Victim of criminal conspiracy

This list is only illustrative and not exhaustive. Undoubtedly, in every case, the trafficked person is a victim of at least one or more of the violations. Oftentimes victims become pregnant as they are subjected to non-protective sex. If the victim has been subjected to miscarriage then the liability of the offender falls under the Sections 312 to 318 IPC.

In some cases, the process of exploitation has proven fatal wherein the victim succumbs to the direct effects of the harm or to the consequential problems arising thereof. This means that the offence of homicide/murder is also attracted. The offences envisaged under the ITPA are specific to the context of CSE.

They are briefly listed out below:

- Keeping or managing a brothel or allowing premises to be used as a brothel
- Living on earnings of prostitution.
- Procuring, inducing, trafficking or taking persons for the sake of prostitution. Even attempt to procure or take would constitute the offence.
- Detaining a person in any premises where prostitution is carried out
- Anybody who carries on prostitution, or anybody

with whom such prostitution is carried on, in the vicinity of public places

- Seducing or soliciting for the purpose of prostitution in any public place or within sight of a public place
- Seduction of a person in custody.

The Juvenile Justice Act, 2000 also has penal provisions. Anybody in control of a child who assaults, abandons, exposes or willfully neglects the child or procures him to be assaulted, abandoned or exposed causing the child unnecessary mental or physical suffering, is liable under S. 23 JJ Act There are so many Human Rights violations that take place on trafficked person.

The list includes the following:

- Deprivation of the right to life.
- Deprivation of the right to security.
- Deprivation of dignity.
- Deprivation of the right to access to justice and redressal of grievances.
- Denial of access to health services.
- Denial of right to self determination.
- Denial of right to return to own community.
- Double jeopardy.
- Denial of right to representation.
- Denial of right to be heard before decision making.

The list of rights violations is long and several such violations can be listed out depending on the provisions of the Constitution/Protocols/Conventions etc.

WHICH LAW TO USE AND WHEN

ITPA, being a special legislation, has comprehensive, stringent and effective provisions to address the issues in trafficking and consequent exploitation. However, there is no bar in utilizing the provisions of ITPA along with IPC etc.

In any given context, the investigating police officer should file charge-sheet against the accused under the graver parts of all laws which are applicable. Do not hesitate to involve the provisions of ITPA along with IPC, JJ Act, and other legislations which would apply to the facts and circumstances of the case under investigation. One has to be careful in applying proper sections of law. Never victimize a trafficked woman u/s 8 ITPA or any other section of any law. When investigation brings home the point that she has been sexually exploited against her informed consent, charge sheet be filed against all her exploiters not only under ITPA, but also under the relevant sections of IPC, dealing with sexual assault. Consent obtained under lure, deceit, duress, coercion, compulsion, force etc is not 'consent' in the legal sense. Furthermore, if the victim is a girl child, the offence is complete even if there was consent.

THE STRENGTHS OF ITPA AND HOW BEST TO USE THEM

ITPA is a comprehensive legislation which gives power and strength to the law enforcement/justice delivery agencies to combat and prevent trafficking. Since its enactment in 1956, the legislation was amended by the Indian Parliament twice, in 1978 and 1986. The latter amendment focused on prevention, a provision which is not so common in the legal regime across the world.

However, for various reasons, the different provisions of this special law are not being used and, furthermore are often misused and abused. One of the main reasons, as research has shown, is ignorance and lack of understanding of these provisions.

Therefore this checklist is a reference guide to the law enforcement agencies and other stake-holders, providing answers to several frequently asked questions and frequently overlooked aspects.

THE LEGAL REGIME RELEVANT IN THE CONTEXT OF TRAFFICKING

- Immoral Traffic Act, 1956.
- The Juvenile Justice Act, 2000.
- The Goa Children's Act, 2003.
- The Indian Penal Code, 1860.
- Procedural laws.

- Preventive Sections of CrPC.
- Other special laws relevant to the context.

THE INHERENT STRENGTHS OF ITPA

General Provisions

- The law applies to trafficking of males and females.
- Commercial sexual exploitation of anybody is an offence.
- The law gives specific attention to women's rights and child rights.
- The law provides a specific mandate for NGO's and civil society in addressing trafficking. Perhaps there is no parallel where NGOs have been given powers in law enforcement on anti human trafficking.
- The thrust of the law is addressing trafficking and not prostitution, as is often misunderstood.
- This legislation gives specific powers to judicial magistrates and also to executive magistrates.
- This legislation gives special protection to the police officers and NGOs taking part in search, rescue etc from any criminal or civil proceedings against them.

The Offences Under ITPA

- *S.3 ITPA*: Keeping or managing a brothel or allowing premises including vehicles to be used as a brothel.
- *S.4 ITPA*: Living on the earnings of prostitution.
- *S. 5 ITPA*: Procuring, inducing, trafficking or taking persons for the sake of prostitution. Even attempt to procure or take would constitute this offence.
- *S.6 ITPA*: Detaining a person in any premises where prostitution is carried out.
- *S.7 ITPA*: Any body who carries on prostitution, or any body with whom such prostitution is carried on, in the vicinity of public places.
- *S.8 ITPA*: Seducing or soliciting for the purpose of prostitution in any public place or within sight of a public place.
- *S.9 ITPA*: Seduction of a person in custody.

Whether "Clientele" is Liable

The answer is yes. Firstly, he should be booked u/s 5(1)(d) and u/s 7(1) ITPA. He is a person who 'causes' or 'induces' another person to carry on prostitution and is, therefore, liable u/s 5(1)(d).

Moreover he is a person "with whom prostitution is carried on" and is therefore liable u/s 7(1). Further subsection IA of section 7 ITPA makes it clear that if the offence of 'prostitution' is committed in respect to a child or minor then the person committing the offence is liable for a graver punishment and fine with a mandatory minimum imprisonment of 7 years.

Besides these provisions of ITPA, he is an abettor to all violations on the victim, which attracts S.114 IPC. If the victim is a child, S.376 IPC should be added to the charges against the "customer". If the victim is an adult, S.376 IPC will come into operation if it can be established that she had not given informed or willing consent. Moreover perverse sexual acts on the victim invite liability under S.377 IPC.

Liability of Traffickers

U/S 5 ITPA, trafficking committed, contemplated or even attempted is punishable, regardless of consent of the trafficked person. The modus operandi could include procuring, attempting to procure, inducing, taking, attempting to take, causing a person to be taken, causing or inducing a person to prostitute etc.

If the offence of trafficking is committed against the will of the person, then the offender is liable for graver punishment. If the trafficked victim is a child, the minimum punishment is 7 years of rigorous imprisonment. Depending on the facts and circumstances of the case, the traffickers are also liable u/s 4, 6, 9 ITPA. Moreover as abettors and/or conspirators they are also liable under IPC.

Jurisdiction of Police and Courts

In which police station can a trafficking offence be registered? Which Court has jurisdiction? Trafficking is a 'continuing offence' and therefore may be tried in either of the following places:

- The place from where the person has been procured, induced to go, taken or caused to be taken or from where an attempt to procure or take the person is made. This means the place where trafficking took place *i.e,* the source point.
- At the place to which the person may have gone as a result of the inducement or to which he is taken or caused to be taken or an attempt to take him is made. This means the destination point or the point of exploitation and the transit points where the exploitation continues.

Since the court of law has jurisdiction in the source, transit and the destination points, the police stations in all these points also have jurisdiction. In this context, the following are the do's and dont's.

- In a case of trafficking, police agencies at the source point, the transit point and at the destination point have a duty and responsibility to register FIR in their police station.
- There is no legal bar in having FIRs registered both at the source point and destination point if the former is only on charge of trafficking and the latter is only on the charge of sexual exploitation. However, the best situation would be to have the FIR at one of the two places and, thereafter, the investigation should cover the entire spectrum of the offences from its origin to the last part.
- In the event of registration of two FIRs at both the source and destination points, the investigation can be clubbed together, as and when the linkage is established in evidence. Thereafter, police is free to file a charge report before the court of law at either place and simultaneously close the investigation in the other place, so as to avoid double jeopardy.
- Since attempt to trafficking is also a specific offence under this section, it gives very strong weapon to

the law enforcement agencies to bring to book the traffickers as well as abettors and conspirators in trafficking.

Law of double jeopardy will not be attracted if the offences alleged are independently acted upon. For *e.g.*, there is no legal wrong if the FIR in one place is u/s 5 ITPA for trafficking and the FIR in another place is for exploitation u/s 7 ITPA, 376 IPC etc, both with respect to the same victim.

The Doctrine of Presumption As a Good Weapon for Preventing and Combating Trafficking

ITPA gives so much strength to the law enforcement agencies by virtue of the fact that the specific provisions of presumption casts onus of proof on the accused. The following are the provisions.

- Section 3 provides punishment for keeping a brothel or allowing premises to be used as a brothel. It shall be presumed, u/s 3 (2A), that the concerned person has knowledge of the same if:
  - A report is published in a newspaper with local circulation that the premises concerned are being used for prostitution, as revealed during a search.
  - A copy of the search list is made available to the person concerned.
- If any person A, over 18 years of age, is proved to have exercised control, direction or influence over the movements of another person B, in such a manner as to show that A is aiding, abetting or compelling B to prostitute, it shall be presumed that A is knowingly living on the earnings of prostitution of another person and is liable u/s 4 ITPA.
- If a person is found with a child in a brothel, it will be presumed that the person has detained the child for CSE and is, therefore, liable for the same u/s 6(2) ITPA.
- If the medical examination shows that the child, who has been detained in a brothel, was sexually assaulted, it will be presumed u/s 6 (2A) ITPA that

the child was detained for CSE and was sexually exploited. This legal presumption is a good tool to establish liability of the person.

- S.6 (3) ITPA, a person shall be presumed to have detained a woman or girl (of any age) in a brothel or upon any premises for CSE, if the person withholds from her any of her property with intent to compel/induce her to remain there. He is also liable if he threatens her with action if she takes away any such property lent/supplied to her by, or on the direction of, such a person.

CSE of Child/Minor

Law views CSE of children/minors as a grave offence and therefore, has the following special provisions u/s 7 ITPA:

- Consent is immaterial.
- Enhanced punishment for prostituting a child/minor.
- Minimum punishment is rigorous imprisonment for 7 years.
- Mandatory fine along with jail.
- If sexual exploitation of a child takes place in a Hotel, the hotel license can be cancelled..

Who can Order Rescue of a Trafficked Person

S.16 ITPA authorizes rescue of any person who is made to carry on prostitution in a brothel. The powers are given to both Judicial Magistrates and Executive Magistrates. Therefore, any of these officials may be moved for an order for the rescue of any such person. The Magistrate can order rescue of any person if he has reason to believe that any person is carrying on or is being made to carry on prostitution in a brothel. S.15 ITPA gives powers to Special Police Officers to search without warrant and carry out rescue u/s 15(4). This gives enormous powers to SPO.

Can Any Civilian Move the Magistrate and Seek Orders for Rescue of Any Person

The answer is yes. u/s 16, the Magistrate has powers to

direct any police officer to rescue any person if the Magistrate has reason to believe that the rescue is required.

The source of information for the Magistrate could be government agencies or otherwise and, therefore, it includes any of the following:

- Police
- Any person authorized by the State Government
- Any NGO
- Any other source

If a Notified Police Officer is Not Available, is Rescue Possible

Yes u/s 16 ITPA, the Magistrate can authorize any police officer provided the police officer is of the rank of SI of police.

How to Prevent/Combat Misuse of Public Places

The legal provisions u/s 7 ITPA envisage a very important role of law enforcement agencies in not only taking action against the offenders who misuse public places, but also in preventing such misuse. In this context, the following aspects be taken note of.

What is a Public Place

Public place, u/s 7 ITPA, includes the following:

- Any premises within an area notified by the Government.
- Any premises within a distance of 200 metres of any place of public worship, educational institution, hotel, hospital, nursing home or other official/public domain.
- Any hotel.
- Any transport or vehicle to which public has access.
- "Any place intended for use by, or accessible to the public" is a public place. "It is not necessary that it must be public property", "Even if it is a private property, it is sufficient that the place is accessible to public". Gaurav Jain vs UOI, AIR 1997 SC 3021.

Can a Hotel Licence Be Suspended if Prostitution is Carried on in the Hotel

Yes, u/s 7(2) (c) ITPA, if the public place which is misused happens to be a hotel, the hotel licence may be suspended for a period not less than 3 months and may be extended to one year. Therefore in such circumstances, the police officer should move the concerned court for the suspension of the hotel licence.

Can the Hotel Licence be Cancelled

Yes, u/s 7(2) (c)ITPA, if it can be proved that the victim of prostitution or CSE in the hotel happens to be a child or minor, then the hotel licence is liable to be cancelled. The police officer has to move the court of the District Magistrate for the same.

Who are All Liable for Misuse of Public Places

U/s 7 ITPA, the persons liable are:

- Any person who carries on prostitution.
- Any person with whom such prostitution is carried on.
- Any keeper of a public place who permits such misuse.
- Any tenant, lessee, occupier or person in charge of any premises who permits the place or part thereof for misuse.
- Any owner, lesser, landlord of any such place, or their agents, who lets the place or part thereof for misuse or is willfully a party to the same.

Closure and Eviction of Brothels After Notice

- The District Magistrate u/s 18(1) ITPA, can act on information from police or NGO or anybody else. The Commissioner of Police or any other official who has been vested with the powers of DM is also empowered to take action under this section of law.
- The information should be that any house, room, place or portion thereof, located within a distance of 200 metres of any public place is being used as a

brothel by any person, or is being used for commercial sexual exploitation of anybody.

- DM can issue notice to the owner, lesser, landlord or their agent, as well as the tenant, lessee, occupier of, or any other person in charge of such house, room, place or portion thereof.
- The notice sent to them by the DM directs that show cause be filed within 7 days of the receipt of the notice stating why the property should not be attached for misuse.
- The DM should hear the party before taking a decision.
- After hearing, if the DM is satisfied about the misuse, he can direct eviction of the occupier within 7 days of the order and direct that prior approval of the DM be obtained before letting out the place again during the following one year.
- The order of the DM is non appealable nor stayable as per S. 18(3) ITPA.
- Since closure of brothel would entail loss of 'income' for the exploiters, and no relief is available by way of appeal, this is a stringent section of law which the administrators, police, prosecutors and NGO's can effectively utilize to combat and prevent trafficking.
- The Sub Divisional Magistrate (SDM) also can exercise all these powers.

Closure and Eviction of Brothels Without Notice

S.18 (2) ITPA, the court convicting a person of any offence under S.3 ITPA or S.7 ITPA, may pass orders of closure and eviction without any notice to any such person. Therefore in the event of a conviction u/s 3 or 7 ITPA, the police/prosecutor should immediately move the court for closure/eviction u/s 18 ITPA. However, the eviction order of the judicial magistrate is a sequel to the conviction of the person to be evicted, and cannot preceed conviction

No Appeal Against Order of Closure/Eviction

S. 18 (3) ITPA, orders passed by the DM u/s 18(1)ITPA

and orders by the convicting court u/s 18(2)ITPA shall not be subject to appeal and shall not be stayed or set aside by any court, civil or criminal. Therefore, the finality of order by a competent court is a very powerful tool to combat CSE.

Special Provisions Against CSE of Child (Under 16) and Minor (Under 18)

Anybody involved in CSE of a child/minor is liable for conviction for a minimum term of 7 years imprisonment which may go upto life imprisonment, u/s 7(1A).

- In such convictions, along with imprisonment, fine is also mandatory.
- If the abuse takes place in a hotel, and the victim is a child or minor, the hotel license shall be liable to be cancelled u/s 7(2) (c) ITPA.

Surveillance of Convicted Persons

S. 11 ITPA, any person, who has earlier been convicted under ITPA or relevant sections of IPC is again convicted under ITPA, for a period of 2 years or more, may be subjected by the court to notify, just as to the rules made by the State Government in this regard, of any change of his residence or any absence from such residence after release, for a period upto 5 years.

If the State rules exist, this is a potent weapon for the law enforcing agencies to keep surveillance on the movement and activity of the convicted person so as to prevent any such crime in future. If there are no rules, the state government be moved for bringing out comprehensive Rules under ITPA.

Externment of Convicted Persons

S. 20 ITPA, the District Magistrate, Sub-Divisional Magistrate, or an Executive Magistrate authorized by the State Govt, has power to extern a convicted person to another place within or outside the limits of his jurisdiction. This is a powerful weapon against convicted exploiters so that they are prevented from carrying on further exploitation. The police has to move the concerned Magistrate immediately after conviction so that the Magistrate can start the externment proceedings.

Finality of Proceedings and Fast-Track Mechanisms

ITPA is a special legislation which has certain inherent provisions to ensure that the legal proceedings are not long drawn.

These provisions and restrictions are meant to be invoked by the agencies concerned so that the trial is expedited and justice is delivered without delay.

The following are the provisions:

- U/s 18 ITPA, there is neither appeal nor stay against the order of eviction by a Magistrate or Court.
- Any appeal against the order for protective custody u/s 17 (4) ITPA, issued by the Magistrate shall go to the Court of Sessions, whose decision shall be final. Therefore, there is no appeal beyond the Sessions Court.
- Special Courts for the trial of offences under ITPA can be constituted not only by State Government but also by the Central Government.
- *Summary Trial*: Whenever necessary, the State Government may authorize the Court to try cases summarily. However, the maximum punishment in Summary Trial is up to 1 year. If the Court thinks that enhanced punishment is called for, then the case can be reverted to regular trial.

Special Police Officer of the State Government

U/s 13 (1) ITPA the State Government can notify one or more police officers, not below the rank of Inspector of Police, as SPO having powers over a specific jurisdiction, which may include the entire state.

Since many trafficking cases have inter-district and even inter-state ramifications, it is better to issue such notifications, without jurisdictional restrictions. The jurisdiction of the SPO is to be at least co-terminus with "that of the offender" so that the SPO can carry out unrestricted investigation.

Shortage of Police Officers in the District, is There any Mechanism Overcome the Situation in Addressing Trafficking

Yes, S.13 (2A) ITPA authorizes the District Magistrate to notify any retired police officer or any retired military officer as SPO.It is advisable that the Superintendent of Police identifies appropriate retired officials and moves the DM for notification.

Is Women Police Officer Essential

U/s 13(3) (a) ITPA, the SPO notified by the State government shall be assisted by an adequate number of Subordinate Police Officers including women police officers, wherever practicable. The best situation would be to notify a combination of male and female police officers for each unit. Wherever women police officers of the rank of Inspector or above are available, they should be notified as SPO.If woman police official is not available, the SPO should take assistance of woman NGO/social worker.

Can Government of India Notify Special Police Officers Under ITPA

U/s 13(3) (4) ITPA, Govt. of India can notify Anti-trafficking police officers with powers throughout India.

Such ATPO can be appointed for investigating offences:

- Under ITPA
- Under any law dealing with sexual exploitation of persons committed in more than one State. Therefore, a notified ATPO will have powers to investigate, crimes relating to not only trafficking but also other such crimes, relating to pornographic rackets, 'sale' and 'purchase' of women etc., which have inter-state and international ramifications.

The Government of India has appointed officers of and above the rank of Inspector of Police in CBI as Trafficking Police Officers having jurisdiction throughout India to investigate any offence under ITPA or any other law dealing with sexual exploitation of persons committed in more than one State.

How to Invoke CBI Investigation

Since CBI derives its strength under the DSPE Act, and since law and order is a 'State subject' under the Constitution of India, the State Govt has to issue notification u/s 6 DSPE Act authorizing CBI to take over such crimes. This is to be followed by a notification of Govt. of India u/s 5 DSPE Act, extending the powers of CBI to carry out the task.

Therefore, despite the notification dated 28 August 2001 by the Govt. of India, CBI takes over investigation of a crime of trafficking when the State Police, having original jurisdiction over the case, hands over the case file to CBI. However, if there is an order by the Supreme Court or any High Court, directing CBI to take over such a case, CBI cannot and will not wait for the notifications by the Govt. Often such directions of the High Court or the Apex Court arise out of Public Interest Litigation.

Role of NGOs in Law Enforcement and Justice Delivery Under ITPA

ITPA is a social legislation which envisages a large role for NGOs/CBOs and social workers.

The following are noteworthy:

- *Advisory Body*: The State Govt. may notify, u/s 13(3) (b) ITPA, a nonofficial advisory body of leading social workers including women social workers. This body has powers to advise the SPO on questions of general importance, regarding the working of ITPA. Therefore, this body can advise and facilitate the police to carry out rescue, ensure that the rights of rescued persons are protected initiate steps for victims' best care and attention, keeping in view victims' best interests, take steps for empowerment and rehabilitation of victims take steps for stringent action against traffickers and other exploiters and initiate and implement steps for prevention of trafficking and network with all concerned government and non government agencies.
- *Accompanying Police during search*: The SPO while carrying out search for victims or even accused

persons should arrange two or more respectable persons of the locality (one of whom should be a woman, as provided u/s 15(2) ITPA to attend and witness the searches. NGOs are the appropriate agencies to be contacted by police in such situations. The male witness should be from the locality, whereas the female witness could be from any where, vide proviso to S.15 (2) ITPA. It would be better to take a lady social activist along. Police officials should maintain a list (ready reckoner) of women activists and NGO's, whose services can be called upon in such situations.This section gives a legal right to NGOs to be part of the rescue process.

- *Interviewing rescued/removed persons*: U/s 15(6A) ITPA, any female person rescued or removed during a search can be interviewed by the police officer only in the presence of a female police officer or a female member of NGO.This gives a legal right to NGOs to be part of the investigation process.
- *Home verification of rescued persons*: A mandatory duty is cast upon the Magistrate u/s 17(2) ITPA to cause home verification of the rescued person before taking a final decision regarding her rehabilitation. Direction is to be given to the Probation Officer. The Magistrate can call upon NGOs to carry out the task. Even the Probation Officer who has been tasked for the same can, in turn, entrust the job to NGOs. This gives a legal right to NGOs to be part of the rehabilitation process.
- *NGOs to advise Magistrate on rehabilitation*: The Magistrate may, as provided u/s 17(5) ITPA. Summon a panel of five respectable persons, three of whom shall be women, to assist him in taking decision in home verification and rehabilitation of the rescued person. It would be better that the Magistrate is provided with a list of NGOs who are working in the field so that their services can be utilized at the appropriate time. This section also gives a legal right

to NGOs to be part of the justice delivery process and an opportunity to ensure that the processes confirm to the principles of human rights and the decisions are in the best interest of the rescued person.

Witness Refuse to Cooperate with Police in Search and Rescue

As per S.15 (3) ITPA, any person who, without reasonable cause, refuses or neglects, to attend and witness a search when called upon to do so by an order in writing, delivered or tendered to him, shall be deemed to have committed an offence u/s 187 IPC. Though, it is a non-cognizable and bailable offence, it entails punishment upto 6 months imprisonment and fine.

Carry Out Home Verification of the Rescued Persons

As per the mandatory requirements u/s 17(2) ITPA, Home verification of the rescued person needs to be carried out. The points of verification include the correctness of age, character and antecedents, the suitability of the parents/guardian/husband for taking charge of the person, the nature of the influence which the condition in the home is likely to have on the person if she is sent home, the personality of the person and the prospects of rehabilitation u/s 17(5) ITPA.

Since the task of verification can be entrusted to NGO's, the law enforcement officials need to network with appropriate NGO's and bring to the notice of the Magistrate the name, address and other details of the NGO's. Once the task is assigned to the NGO's, it needs to be facilitated and followed up so that the verification is expedited. Objectivity is called for in the process of verification.

The verifying authority should consult the victim, her well-wishers, friends, parents, guardians, neighbours and all persons who can share information. There are instances where the guardians themselves have indulged in trafficking. Therefore extreme care is called for in arriving at conclusions.

Protection and Safety for Police Officers and NGO's against Litigation

S. 15(6) ITPA provides a safety clause for bonafide work.

The authorized police officer, the witnesses, and the NGOs who take part, attend, or witness a search shall not be liable to any litigation, civil or criminal proceedings, against them for any bonafide work in connection with or for purposes of the search being carried out u/s 15 ITPA.

POLICE RESPONSE TO TRAFFICKING IN WOMEN AND CHILDREN: DO'S AND DON'TS

RESCUE: DO'S AND DON'TS

- Special police officer can search without warrant u/s 15 ITPA and carry out rescue. Therefore the SPO is free to act on his own and promptly.
- The Magistrate can authorize any police officer u/s 16 ITPA to rescue anybody any time. If SPO has not been notified, the available police officer should feel empowered under this provision. He/she should go to the Magistrate, get orders and then move for rescue.
- Do not delay rescue at any cost. Delay denies justice delivery and also exacerbates exploitation. Do gather intelligence and act in time.
- Information source for rescue could be anybody, although NGOs play a significant role.
- Magistrate can take cognizance of report by anybody including NGO.
- Magistrate can be anybody from the categories of JM/MM/SDM/DM having jurisdiction over the area.
- The search/rescue party should have two women police officers as required u/s 15(6A). Maintain a list of WPOs residing in the jurisdiction of the PS, neighbouring PS and other nearby locations. If there is shortage of WPO, get retired WPO notified as SPO u/s 13 (2 A) ITPA.
- Two respectable persons are required as witnesses during search and one of them shall be a women u/s 15(2) ITPA. Utilize the services of local NGO's. Do network with NGO's in the area.

- Interview of rescued person should be done only in presence of or by WPO or woman from an NGO, as per Section u/s 15 (6A) ITPA. Maintain list of NGO's in the P.S.
- Rescued persons are to be produced before the Magistrate forthwith.
- Keep the victims segregated from the accused and suspects, so that they do not intimidate or violate the rights of the victims.
- Rights of rescued persons are to be ensured during rescue and post rescue situations.

This includes the following:

- Facilitate the rescued person to carry along with her all her possessions like clothes, money, jewellery, etc.
- If the rescued person has children, they should be allowed to accompany her. Extra care should be taken to see that the children are not left behind in the brothel.
- One should be careful in the use of language/ gestures/demeanors. They should not be abusive or intimidatory and should no way violate her rights.
- Avoid publicity of the victims so that anonymity is maintained.
- Carry out a brief interview of the victims at the place of rescue to know their age and to locate their assets and possessions. One or two officials should be earmarked exclusively for this purpose.
- Ensure proper handing over of victim's possessions to her at the appropriate place and time.
- Provide counselors for trauma counseling. Keep a list of NGOs and trained counselors who are willing to work in this field.
- Legal counseling be provided to the victim. Keep a list of lawyers willing to work for the victims.

  - Immediate medical relief be provided. Medical relief should include mental health as well. As per s.15(5A) ITPA, the Magistrate has to order medical examination for –
    (a) Age determination
    (b) Injuries
    (c) Sexual assault
    (d) Presence of STD
- Children are to be dealt under JJ Act. Therefore, while rescue is going on, please do segregate the children from the adult victims and proceed with them under JJ Act. They are children in need of care and attention and, therefore, are to be handled by the Child Welfare Committee set up under the JJ Act.
- The police officers need to know before hand as to where the Rescue Home is available. If there is a need for such Homes, it should be taken up with the concerned authorities. Of late many NGO's have set up such Homes. Keep a list of their address, telephone, contact person, etc.
- As and when the rescue is done, please notify the authorities of the concerned Home regarding the number of persons going to be lodged so that they could be prepared to receive them and organize themselves.
- Rescue Party should have adequate number of vehicles so that the rescued persons could be transported without publicity and glare. Accused and suspected persons should never be allowed to mix up with the rescued persons.
- Search and seizure of all material evidence, including documents in the brothel, is an important job. This should be done at the first available opportunity so that evidence is not destroyed or made to disappear by anybody, especially the exploiters.
- Training of police officials on victim protocols is a pre-requirement to see that they are aware and sensitized to the issues concerned.

- Ensure accountability of all the officials taking part in the rescue. Brief them well in advance on all the points and ensure compliance. Accountability demands appreciation of good work as well as condemnation of all wrong-doings, including acts of omission and commission. Utilize the services of reputed NGOs, as independent agency, to understand and assess how things are and were during the search so that appropriate steps could be taken accordingly.

POST RESCUE: DO'S AND DON'TS

- Interview the rescued persons to know about their personal details like age, nativity, health status, family history, etc and also to identify their best interests so that actions can be oriented accordingly. Interview is essential in the investigative process to identify the traffickers and other exploiters so that they can be brought to book. NGOs and trained counselors are useful in de-traumatizing the person and helping in ice breaking so that the police officials can carry on with the interview. Interview must be carried out by a female police officer or in the presence of a female NGO worker as mandated u/s 15(6A) ITPA.
- There can be one or more statements u/s 161 and 164 CrPC. Hence do record statements as the story unfolds and when the victim is comfortable to speak, especially after counselling.
- Do not delay production of the rescued persons before the Magistrate.
- SPO can produce the rescued person before any Magistrate.
- Intermediate custody can be obtained for a period not exceeding 10 days by which time the person has to be produced before the appropriate Magistrate.
- Rescued children should be produced before the Child Welfare Committee constituted under the JJ Act.

- During the pendency of verification the person can be kept in a recognized rehab institution after obtaining orders from the Magistrate concerned.
- Home verification is to be done by Probationary Officer, who can utilize services of NGOs.
- Suitability of the rehabilitation home should be verified before the person is lodged.
- Magistrate may utilize the services of five NGOs for home verification and also consult with them in the process of decision making u/s 17(5) ITPA.
- For trauma counseling of victims, it is ideal to utilize the services of NGOs. A list of such volunteers/NGOs, who have specialization in this field, be maintained at the police station. The Family Counseling Centres available at certain police stations in certain states have trained counselors whose services can be utilized.
- For legal counseling, networking with lawyers/NGOs is advisable. A list of willing lawyers should be maintained at the police station. Contact Bar Council and District Legal Services Authority for the same.
- Medical care and attention should be provided immediately after rescue. Also make arrangements for expert care, if required. Besides specialist doctors in hospitals, Medical Associations can be contacted for such services.
- Network with appropriate agencies for rehabilitative steps.

Can an Adult Person be Sent to Protective Custody

The answer is yes. S. 17 ITPA applies to children and adults. If the inquiry reveals that the person, irrespective of age, is in need of care and attention, the Magistrate, as provided u/s 17(4) ITPA, should direct protective custody in a protective home.

REGISTERING THE CRIME (FIR) AT THE POLICE STATION (PS): DO'S AND DON'TS

- There should not be any delay in registering FIR.

- The FIR has to be on the statement of the complainant. The statement cannot be altered or amended by the police. If the complainant is the victim herself, she may be traumatized and, therefore, may not be able to recall the events which constitute specific offences. The police officer can help her to recall such events. Even otherwise, the statement of the victim u/s 161 or 164 CrPC, recorded in due course, should bring in all details, including those which have been missed out in the FIR.
- Anybody can be the complainant. If nobody comes forth, the police official should be the complainant.
- Jurisdiction of the PS need not be disputed. As trafficking is a continuing offence, the FIR can be lodged at the source or destination. Both courts have jurisdiction. This has been specifically provided u/s 5(3) ITPA. However if two or more FIRs are lodged at different PS on the same issue, the police officials can consult each other and transfer the evidence and case documents to one of the PS, who can follow it up thereafter.
- The copy of the FIR has to be given free of cost to the complainant.
- Female witnesses/victims are to be interviewed at the place of their choice. Police should go to them for the interview, and not vice versa.
- No female witness should be summoned to the police station after sunset.
- Do not deny the right of the victim/complainant to know the progress of information.
- Do maintain proper and regular contact with the victim and her well wishers, including the NGO who is attending to her.
- FIR is the first document in the process of justice delivery. The steps that follow are mostly dependent on the FIR. Distorted FIR where the victim has been shown as accused entails further violations and harm to the victim. Therefore, victim must be projected as

victim and this be done loud and clear from the FIR onwards.

- Do register cases under the relevant provisions of ITPA and other laws which are applicable, IPC, special legislations like Bonded Labour System Act,1976, Child Labour Act 1986, Children Act 1933, Maharashtra Control of Organised Crime Act 1999 etc.
- All cases of trafficking be treated as 'Grave Crimes' or 'Special Report' Crimes and be investigated and supervised by senior police officials, specially those who are sensitized and trained for the same. The SP/ DCP can take initiative in this.
- Do understand the abuser-abused dynamics involved. All steps should be oriented accordingly.

INVESTIGATION OF TRAFFICKING CRIMES: DO'S AND DON'TS

Salient Features

- Distinguish victim from the suspect/accused by a process of intelligence collection and interviewing. Do not treat victims as suspects or accused.
- While ensuring that the rights of accused are protected, do not forget to ensure that the victim's rights are ensured. This includes the following:
  - Do not allow suspects and accused to mix up with victims.
  - Do not intimidate or abuse victims by words/ action/gesture/demeanor.
  - No publicity should be allowed. Ensure anonymity.
  - Support the victim. Validate the harm done to her. Make her feel and realise that she is a victim, that she has been harmed and that she is never at fault.
  - Empower the victims. Make them aware of their rights so that they can also ensure that their rights are not violated further.

- See that the victim gets possession of all her belongings, assets, etc and without any delay.
- See that the children of the victims are provided due care and attention and are not separated from the mother, if they were living together before rescue.
- Help the victim to get all her dues and rightful claims, as most brothel keepers are reluctant to part with her earnings.
- Ensure physical safety of victims during rescue and post-rescue transfers and movements.
- Get the medical examination of the victim done without delay. Utilize the services of female doctors/para medical staff, as far as possible. Do provide lady constables to accompany the victim. Age verification is also a part of the medical exam. If any malafide is suspected, especially with reference to age assessment, do get the matter referred to a Medical Board after obtaining orders of the competent judicial authority.
- Utilize the services of female social workers/ NGOs in these activities. Do get them notified in the Advisory Body as envisaged u/s 13(3) (b) ITPA. Even if they are not notified, nothing stops the police in associating them in their activities.
- Considering the social stigma attached to prostitution, there is a tendency to look down upon trafficked persons by branding them as 'prostitutes'. This should be condemned and not allowed to happen, as the victim of trafficking is neither accused, accomplice nor abettor. The victim's status should be maintained and ensured all through. All protection and care be extended for the same.

• The process of investigation should not be intimidatory or violative of victim's rights. For example, avoid repeated interviewing by several levels of police officers as the victim is made to recall and relive the trauma repeatedly.

- If the statement of the victim is to be recorded u/s 164 CrPC, do it at the earliest so that restoration/ repatriation is not held up. Additional statements u/ s 161 and 164 CrPC are possible, hence do not hurry to close down, especially when the victim is still in trauma.
- Investigation be based on a plan of action which is to be drawn up, keeping the victim's rights in focus.
- Dissect the law and list out the elements of the offence. Thereafter attempt to check out the contents of each of these elements. Carry out investigation into each element so that none of the elements is missed out. The evidence be marshaled element-wise so that the presentation is cogent and convincing. The elements vary with the offence alleged, though there are certain common points in all the offences. A check list will ensure that no aspect is omitted.

Scene of Crime Investigation: Do's and Don'ts

The investigating officer should see that the investigation is not perfunctory or superficial. Usually the SOC is perceived to be a room in a brothel. This is incorrect. The scene of crime extends to the place from where the person was trafficked, the places where she was taken to, the transit places, the final destination where she was exploited, etc.

Therefore the SOC should include:

- The source point
- The trafficking routes
- The transit points
- The destination point
- The points of exploitation
- The places where the 'products' of exploitation were transferred to
  - A trafficking map should be developed and kept as part of the case diary. The map should link up the source-transit-demand places.

- Documents at the SOC: Investigation should be caused into the records maintained in the various SOC. Role of the various exploiters whose names may find mention in the register are to be investigated and evidence extracted against them. These documents have tremendous value, informatory and evidentiary, if investigated properly.
- Photograph/video graph of the SOC: Electronic documents can make a visible impact of the extent and intensity of exploitation and therefore, are advisable. Care should be taken to see that the photographs and videographs do not violate the rights of the victims..

Identification and Arrest of Offenders: Do's and Don'ts

Their roles are linked and, therefore, sustained investigation will open up the linkages one by one and will bring out the role of each. Do use the 'organized crime approach' and investigate into the cross linkages of crimes in the past and elsewhere.

It is a real challenge for investigators to dig out evidence, present them in the charge sheet and get them convicted in the court of law. Conviction, no doubt, is the true test of professional investigation. In this context, the following are the do's and don'ts.

Who are the exploiters who should be investigated:

- The traffickers.
- The transporters.
- The conspirators.
- The abettors.
- The financiers.
- The abusers.

These are only some examples of the many exploiters involved. As and when investigation unfolds, furthur linkages of these persons and many others will also come up. The task of the investigator is to go into the depth of the case, covering all aspects and to dig out the evidence.

This calls for the following efforts:

- *Search of SOC*: The scene of crime provides a lot of evidence for a discerning eye. Search should be systematic and scientific. Secure the place beforehand to avoid disturbance. The victim can lead the IO to the various locations especially the places where trafficked persons are kept hidden. Chain of custody has to be ensured while seizing, labeling and transporting.
- *Linking up role of suspects*: Statement of victim and other witnesses are to be recorded in detail to link up the role of the various suspects involved in the entire process of trafficking and exploitation. Record the statement in the language in which the person speaks. Do not miss the emotions, feelings and other expressions conveyed by the person.
- Medical examination of the suspects be carried out at the earliest. In a crime where the accused has been caught in a compromising position, the medical examination can reveal the level of exploitation. Medical examination should be followed by other scientific examination such as forensic examination of the materials recovered from the SOC.
- Interview of the suspects: Interviewing helps to identify the suspects' background, and to understand the strengths and weaknesses of the person, which can be utilized to develop themes during interrogation. Interrogation should be scientific to lead the accused through the various events. As per the Indian Evidence Act confession before police officer is not admissible in the court of law unless it leads to a recovery. Therefore IO should strive for recoveries and discoveries during interrogation. However admission and confession of accused before police do provide a lot of inputs for further investigation. The alibi of the accused should be further verified and, if found wrong, should be negated by facts. Evidence to rebut the same,

including oral statement of witnesses, should be incorporated in the case diary.

- Interrogation of suspects should be in detail, with an aim to bring out the role of other suspects, the extent of the crime, involvement in other crimes, the various dimensions of not only the process of trafficking, but also the exploitation, the money generated, the expenditure, the assets created and the investments made etc. All these should be brought on record so that in the event of conviction, these illegal assets could be forfeited and confiscated. Therefore, the IO should question the suspect on all dimensions of the crime,
- Arrest of offenders should be done at the appropriate time. There is no point in rushing to arrest, as it will delimit the time available for filing a charge sheet. As per S. 167 CrPC, if the charge sheet is not filed within 60 days of arrest, the arrestee will be bailed out. It is worth mentioning here that in most of the cases, CBI carries out arrest only at the end of the investigation. If the evidence could be adequately built up and marshaled before arrest, it would be useful for opposing his bail in the court of law. However, in certain situations, arrest has to be done without any delay.

Under ITPA, even attempt for trafficking is an offence. Therefore the IO has a long list of persons who can be brought into the trafficking net. Anybody who is involved in any act, even partly, or contributes to, or leads to the process of trafficking, should be investigated and brought on record.

The offender's intention and knowledge are two relevant aspects to establish the offence. Even if the person had no intention, but had the knowledge that the act indulged in by him contributes to trafficking, it would suffice to bring him under the realm of offender.

Therefore investigators should probe not only into the acts of omissions and commissions by the suspects but also into the frame of mind behind such acts.

Arrest of Accused: The Legal Provisions in ITPA

- The cognizable offences are S.3, 4, 5, 6, 7, 8 and 9 ITPA. Utilize appropriate sections of ITPA and also IPC as well as other laws which are attracted. Graver sections of law will act against easy bail. Invoke the provisions of special laws wherever applicable.
- A notified SPO is fully empowered to arrest without warrant (u/s 14(i) ITPA.
- SPO can authorize and order any police officer in writing for arrest (u/s 14(ii) ITPA.
- SPO can authorize any police officer u/s 14(iii), even without a written approval, in case of urgency if:
  - The accused is likely to escape.
  - The identity of the accused is suspect.
- The grounds for authorization should be specifically recorded in police documents.
- The authorization should be by name and not a general authorization.
- Authorization for arrest is distinct from authorization for investigation.
- Only the competent and notified official can take up the investigation of the crime. Technical errors often lead to discharge of the case in the court.
- The arrest of the accused is guided by the provisions of CrPC and Evidence Act, as it applies to any other offence.

Mapping the Harm Done to the Victims

This is an area usually neglected in the present day investigation process. Do map and document the entire harm and damage done to the victims. This includes

- Injuries of physical assault.
- Injuries of rape and other sexual assaults.
- Injuries consequential to the various act of exploitation.
- Injuries consequential to the denial of medical care and attention.
- The medical status including STD, HIV etc..

- The psychological harm not only due to exploitation, intimidation, and denial of privacy and dignity but also as a result of neglect of oneself, one's children, and abuse of children.
- Physical and mental harm to the children of the victim, especially those who are staying with them.

The mapping of harm could be professionally done with the expert assistance of doctors, forensic experts, psychiatrists, and psycho-social experts. However, documenting the victim's own experience and the observation of the NGOs, counselors, etc associated with the victim are also relevant.

They should be well recorded and presented in the case records. Record the statement in the language spoken to by the victim. Do not ignore the emotions, the feelings, etc conveyed by the victim.

Do document them all. As regards child victims, their own version of the events be appropriately recorded without editing the language and content.

Mapping the Exploiter's Profit

This is another investigative component, usually neglected. In cases of trafficking, the exploiters gain monetarily and otherwise, while the victim continues to be harmed and exploited. Additionally younger the girl, higher the level of exploitation and, consequentially, more 'earning' for the exploiter. The NHRC study has brought out the unbelievably high profits that the traffickers and other exploiters have made at low or no cost to themselves. Therefore it is essential to map these assets and take appropriate action to prevent and combat trafficking.

The following are the dos and don'ts in this context:

- Investigate into and bring on record all assets, incomes, earnings, profits and expenditures related to trafficking.
- Establish the linkage of the crime of trafficking to the "fruits of crime" through documentary and oral evidence.
- Collect intelligence regarding these aspects from the

trafficked victims, their parents/wards, etc through careful interviewing.

- Conduct sustained interrogation of the accused and suspects to bring out the details of profit, places of deposit, utilization of money/assets,etc.
- Investigate into the assets and profits of the traffickers to expose the linkages with other exploiters and profiteers. This will also bring to focus the gravity and extent of the exploitation.
- The case diary should specifically list out the details of investigation in this regard and should invite the attention of the court during trial so that in the event of conviction, the court could be moved to attach and confiscate the properties.

Interviewing Victims: Do's and Don'ts

- Female victims should be interviewed by WPO. If WPO is not available, involve women NGO's or counselors during interview.
- Ensure that the accused/suspected offenders are nowhere in the vicinity.
- Conduct the interview at a place where she is comfortable. It should be a place of her choice.
- Keep the ambience child friendly, if the victim is a child.
- Do associate the person whom she is comfortable with. A 'child minder', a counselor etc would be appropriate.
- Avoid onlookers, interventions and interruptions during interview.
- Include psychiatrists and forensic experts, as and when required.
- Avoid repeated interviews, unless essential. Senior officers and supervisory officers should ensure that they participate in the interview alongwith the IO. Repeated interviews be avoided so that the victim does not have to relive the trauma.
- Effort should be made to help the victim come out of trauma so that she is able to recall events properly, logically and fully.

- Support the victim. Validate the harm done to her. She should be made to feel and realise that she is a victim, that she has been harmed and that she is never at fault.
- Listen to the victim carefully and empathetically. Do understand her from her perspective. A child victim may not know the adult language and terminology. I.O has to go to her level of understanding.
- Avoid making value judgements, comments and criticisms.
- Remember that the victim is the best witness to speak about all aspects of trafficking and exploitation. Therefore her statement should be logical, detailed and should incorporate all aspects of the trafficking process, such as the exploitation, the role of various persons involved and the entire chain of events.
- Prepare a check list of events, facts and themes on which the victim needs to be interviewed. As the interview progresses, new events, facts and themes will emerge and the interview has to be logically oriented to bring out all the relevant details.
- Interviewing of victims must be carried out with care and caution. See that the investigative processes do not traumatize her any further. It is essential to adopt sensitive techniques to help the victim recall all the facts which are of evidentiary value. The victim may not know about the significance of these facts, whereas the police officers ought to know. The interview processes should be done keeping in mind her best interest and not anybody else's.
- With the victim's informed consent, electronic documentation of the recording of the statement can be arranged which can be eventually used in the court of law. However, every effort should be made to protect her anonymity.
- Facilitate the victim to ask questions and raise doubts. It will open up the conversation.

- Record statement in the victim's language. Translation can be done later. Do not forget to include the emotional content and body language as displayed during the interview.
- The police officer recording statement should sign and record his full name, designation and address.
- There should be no publicity of the victim and her statements.Ensure anonymity at all occasions, including the period of transfer to court and back.
- If re-examination is required, do seek her consent and convenience.
- Do not delay in recording the statement of the victim u/s 161 and 164 CrPC as it would delay restoration/ repatriation. However one should not be in an unusual hurry. There is no bar in having additional statements recorded, as and when the victim desires to speak.
- Provide proper escort by WPO at all places of stay and movement.
- Do look after victim's comforts. Ensure that there is place of rest, easement, etc. Provide food, water, tea, etc. as and when required. Child victims need special attention regarding choice of food.
- Ensure that the actions taken by police are in the best interest of the victim. The thumb rule for decision making should be "victim's best interest".
- Do not forget to thank the victim after interview.

Medical Care and Attention of Victims: Do's and Don'ts

- All examinations should be done by a female doctor. If no female doctor is available, do associate other female persons like nurses/counselors/NGO workers during medical examination.
- Male police officers and attendants should keep away, if female officials are available.
- The doctor should do a mapping of not only physical injuries but also the psychological harm. If required associate a psychiatrist.

- Medical exhibits should be carefully preserved and the chain of custody be ensured.
- Do not delay medical attention. Timely care helps to de-stress and detraumatise the victim.

Psychosocial Care of Victim: Do's and Don'ts

Mental health care is an area often neglected by the police and other after-care agencies, despite its crucial role in victim care and rehabilitation. Do associate appropriate government/non-governmental agencies to attend to this issue. As an untrained counselor can cause further damage and trauma to the victim, it is very important to associate a trained and qualified expert, from the very beginning itself.

Trauma counseling should be ensured even at the home/lodging house. This should be a continuous process as the victim will take time to get over the trauma. Moreover the counselor/psychiatrist will be an important witness in the court of law. Hence he/she should be cited as an expert witness in the charge sheet filed against the accused persons. There are many strategies available for psychosocial counseling. However the focus should be to empower the victim. Therefore it needs to be ensured that all steps and initiatives are Rights-based and are in the best interest of the victim.

Age Verification/Assessment

The Magistrate, before whom the rescued person is produced, shall u/s 17(2) ITPA, cause verification of the age of the person. Age is crucial in deciding on the application of IPC Sections like 372, 323, 375, 366 A, 366 B etc and that of JJ Act. If the person is less than 18 years of age, JJ Act comes into effect and the Magistrate should refer the person to the appropriate authority, ie, the CWC.

Therefore, correct assessment of age of the rescued person is an important step. Though u/s 49 JJ Act the competent authority is authorized to take steps in determining the age, in practice, it is left to the rescuing officials to take a prima facie decision as to whether the rescued person is an adult or a child. The following are the dos/don'ts in this regard.

- Presumption of age, at first sight, be drawn in favour of the rescued person.
- Interview the person to arrive at objective yardsticks, like date of birth in school records etc. There are several events in the life of a person which can reveal her age.
- Associate social workers, CWC members etc, in assisting the police official in age determination.
- Do not go by the age spoken to by the brothel 'madam' or the exploiters. They will confuse.
- The victim may be under pressure by the exploiters to speak out wrong age. Careful interviewing of the victim can bring out the truth.
- Age verification by the medical/professionals and forensic experts involve ossification test and other parametres. Do involve these professionals as early as possible.
- If the expert is not able to categorically state the exact age, but opines it to be falling under a range the benefit of doubt should go to the person.

Investigating the Organized Crime of Trafficking

Trafficking is an organized crime. Therefore all principles of investigating other organized crimes should be invoked into the investigation of trafficking.

In this context, the following are important:

- Intelligence on traffickers and exploiters in one case of trafficking can be appropriate inputs for investigating another crime of trafficking. One case can lead to another. Therefore, such intelligence should be shared at once with all concerned and, as far as possible, documented.
- Data base on traffickers, and exploiters, including their modus operandi, origin, place of activity, movements and influence, the communication linkages, the income generated, transmitted, invested etc, the expenditure patterns, the operational linkages among the exploiters, the linkage between the source area the transit area and the demand area etc., be developed.

- Searches conducted earlier at the scene of crime, documents in this regard including police documents and even media reports are relevant not only as evidence but also as clues for investigation into the organized linkages.
- In case of inter district crime, the SSP should take initiative for follow up. In case of inter state crimes, the police managers and CID wing should take initiative to provide support to the investigators. Nothing legally stops an IO to investigate anywhere in India.
- Involve NGOs for intelligence collection. As of today, NGO networks like ATSEC, CBATN, SAPAT etc have developed net works across the boundaries and do have intelligence sharing on trans-border traffickers. Their services could be effectively utilized by the Law Enforcement Agencies. Nothing prevents the Law Enforcement officials from associating competent NGOs.
- Recording of statements of witnesses: Do get the witness statements, especially the important ones, recorded and/or video-recorded by a Magistrate u/s 164 CrPC, so that do not turn hostile. If they do so, it would invite prosecution for perjury.

In case of a transnational crime like AHT, investigations may have to be caused abroad. For legal and officials transfer of evidence, Letters Rogatory are to be prepared, sent and followed up. Electronic documentation of the material exhibits will be of immense help in transfer of evidence in such crimes. However, the services of NGO networks having linkages across the borders could be utilized for collection and collation of information which can, if required as legal evidence, be brought over through official channels, by sending LR.

PROSECUTION OF TRAFFICKING CRIMES: DO'S AND DON'TS

EXPEDITING TRIAL

- Ensure timely intimation to witnesses and facilitate

their appearance in the court. Delayed trials are mostly due to non-appearance of witnesses.

- Witness care requires that transport and other contingencies are taken care of.
- Provide protection to the witnesses against undue publicity
- To encourage experts to appear in the court as witnesses, it is essential to maintain their address, contact telephones, e-mail and networking. Maintaining regular personal contacts is advisable.
- Police officials who are witnesses do get transferred out. Therefore, keep an update of their addresses and contact numbers.
- Ensure liaison with the prosecutors and court staff for timely redressal of the problems and issues which come up in trial.
- Liaison between the Presiding Officer of the court, the Prosecutor and the Police official concerned is a sin-qua-non for removing all bottlenecks and ensuring early and prompt delivery of justice. Prosecutor is the officer of the court and, therefore should take initiative in ensuring this liaison.
- Prosecutor has a large role to play in the delivery of justice by bringing to the notice of the court any major flaw or deficiency in investigation. This would facilitate the court to take an appropriate decision whether to proceed further or to refer the case back to police for further/fresh investigation or draw the attention of senior police officers/or refer the case to specialized agency like CID etc for investigation.
- S.22 ITPA provides for special courts to be constituted by the State Government or the Central Government. Prosecutor should take initiative in this direction as this is an important step in delivering justice expeditiously.
- Ensure that all facts are brought to the notice of the court. "It is as much duty of the prosecutor as of the court to ensure that full and material facts are

brought on record so that there might not be miscarriage of justice".

VICTIM AND WITNESS CARE AND PROTECTION DURING TRIAL: DOS AND DON'TS

- Victims are wary of the court ambience. Do orient and counsel them. Assure them that their rights will not be violated and that their truthful version of all facts is essential for delivery of justice which is in their interest and also in the larger public interest.
- Victims require briefing on the facts of the case, especially to recall the events in a logical way. This should be done before she is put in the witness box.
- Prosecutors ought to ensure that the defence-side does not violate the rights of the victim. Embarrassing questions need to be avoided. Intervention of the court should be sought immediately to prevent any such violations.
- All efforts should be made to ensure the anonymity of the victim. Anonymity provides strength and confidence to the victim.
- Move the court for allowing in-camera trial. The Supreme Court of India has directed that in-camera trial should be extended to all cases of sexual assault on children. A screen has to be provided in the trial court so that the child victim is not exposed to the suspect and accused persons. A child counselor should be provided to assist in the court. Adequate recess should be allowed during trial proceeding so that the child victim gets rest. This is a landmark judgement in ensuring child rights and, therefore, needs to be implemented in letter and spirit. The police and prosecutors should move the trial courts for the same. _ Video conferencing is an ideal mechanism to prevent victimization of the trafficked victim. It should be done whenever possible. The Supreme Court, in its landmark decision, in State of Maharashtra vs Dr. Praful B. Desai 2003 (4) SCC 601,

has underscored the validity of video conferencing and enumerated the safeguards to be ensured during the trial of cases.

- *Victim care and protection also requires the following*:
  - Depute a sensitive liaison officer with the victim, preferably a WPO.
  - Brief the victim on the facts of the case before trial starts.
  - Orient the victim to the court scenes before the trial.
  - Debrief the victim immediately thereafter.
  - Follow up on the debriefing and make required amendments.
  - If the victim speaks a different language, make arrangements for appropriate translators.
  - Ensure transportation of the victim to and fro.
  - Provide for contingency expenditures. Court has funds for this. In some states like Tamil Nadu, Government has provided special funds for this work.
  - Take care to return the victim to the concerned destination.
  - Do look after other logistics and contingencies such as providing facility for rest, easement, etc.
  - Do not forget to thank the victim/witnesses and all those who assisted in getting the victim to the court. Do ensure their safe and comfortable return.
- Post Conviction Matters requires special attention by the prosecutor. This includes the following major steps.
- Seeking enhanced punishment for repeated offences/ offenders.
- Moving the court to impose fine alongwith punishment.
- Seeking compensation for the victim from the offender.
- Seeking compensation from the state.

- Taking steps for closure and eviction of brothels u/s 18 ITPA.
- Taking steps for surveillance of convicted person.
- Initiating steps for externment of the convicted person.

VICTIM/WITNESS PROTECTION SYSTEMS

There are several constitutional, legal and administrative provisions in India for ensuring the rights and protection of witness/victim.

Some of these are listed below which can be of ready reference to the law enforcement agencies:

- Right to anonymity is a legal right
- In camera trial, u/s 327 CrPC is essential in rape crimes. The provisions of in camera trial have been extended to all crimes of sexual assault against children Therefore in camera trial should be invoked in all crimes of trafficking of children for CSE.
- Video Conference is allowed in the trial of crimes. This ensures not only anonymity but also protection to the victims and witnesses.
- *Provision of free atmosphere*: In Sakshi vs UOI, it was held that "the whole inquiry before a court is to elicit the truth. It is absolutely necessary that the victim or the witnesses are able to depose about the entire incident in a free atmosphere without any embarrassment. .... A screen or some such arrangements be made where the vctim or witnesses do not have to undergo the trauma of seeing the body or the face of the accused".
- *Recess during court proceedings*: In Sakshi vs UOI the Supreme Court directed that whenever a child or a victim of rape is required to give testimony, sufficient brakes should be given as and when required.
- Legal representation is a legal right. In Delhi Demostic Working Womens Forum vs UOI, 1995 (1) SCC 14.) The requirement of legal representation and

counseling has been extended to the victim right from the Police Station itself.

- Victim can have Private Lawyers who can assist the Public Prosecutor and even submit written arguments, nevertheless functioning under the public prosecutor, vide Section 301(2) CrPC.
- Victim is never an accomplice.
- Right of accused to cross examine the victim/witness, though a legal right, is restricted by Sakshi judgt, in such a way that in a case of sexual assault of children, the defence cannot question the victim directly, but has to furnish the questions to the court and the court will, in turn, communicate it to the victim.
- Compensation is an entitlement of the victim for injury/loss, u/s 357 CrPC.
- Compensation can be awarded to the victim from the convicted person even if there was no fine as part of the sentence.
- Compensation can be awarded to the victim even without conviction and even during pendency of trial.
- Age assessment of the victim should be done, when in doubt, in favour of the victim. In State of Karnataka vs Majamma, it was held that even if the prosecution has not proved that the girl was less than 16 years, her own statement should be trusted and accepted.
- Delay in reporting of the case will not affect the case if reasonable explanzation is given/brought out during investigation.
- *Defective Investigation*: Flawed investigation is no ground to deny justice to the victim. "It would not be right to acquit an accused person solely on account of defect; to do so would tantamount to playing into the hands of the investigating officer if the investigation is designedly defective".
- *Prosecutrix need not be examined*: in State of Himachal Pradesh vs Mohan Misra, 1995 CrLJ 3845, the Supreme Court held that "merely because the victim girl is not examined, this can never be a ground to

acquit an accused if there is evidence otherwise available proving the criminal act of the accused.

- Character and antecedents of the victim has no bearing or relevance... and can never serve either as mitigating or extenuating circumstance. No stigma should be implied against the victim/witness. 'After all it is the accused and not the victim of sex crime who is on trial in the court'..
- *On reliability*: The evidence of a victim of sexual offence is entitled to a great weight, absence of corroboration notwithstanding The rule of prudence that the evidence of a victim of sexual assault must be corroborated in material particulars has no application.
- *On corroboration*: In Punjab vs Gurmeet Singh it was held that the statement of the rape victim who was between 15-17 years, inspired confidence for acceptance and, therefore corroboration of evidence was not needed. Held that there is no legal compulsion to look for corroboration of the evidence of the prosecutrix before recording an order of conviction. Evidence has to be weighed and not counted. There is no rule of practice that there must in every case be corroboration before a conviction can be allowed to take place.
- *On discrepancy in the statement of victim/witness*: In cases involving sexual assault minor contradictions or insignificant discrepancies in the statement of the witnesses should not affect the case. It was held that the court must appreciate the evidence in totality of the background of the entire case and not in isolation.
- *On medical report*: In Rampal vs State of Haryana, 1994 Supp(3) SCC 656, conviction was based on the sole testimony of the prosecutrix. Though the doctor did not find any visible injuries, the court held that, there was no reason to suspect the testimony of the victim and upheld the conviction of the accused.
- Expeditious trial is an essential ingredient of

reasonable, fair and just procedure guaranteed by Article 21. It is the constitutional obligation of the state to devise such a procedure as would ensure speedy trial.

- Courts need to take participative role to deliver justice to victim. "The Courts have to take a participative role in a trial. They are not expected to be tape recorders to record whatever is being stated by the witnesses. S.311 of CrPC and S.165 of Ev. Act confer wide and vast powers on presiding officers of Court to elicit all necessary materials by playing an active role in the evidence collecting process".
- *Witnesses to turn up in trial*: In order to ensure fair trial, a duty has been cast on the prosecution to produce witnesses on time. "The presence of the Investigating Officer at the time of the trial is must. It is his duty to keep the witness present. If there is a failure on the part of the witness to remain present, it is the duty of the court to take appropriate action".
- *Right to be rescued*: Section 16 ITPA provides powers to Executive Magistrates and Judicial Magistrates for directing any police officer of the rank of SI and above to rescue a person based on information received from any source. This accrues a right to the victim to notify the Magistrate, by whichever means possible, and a duty is cast on the Magistrate to ensure steps for rescue.
- *Right to restoration to a safe place after rescue*: Section 17 ITPA provides that a rescued person shall not be restored to or placed in the custody of a person who may exercise a harmful influence over the person. This section of law calls for Home verification to verify whether the original home of the rescued person is safe enough for her return.

PROSECUTOR ROLE IN PREVENTION OF TRAFFICKING

The prosecutor has a large role to play in preventing trafficking.

- If the trafficker is convicted and kept behind bars, as a corollary, the trafficker is being deprived from indulging in trafficking. Therefore, by aggressive law enforcement, prosecutors can ensure prevention of trafficking.
- If the post conviction measures are taken properly against the trafficker and other exploiters, it will make a tremendous impact in preventing trafficking.
- Eviction of brothels and such other places of commercial sexual exploitation carried out effectively, is another method of preventing trafficking. Prosecutor should take initiative u/s 18 ITPA.
- Post rescue care and attention of victims and survivors, if carried out properly, in such a way that they are rehabilitated just as to their best interest, would mean prevention of re-trafficking. Prosecutors can play a role in such post rescue activities by involving the government department or the civil society either directly or by taking up with the concerned Magistrate depending on the issues concerned and getting an appropriate direction issued by the Magistrate to the concerned government agency/NGO.

PREVENTION OF TRAFFICKING: DO'S AND DON'TS

Prention is the sumum bonum of all activities that one can do to address trafficking. It includes prevention of re-trafficking too.

- Law enforcement processes should be integrated and comprehensive. There should be a combination of steps for Prosecution, alongwith Protection and Prevention. An integrated P-P-P model is essential. Adequate attention should be paid to all the three legs and the efforts should be dove-tailed.
- Prevention of trafficking requires attention at all the scenes of crime. Accordingly they can be classified into three:

- Prevention at the demand point: This requires proper investigation, prosecution, conviction, addressing the demand effectively and all post conviction measures. This also involves proper care and protection of victims to ensure prevention of re-trafficking.
- Prevention at the transit area: Trafficking when carried out from one place to another involves transit places. The major hub of such transit are railway junctions, bus stops, ports, border entry posts etc. 'Rights intervention centre' started by the NGO 'SEWA' of Gorakhpur at Sanauli, with the partnership of local police, is a classic example of prevention of trafficking. In a span of nine months, 65 girls could be prevented from exploitation, by interception at the transits place. Effective surveillance and watch on suspects at the transit places by deputing spotters in association with NGOs can be a good method. The details of transit routes, mode of transport and the names of persons involved could be gathered on careful interviewing of victims and interrogation of suspects.
- Prevention at the source point requires several steps, like addressing vulnerabilities, attending to missing persons, networking with the civil society and Panchayati Raj institutions, empowering the vulnerable sections along with other police strategies on prevention. The details of these strategies are discussed below:
  - (a) Do ensure conviction, punishment and stringent action against traffickers and all exploiters.
  - (b) Do ensure post conviction steps. This includes closure and eviction of brothels and other places of exploitation, externment of the convicted persons, surveillance and dossiers on convicted and suspected persons, confiscation of illegal assets etc.

- Address the demand factor effectively. This calls for a strategic intervention, depending on the persons who 'demand'.
  - All traffickers and intentional abusers, who are usually called "customers", should be prosecuted and firmly dealt with. Further, all those who perpetuate the demand, including financiers, colluders, conspirators, abettors etc be prosecuted.
  - Adolescents/youths also come in as 'customers' and contribute to the demand. They require a different treatment, as they have the knowledge but may not have the intention to exploit. Advocacy and orientation of such persons, with the help of NGOs, on issues of sexuality, gender, women's rights, child rights, etc. be carried out to address the demand in this sector.
- Protection and care of victims commence with proper rescue processes. Do not criminalize them. FIR should be only against traffickers and abusers, but never against the victims. All further steps in investigation and justice delivery should follow this principle. Simultaneously, do see that the victims are empowered and properly rehabilitated. Often police officials think that they have nothing to do with the rehabilitation of the victims. This is a mistaken notion. Prevention of crime is a mandate to police under the Police Act. To prevent re-trafficking, it is essential to rehabilitate the trafficked victim.
- Preventing re-trafficking The NHRC study has established the fact that a large number of rescued persons are re-trafficked. The reasons are many. Victimization of the victims, arrest of trafficked persons as accused and their criminalization are some of the reasons. Improper/inadequate rehabilitation/ empowerment lead to lack of livelihood options which, in turn, make these persons highly vulnerable and subjects of prey by traffickers.

- Therefore the following can be done to prevent re-trafficking.
  - Provide proper counseling, right-based empowerment and appropriate livelihood options, including adequate resources, skills and marketing facilities, to the rescued persons.
  - Police should network with other departments of government as well as with NGOs and INGOs working in the related fields, in addition to Corporates who would like to be associated, and involve them in the various processes of empowerment..
  - Ensure that the repatriated/rehabilitated person is reintegrated properly by taking regular feedback.
  - Accountability be cast on the village-level functionaries to monitor the same. Do involve Panchayat Raj Institutions in this task.
  - Do remember that re-trafficking is more often done by known traffickers and their coteries. Hence strict action/surveillance on such persons can be an effective tool to prevent re-trafficking.
- Addressing vulnerable persons/areas is an important strategy in the prevention of trafficking. Police should develop synergy with the concerned governmental and non governmental organizations and undertake the following steps:
  - Identify the vulnerable persons/areas and focus attention on them. Empower them. Let this be a priority.
  - Pay special attention to the most vulnerable persons. This needs to be top priority.
  - Mount surveillance for suspects and look-out for victims at possible transit/transfer points like bus stands, railway stations, wayside hotels, beach resorts, etc.
  - Facilitate empowerment programmes by networking with government departments, MNCs etc.

- Involve multiple agencies to provide sustainable livelihood options.
- Adopt a "Human Rights approach" in all activities and programmes and discard the "welfare act" orientation. This requires change of mind-set. Proactive policing, with the support of NGO's, can stimulate such a change.

• *Networking with other government agencies*: Partnership with the departments of women and Child Development, Social Welfare, Paramilitary agencies manning the borders, BSF, SSB, ITBP etc is essential, depending on the area of functioning. In fact, it should be a process of mutual assistance. Agencies like BSF should have anti-trafficking cell with its network extending to State Police Systems, Human Rights agencies, NGO's etc. Similarly police agencies should network with Human Rights Commission, Women Commission etc so that preventive steps could be meaningful, effective and institutionalized.

• *Networking with Civil Society Members*: Since concerted efforts are called for, the law enforcement officials should develop synergy with NGO's, CBO's, Social activists, academicia, lawyers etc. Panchayat Raj Institutions can play a large role in identifying and addressing vulnerabilities, keeping surveillance on exploiters and in public awareness/empowerment programmes. Tamil Nadu has developed a good model in this direction.

• *Issue of Missing Persons*: There is a strong linkage between 'trafficking' and 'missing persons'. The research report of NHRC on trafficking shows that in one year more than 30,000 children are reported missing and one-third of them remain untraced. This study has established with examples that many of these 'missing children are, in fact, trafficked. Hence prevention of trafficking requires the following:

  - Do realise the linkage between 'missing' persons

and 'trafficked' persons, because many who are 'reported missing' have been, in fact, trafficked.

- Do cross-check the list of persons rescued from brothels and other places of exploitation with the list of persons reported missing from anywhere in India.
- The linkage will also help to expose the traffickers, trafficking routes and trafficking processes.
- Do follow up missing women and children till a logical conclusion is arrived at. Constitute special teams to go into the root of the issue and ensure rescue/return/recovery of the missing person. Follow-up all the leads in this process to ensure that those responsible for making the person missing are brought to book. Any slight suspicion should immediately be taken cognizance of a proper FIR registered, followed by sustained investigation.
- It is often seen that the trafficked person is blamed 'as if he/she is responsible for being 'missing'. One should realise that more often children who were missing are from the vulnerable sections of the society and are essentially 'children in need of care and protection'.
- Provide the details of missing children to the police agencies and NGOs who are working in the rescue of trafficked persons so that they could also follow up.
- Network with NGOs/Helpline/Child line, etc. to identify the linkage. Expand the database of missing persons to link it up with trafficked and rescued persons.
- Do a mapping of missing persons for a specific time in a particular place and undertake special operations to locate them. One linkage to a brothel elsewhere in the country could be a clue for locating many who are still missing.

- *Utilizing preventive sections of CrPC*: Section 110 CrPC provides enough scope for preventing offences. Executives Magistrates are vested with the powers. The Magistrate can bind down the persons for ensuring good behaviour. Steps u/s 111, 116, 121, 122 CrPC will further affirm the preventive actions against likely offenders.
- *Helplines*: The Police Managers should establish proper and functional networks with the existing help-lines like child-line, Women's helpline etc. Such help-lines should be linked up to the police control rooms and police stations for prompt response.
- *Strengthening Police Stations*: Institutionalization of the response systems requires that the police stations, being the fundamental unit of police administration and public service, be strengthened. Besides empowering the police stations with the required human and material resources, their capabilities need to be enriched by regular training and discussions. The methodology prescribed for the functioning and training of STF are applicable here too.
- *Involving local self government agencies*: The Panchayat Raj Institutions have lot of sway over the local public. Therefore their services can be effectively channelised towards the prevention strategies. Tamil Nadu has started this process through a Government order issued in 2002 followed by training/orientation programmes for PRI members on preventing trafficking. This model could be adopted by others too. Police officers should network with the PRI's, orient them, sensitize them and involve them in the anti trafficking processes. District level and village level Monitoring Committees could be set up by the DM/SP, involving all stake holders and PRI's.
- *Data-base*: One of the essential ingredients of crime management is to develop a proper data base. It is utmost essential for not only combating trafficking but also prevention of trafficking. As of today lack

of database is one of the major impediments in law enforcement. Since theInvestigating officials are more or less confined to their limited jurisdictions, the police managers like SP/DCP and other higher formations should take initiative in developing the data base, not only on traffickers and exploiters, but also on victims and survivors. The data should include the profile of the offenders, the area of operations of the traffickers, their networks, the details of source, transit, destination etc. This should be regularly updated. The second aspect of data base is data analysis. This would facilitate in developing criminal intelligence. The third aspect of data base is sharing of criminal intelligence with all concerned and initiating appropriate action for combating and preventing trafficking. Collation, analysis and dissemination of data and intelligence are professional aspects of policing and therefore the responsibility for the same is with the police managers. It is advisable to involve appropriate NGOs working in the field and associate them fully in all activities.

- *Anti Human Trafficking Unit*: An in-depth understanding of the dimension of trafficking will clearly bring to focus the essentiality of multi stake holder partnership in preventing and combating trafficking. The law enforcement agencies need to have close association with other departments like health, social welfare, labour, department of women and child, department of correctional administration, development department, panchayati raj institutions etc. These government agencies need to have symbiotic partnership with the NGOs working in this field. The police managers especially the SP/DCP should take initiative in setting up an AHTU by developing close partnership of the police with all these responders. Such an AHTU will be the best mechanism in the given situation to prevent and combat trafficking. The officials and NGOs who are put in the AHTU should be specially trained and oriented. Protocols should be drawn up to demarcate the role of each stake holder. The scope of AHTU can be widened to include Corporates so that they could lend the services of their corporate social responsibility for not only funding the programmes but also giving appropriate back up support in empowering the survivors, utilizing the services for productive activities, marketing their produces etc.

4

Stranger Danger: Explaining Women's Fear of Crime

Although not everyone has been the victim of a crime, criminal acts may touch upon everyone. Those fortunate enough not to have been victimized, nor to know someone who has, will have probably read, watched, or listened to news, film, television, or radio stories about those who have been victimized.

Repeated exposure to criminal events and the after-effects of such events, on the whole, may come to be a powerful socializing force affecting people both directly and indirectly. Research on criminal victimization indicates that many people fear crime and engage in a variety of activities to prevent crime, yet may also choose not to report crimes to police.

For example, women who are physically abused at home, or who have been sexually assaulted, tend not to report the crimes to police. The hidden nature of women's victimization necessarily means that there is much about violence against women that we do not understand. The primary focus of this study is women's fear of victimization. This work expands on the work by Keane by extending the analysis to two other fear variables: fear while using public transportation, and fear while using a parking garage alone.

Unlike Keane, this study also examines self protective behaviours and their relationship to fear. Given the growing awareness of the hidden nature of women's victimization, research at this point in time is particularly appropriate. A statistical analysis was undertaken, using the 1993 Violence

Against Women Survey conducted by Statistics Canada, in order to estimate the nature and extent of women's victimization, and how women react to it given certain life experiences.

LITERATURE REVIEW

FEAR

Stanko noted that although traditional victimization surveys demonstrate that young men are at the highest risk for victimization, women consistently report, on average, fear of crime that is three times higher than males. One would expect that fear of crime is related to likelihood of victimization. Yet, women report higher fear even though official reports indicate they are less likely to be targets of crime than males.

This paradox has led Skogan to observe that fear of crime has often been perceived as "irrational." Stanko agrees with Smith that this fear of crime paradox may fail to capture the lived experiences of women's physical and sexual violence. Stanko argues that conventional criminology tends to look at street crime and not crimes happening behind closed doors between non-strangers and thereby undermines the detection of crimes of violence against women. Statistics indicate that men are roughly eleven times less likely than women to experience "being forced to do something sexual" over their lifetime.

Research investigating women's fear of victimization led Warr to suggest that women report more general victimization fears because of an intertwining of general fear with their fear of sexual assault. Therefore, he suggests that women's fear of victimization may be founded on a different basis than those fears held by men, as men rarely fear sexual assault. Ferraro's research observes that women and men reported the same fear levels for nonviolent crime.

However, when the crime of rape was added into the fear category, women's reported fear rose significantly. Gordon and Riger argue that this is because women fear not only the violent act of rape, but the aftermath of rape as well. Alternatively, Keane argues that there is a dual nature to women's fear: concrete fear and formless fear. Concrete fear is the fear associated with certain crimes. The implicit assumption here is that some criminal activities elicit more fear than others.

For example, rape elicits more fear than theft. Formless fear, however, is a more generic or less specific fear of crime. Keane found that women who were younger reported higher levels of both types of fear. In particular, his results indicate that younger women reported highest results for concrete fear, or fear of specific crimes. To this end, his work supports research that women perceive the seriousness of rape as almost equal to or exceeding the perceived seriousness of murder.

The purpose of this document is to establish whether women with certain demographic characteristics, experiences with criminal victimization, who avoid risky situations, and/or use risk-management in potentially dangerous situations, will report higher levels of fear.

DEMOGRAPHICS AND FEAR

Results of research examining the age/fear of victimization relationship have been mixed. Simply, studies confirm that both older and younger individuals have high levels of fear. Ferraro in an extensive review of this literature, concludes that the relationship between age and fear is actually curvilinear. That is, both the youngest women and the oldest women queried in various surveys report the highest levels of fear. Emerging evidence suggests that older women and younger women may have different bases for their fear of victimization, respectively.

In 1996, Ferraro's continued research examining the age/fear of crime paradox revealed that although women rank consistently higher with respect to fear of all victimization types, that most of the variance explained diminishes or is reversed when fear of rape is taken out of the equation. Ferraro further asserts that the fear women hold, especially by those who are young, operates in the shadow of sexual assault. These findings again support Warr's research: younger women fear the act of sexual assault most. As young women age, their fears subside to some degree. However, as women get older their fear begins to resurface as they become increasingly more vulnerable, physically. Elderly women are more concerned with personal injury during the course of any crime, because they are physically weaker and the potential for harm is greater. Using the variables of education and income as proxies for socio-economic status, Keane found that women with lower SES were more likely to worry about walking alone outside the home after dark and about being alone inside the home at night.

Keane suggests that fear was stronger for single women than for married women. The Statistics Canada, single women generally have the lowest average yearly income when compared to other groups. Single women, typically having fewer financial resources than men or married women, are more vulnerable. Research conducted by Pantazis reveals that the financial constraints are not the only obstacle to those in poverty. Poverty is associated with physical situational correlates that accompany low-income living such as poor living and working conditions, which contribute to an increased risk of victimization.

Therefore, not only do women who live in poverty have fewer financial resources to deal with victimization, they must also continue to live and work in conditions that may put them at higher risk. Women in poor working and living conditions may have to take public transportation more often, and after dark, as they are less likely to be able to afford and insure an automobile. They are probably less likely to have choice about where they can afford to live, fewer resources to ensure self protection such as adequate locks on doors, etc., and may have to take jobs that are more likely to put their personal safety at risk.

PAST EXPERIENCE

Warr reports that there is an increased sensitivity to fear of victimization depending on both the type of crime and the characteristics of the individual. Previous experience with victimization may indirectly affect fear of crime. Keane finds that experiencing specific offences may be a better predictor of fear than others. In particular, along with more serious personal offences such as sexual assault, crimes that posed even the threat of sexual assault; such as being followed, getting obscene phone calls, or indecent exposure also elicited high fear responses.

Macmillan, Nierobisz, and Welsh report that harassment from strangers is not only more common but more extensive than non-stranger harassment, and it results in high fear of victimization. An implication of this finding is that threatening behaviour from an unknown source will elicit more potential for sexual violence and that more fear is generated.

AVOIDANCE AND RISK-MANAGEMENT BEHAVIOUR

Skogan and Maxfield have suggested that routine crime prevention behaviours can be broken down into two major categories: avoidance and riskmanagement strategies. They argue that one can reduce the risk of victimization by avoiding dangerous situations and settings, thereby reducing the risk of running into a potentially threatening situation. Riskmanagement practices are used when one finds oneself in a potentially dangerous situation and/or location and takes precautionary measures to be a less suitable target for victimization.

After a considerable search, no studies were found that specifically looked at the effect of utilizing these techniques on resulting fear levels. However, it stands to reason that those who use these strategies more frequently are enacting them as they feel less safe and, therefore, are more fearful generally.

PROPOSITIONS AND HYPOTHESES

From the literature, three general propositions are made. First, demographics, or core characteristics, will have an effect on fear. Given that women predominantly fear sexual violence, it is hypothesized that those demographic factors that leave women more vulnerable to potential victimization will predict higher levels of fear. Therefore, women who are younger, have lower incomes, less education, are single, living alone, and/or living in an urban environment will report higher levels of fear. Second, those women who report past experience with victimization or negative experiences with strangers will report higher fear levels. Third, women who actively engage in situational specific avoidance and risk-management strategies or who have had no previous training in self-defence will report higher fear levels.

METHODOLOGY

The data source for this document is the Violence Against Women Survey. Random Digit Dialing telephone interviews were conducted by Statistics Canada from February through June of 1993. The sample population included women in Canada who were 18 years of age and older. In all, 12,300 women were interviewed by telephone representing a 67.3% response rate.

INDEPENDENT VARIABLES

Respondents were 18 years of age and older. However, the VAWS public use microdata file coded all respondents over the age of 75 as 75 to protect identities. Educational attainment of the respondent was recoded as: some elementary education or no schooling, elementary school diploma, some high school education, high school diploma, some trade, technical, or vocational training, some community college, some university, receiving a trade, technical, or vocational diploma, receiving a college degree, receiving a Bachelors, undergraduate, or law diploma, and having a medical degree, Masters, or Doctorate.

As with the Keane study, the respondent's personal income was measured as: having no income, less than $5000, $5000 - $9999, $10,000 - $14,999, $15,000 - $19,999, $20,000 - 29,999, $30,000 - $39,999, $40,000 - $49,999, $50,000 - $59,999, $60,000 - $69,999, and $70,000 or more. Additional demographic measures such as being single, living in an urban area, and living alone are recorded as yes or no. The VAWS survey asked about victimization experiences in the last twelve months and since age 16. If the respondent reported having experienced an assault in the last twelve months, had received an obscene phone call, had reported being followed by a male stranger in a manner that frightened them, or had received unwanted attention from a male stranger, each response coded as yes or no.

The total number of violent incidents a woman reported over her lifetime is also coded from 0 to 7. Respondents were asked about self-protective behaviours. Whether they had taken a self-defence course in the past year was coded as yes or no. How frequently they did any of the following when alone: a) carried something to defend themselves or to alert other people, b) avoided walking by teenage boys or men, c) locked car doors for personal safety, and d) checked the back seat for intruders before getting into a car were coded as never, sometimes, usually, and always.

Respondents were further asked how often they engaged in three activities when they were alone: a) walked in their neighbourhood, b) used parking garages, and c) used public transport. Response categories were: never, less than once a month, at least once a month, at least once a week, and daily.

DEPENDENT VARIABLES

Respondents were asked to rate how worried they would feel if alone at night in four situations: a) walking in their neighbourhood at night, b) taking public transport, c) using a parking garage, and d) being home. The response categories were coded as: not at all worried, and worried. Logistic regression was utilized to determine the effect of demographic, experiential, and behavioural variables on fear in four situations.

RESULTS

Women's age was normally distributed. Most women reported having some post secondary education. Nonetheless, for the sample, women's average personal income fell below $15,000. For living arrangement, about 1 in 7 women reported living alone, and almost 7 of 10 reported living in an urban area. Approximately 1 in 5 women reported being single at the time the survey was conducted. Considering victimization experiences, about half of women reported at least one incidence of violence. Approximately 7.9 per cent of Canadian women said they had experienced a violent crime in the last 12 months. Almost two thirds of respondents reported receiving an obscene phone call, while three out of five reported receiving unwanted attention from a stranger. Almost one third reported being followed by a stranger in a way that frightened them.

With respect to protective behaviour, about 1 in 10 women stated they had taken a self-defence course over their lifetime. Almost one third of women reported instances where they avoided walking by boys or men, and almost two of every three women surveyed stated that they walked alone at night in their neighbourhood after dark less than once a week. Of those who reported using public transport, the majority stated they used it less than once a week after dark when they were alone.

Of those who reported using or owning a car, the majority of these women reported usually or always locking car doors, usually or always checking the back seat of the vehicle and reported using parking garages less than once a week. A large proportion of women reported being somewhat or very worried walking in their neighbourhood at night. Of those who reported using public transport, 3 out of 4 stated they were somewhat or very worried using this service after dark when alone.

Approximately 4 out of 5 women who used cars stated that they were very or somewhat worried when using them at night when alone. Almost 2 out of every 5 respondents reported being somewhat or very worried when home alone in the evening. In estimates of the bivariate correlations between the four fear of crime items and the independent variables. Given the large sample size of the VAWS, fear is significantly correlated with almost all of the independent variables. Substantive results are women's past experiences with violence and are associated with higher fear in each of the situations. Additionally, having negative experiences with unknown men raises fear. Factors associated with reduced fear among respondents are increased age and walking alone more frequently alone at night in one's neighbourhood. Living alone was associated with higher fear levels in all situations except fear when walking alone in one's neighbourhood at night.

Being single had only a weak and positive association with walking alone in one's neighbourhood at night. The effects of education and levels of personal income had mixed effects across situations. The logistic regression coefficients, standard errors, Wald statistics, and odds-ratios for fear in four situations. The Wald statistic is used to estimate the significance of relationships between variables. Odds ratios greater than 1 indicate an increase in the likelihood of fear with a one unit increase in a predictor variable.

Odds ratios less than 1 show that odds are less likely with a one unit change. The Wald criterion, in each of the models, age had a significant effect on fear. The unstandardized coefficients show that there are negative or inverse relationships as fear in each situation decreases as age increases. The odds ratio show a proportion decrease of 0.7 per cent less likely to report fear while walking alone in their neighbourhood, and 0.8 per cent less likely to report fear in all other situations.

Although these may appear to be small changes, notice that this is an estimated change for one unit of age. There would be substantial differences in reported worry levels if we compared estimated change in odds between a 20 and a 70 year old. In this instance one would multiply these odds by 50 times. Moving to the respondents' education and income, the Wald criterion shows mixed effects across situations. Significant results were detected in all scenarios except worried while walking in one's neighbourhood at night.

Reported personal income was not a significant factor in predicting fear while using public transportation alone at night. Looking at the odds ratios, women with higher levels of education were 5.2 per cent more likely to be worried while in the transportation situation, 5.1 per cent more likely to report being worried while in a parking garage alone at night, but 3.2 per cent less likely to report fear while home alone in the evening. As personal income levels rose fear changed across situations. Women were 2.9 per cent less likely to report fear walking alone in their neighbourhood and 2.7 per cent less likely to report fear for home in the evening, but they were 3.8 per cent more likely to report fear while using the parking garage alone in the evening. Being single significantly increased the odds of reporting worry when out in one's neighbourhood at night by 18.5 per cent, but had no other significant effect in these models.

The odds ratios show living in an urban environment had substantially increased worry in all situations except worry while being home alone. Living alone increased the odds ratio of reporting fear while walking alone by 27.4 per cent but decreased odds of reporting fear by 27.3 per cent while home alone at night. Living alone had no significant effect on either the parking or public transit situations. Looking at women's past experiences, the strongest predictors of fear are negative experiences that women reported having had with strangers, but not necessarily the number or recency of victimization experiences. If respondents reported higher numbers of victimization experiences since age 16, they were seven per cent more likely to report fear in a parking garage and 7.6 per cent more likely to report fear while at home alone at night.

If women had reported a recent victimization within the last year, they were 37 per cent more likely to report fear while using public transport alone at night, but not significantly more likely to report worry in the other three situations asked about in this survey. Across all fear situations, having received an obscene phone call, having been followed by a male stranger, or receiving unwanted attention from a stranger significantly increased respondents' reporting of worry.

Having received an obscene phone call increased reported worry from 19.9 to 34.2 per cent depending on the situation. Likewise, having been followed by a male stranger increased reported worry from 25.5 per cent to 37.4 per cent across situations. Receiving unwanted attention from a male stranger increased the odds of reporting fear from 11.2 per cent to 48.2 per cent. Looking to current behaviour, if respondents reported engaging in risk reduction protective measures they were more likely to have high levels of fear with the exception of having received self-defence training. Having this training served neither to significantly increase nor decrease worry in any situation asked about in the survey.

However, carrying a weapon significantly increased the odds of women reporting worry in these situations by 7.9 to 23.9 per cent with the highest odds being reported while using public transportation while alone at night. Changing one's behaviour strongly and significantly increased the odds of reporting fear. Women who frequently reported avoiding walking by boys or men in these situations were anywhere from 43.5 per cent to 66.5 per cent more likely to report being worried in these situations with the highest odds being fear while walking in one's neighbourhood or using public transportation at night.

Women who reported fewer incidents of walking alone at night were remarkably 39.5 per cent less likely to report worry in these situations. Walking alone less frequently also decreased the odds of reporting worry in the other situations, but to a lesser extent, from 15.4 per cent to 26.5 per cent. Of those who reported using public transport, those who used it less frequently were 12.1 per cent less likely to be worried when using it. Of those who reported using or owning a car, worry increased by 29.3 per cent if they reported locking their car doors while in the vehicle, and by 29.2 per cent if they checked the back seat of a car before getting into it.

However, worry decreased by 9.4 per cent if they reported using parking garages more frequently. The Nagelkerke measure of explained variance adjusts the Cox and Snell R-square statistic so that a value of 1 can be achieved. It is similar to an R-square statistic in regular OLS regression. This study shows that there are substantial differences in explained variance depending on location. Fully 23.4 per cent of variance is explained in reported fear levels for walking alone in the respondent's neighbourhood at night. Using these variables this study accounted for 49.9 per cent of "not worried" responses and 83.3 per cent of the "worried" responses, for an overall prediction rate of 70.4 per cent. When looking to more situationally specific fears for those using public transportation or parking garages, the explanation of variance for these situations drops to 20.5 per cent and 19.2 per cent, respectively. This second analysis was only able to predict "not worried" responses in the public transit situation 23.1 per cent of the time but was able to predict "worried" responses 95.6 per cent of the time, allowing for a 78.5 per cent accuracy rate.

The third analysis was unable to predict "not worried" responses in the parking garage situation, yet 100 per cent of all "worried" responses, for an overall accuracy in prediction of 82.2 per cent of cases. Fear at home when alone at night has the lowest level of variance explained at 10.7 per cent. In opposition to the third analysis, this final analysis could predict all of the "not worried" responses but none of the "worried" responses for an accuracy of prediction of only 59.8 per cent.

DISCUSSION

Contrary to the first proposition made, the effects of demographic variables on predicting fear were mixed. Overall, the first hypothesis stating that demographic variables indicating potential vulnerability are more likely to predict fear when alone in various situations is strongly supported in only one of four conditions: walking alone in one's neighbourhood at night. There is only weak support for the first proposition while using public transport or parking garages, in which younger respondents and those living in an urban area were most likely to report higher levels of fear.

There was slightly stronger support for this proposition in the home situation, with the exception of those who reported they did not live alone. These findings suggest that certain demographic variables come into play in different situations. Where many demographic variables increase fear while walking in one's neighbourhood or being home alone at night, some of these variables have the reverse effect where women reported using other public spaces such as using public transit or parking garages. Given that most of our understanding of fear of crime has centered around findings using respondent's feelings of fear or worry while walking in their neighbourhood at night, it is not entirely unexpected that situationally specific fear questions may challenge some of these findings. Although most of the variables placed into the logistic regression analysis were associated with fear, at a bivariate level, the nature of many of these associations changed when other variables were held constant.

For example, taking self defence training was significantly and positively correlated with increased worry in these four situations. However, this variable ceased to have any significant effects in the model, once other variables were held constant. Personal income and education levels were significantly and positively correlated with worry while walking alone in one's neighbourhood in the evening, but had a negative causal relationship when other variables were held constant.

Odds of reporting fear increased significantly in the home alone situation or walking alone in their neighbourhood alone at night if personal income was lower. Also interesting is that being single is positively associated with fear, and only significantly in the first situation. Use of logistic regression techniques, however, reveals that only the neighbourhood situation maintains directionality and significance with respect to fear. In fact, what becomes clear, many of the demographic variables that have been predictive of fear in other research projects are only predictive of fear in one's neighbourhood. One exception is the rather strong and positive effect of living in an urban environment on fear in situations outside the home. The role of past experiences also had mixed effects on predicting fear.

Only a weak and positive relationship exists between using public transport if the respondent had been reported being assaulted in the last 12 months. What is telling is that those who reported one or more incidents of violence since age 16 were significantly more likely to report feeling worried while at home than in any other situation. This result may be tapping into experiences of repeated violence, which may be at the hands of someone who lives within the home, such as a spouse or other family member. Women in this survey who reported not living alone were also more likely to report fear while home alone in the evening. It is suggested here that repeat victimization of someone who the offender has access to in a controlled environment, such as the home, is far more commonplace than repeat victimization by unknown men.

Women who report higher numbers of violent incidents are not significantly more likely to report higher levels of fear while in the other more public situations. This suggests that their source of fear may actually lie within the home. When comparing the specific locations of waiting for public transport, or using parking garages while alone in the evening, some interesting patterns emerge. In many cases there was a stronger predictive effect of behavioural practices on fear while using public transportation, when compared with those who report using parking garages.

This is somewhat commonsensical. If one uses public transportation, a woman's routines would place her out in the open, and for longer periods of time while waiting for transportation to arrive. Transportation stops are placed along busy corridors which increase the potential for becoming a suitable target. Further, particularly remote transportation locations may also produce anxiety and fear, due to the lack of capable guardianship. Automobiles allow more accessible, and safer modes of transportation, as the driver must only be concerned with getting to the car, rather than walking comparatively longer distances to bus stops and waiting for the transportation vehicle to arrive.

Further, these automobiles can be parked on residential streets, which can provide less exposure to potential predators when compared to a busy thoroughfare. Therefore carrying a weapon, controlling when and how one walks alone, and avoiding unknown groups of boys and men may serve to allay more tangible safety concerns for those using public transportation, than those who use cars as a principal mode of maneuvering around their environment. The strongest effects on the reporting of higher levels of fear are past experiences that women have had with unfamiliar males, thus partially confirming the second proposition tested. Receiving obscene phone calls, or having been followed by an unknown male, and/or receiving unwanted attention from unknown males were all strongly and significantly predictive of higher levels of fear in all situations.

What this suggests is that experience with male strangers plays a stronger formative role in fear production in the lives of women than how old they are, whether they are single, what their financial resources may be, and to a lesser extent what educational achievements they may have made over their lives. This fear of strangers has been aptly referred to as "stranger danger." As young children, many of us are told to be wary of strangers. Children in schools are taught how to cope with strangers through various programmes including verbal rehearsing, modeling, and feedback programmes. These programmes, which are also to be backed by reinforcement of parents, serve to equip children with identifying verbal and physical ruses that predators may use as well as to educate children about verbal and physical resistance strategies they can use in such situations.

Children are less likely to be taught to be fearful of people they know. This taught fear of predators, or strangers, has had repercussions into adult life. These repercussions are so widespread, that effects have been noted in the political sphere. Websdale has argued that implementation of sexual predator laws through the United States has created a moral panic around violence against women and children by people identified as predators.

He argues further that this has served to limit women's participation in public spheres. Most striking are findings in this analysis that reveal that women who restrict their behaviour, avoiding walking by boys and men, not walking alone at night, not using public transportation in the evening, and not using parking garages after dark, have the highest odds of reporting fear. These types of self-protective behaviours are obstacles to participation in evening activity, and thereby reduce women's ability to leave the home. Women who report avoiding walking by boys and men are especially fearful, being roughly one and a half times more likely to report being worried in all situations than those who do not avoid these groups. In fact, all techniques with the exception of taking a self-defence course, regardless of the situation, held the strongest predictive effects on fear. In essence, with the exception of self-defence training, women who altered their routines in order to carry out daily living tasks were estimated as having the highest fear levels.

This is almost an overall confirmation of the third proposition tested. Women who accommodate feelings of lack of safety, and take measures to enhance their security, have the highest fear levels. What is telling is that those who reported using public transportation or parking garages more often were more likely to report lower levels of fear. While this finding is commonsensical, future research into the area should look not only for what generates fear, but for situational factors that generate feelings of safety.

CONCLUDING REMARKS

This document has examined the relationship between demographic, experiential, risk management and avoidance techniques, and fear. Most important for predicting fear were women's reports that they had altered their routines to avoid or manage risky situations. Less strong, but still highly significant across all situations was the power of having frightening experiences with unknown men. When the effects of these experiences are held constant, the predictive value of demographic variables, such as the age of the victim, almost disappears.

It is argued that the past experiences that women have had with strangers, and the daily protective routines women engage in, are more salient predictors of fear than more basic demographic variables. This analysis served to explain higher levels of variance than one done earlier by Keane which looked at fear of crime using the same data set. Future research into fear of crime should seek to more fully understand the role of experiences, especially those with strangers, in generating fear. Finally, it is ironic that this study demonstrates, for the most part, that women fear the danger posed by strange men even though statistics show that women are more likely to be victimized by individuals they know. It would appear that they are most afraid of the surprise sexual attack by the unknown assailant, despite the fact that statistics and public service media campaigns are making women aware of dangers of dating and marital situations.

It is argued here that there is something more at stake with the unknown assailant: predictability. Level of intimacy between the victim and the offender, with few exceptions, offers a buffer to thoughts of victimization. If a woman is approached by an unknown man from behind, and he grabs her arm in this process, she is likely to become alarmed. However, if she turns around to find that it is her neighbour, a friend, or an intimate, her anxiety will probably lessen.

The fact remains that she is more likely to be assaulted by someone she knows, but it is her very relationship with the potential assailant that will allow her to let her guard down. In essence the author is suggesting that knowing someone allows for a false sense of security in that one may feel that they can predict more accurately, and thereby possibly control, the behaviour of someone if they have met in the past. Future research on fear of crime should assess what allows people to have a heightened sense of vulnerability around strange men, while feeling more at ease around those whom they have met before.

5

Women, Crime and Informal Economy

INTRODUCTION

The aim of this stage is to revisit the literature on the informal and criminal economies and provide a critique which builds upon this work by investigating women's contribution to a criminal economy. The discussion is organized around three broad headings: Women and Crime, the Informal and Criminal Economies and Women, Crime and an Informal Economy. There is a considerable literature in two of these areas.

The literature addressing women and crime has proliferated since the publication of Carol Smart's book Women, Crime and Criminology: A Feminist Critique and since then several notable authors have become well established contributors to this area. With respect to the informal and criminal economies, there is also a history of literature with contributions from various disciplinary areas. The informal economy in particular is attracting a recent resurgence in interest.

The third area, women, crime and an informal economy is less well served by the literature. If crime were excluded and women and the informal economy were the focus there is more evidence of published work particularly in the Third World countries. Before the discussion directly addresses the three areas identified, two points are made which are important to bear in mind. The first concerns the so-called 'generalisability problem' and the second related point concerns timing. The 'generalisability problem' is concerned with whether or not general theories take account of both women's and men's criminality. In essence, the question is whether or not the same theories can be used to explain female and male crime.

The Gelsthorpe and Morris, this idea 'has profound significance for theory construction'. My argument is that there are rational choice theories to which this test needs to be addressed. The problem was identified after the first phase of feminist criminology particularly in the UK following Carol Smart's 1976 publication which spawned a feminist critique concerned almost exclusively with the legacy of sexism, with man-made constructions and social control issues. Amongst the few authors who provided exceptions to this are Dorie Klein and previously with June Kress, and Pat Carlen whose works will be addressed below.

Since this first phase, usefully summarized by Daly and Chesney-Lind's posing of the 'generalisability problem', two of the most important theoretical developments are rational choice in the 1980's and doing gender - doing difference in the 1990's. The 1980's saw the domination of the rational choice perspective in mainstream criminology. Whether or not this perspective can be generalized to females has yet to be fully explored.

The 1990's saw the influential body of work 'doing gender - doing difference' emerge. Whether or not rational crime for economic gain is part of 'doing femininity' has yet to be explored. Both the rational choice perspective and doing gender - doing difference are important issues that must be confronted when the focus of research is on female offending and crime for gain. These important theoretical developments of the 1980's and the 1990's must be thought about in relation to the generalisability problem.

WOMEN AND CRIME

This part considers the literature on women and crime that has specific bearing on those women who commit 'economic crimes'. Most female crime, just as to any measure of female offending, is property crime, it is economic. Despite this, economic rationality, the dominant way of accounting for property crime generally, is the one explanation seldom offered when women enter the equation. This stage suggests that explanations for female offending are partial and incomplete. The following discussion begins to show how and is organized in five parts:

- Explaining women and crime
- Doing gender - doing difference
- Rational Choice
- Shoplifting
- Rational or Willful women ?

EXPLAINING WOMEN AND CRIME

The purpose at this stage is to re-consider the work of Dorie Klein and June Kress and Pat Carlen, during that early wave of feminist criminology. As Klein and Kress observe women offenders have rarely been seen as either rational or willful: Women criminals have rarely been accorded even the grudging respect shown male criminals, who are at least seen as a threatening force with which to be reckoned. Instead, women have been the target of voyeuristic studies concerned only with their sexuality.

In a later review entitled the 'Etiology of Female Crime', Klein again makes reference, in her critique of authors who contribute to the 'legacy of sexism', to the way in which boys are 'instrumental' whilst girls are 'expressive' and that even; 'Economic offences such as shoplifting are explained as outlets for sexual frustration'. Men and boys have always been credited with committing crimes for a whole variety of reasons. In addition to being lead astray, being sick or evil, males have also been viewed as rational.

Male offenders have been credited with the faculty of reasoning, women offenders have not. As with the popular stereotypes of women in society generally women offenders are portrayed as hysterical, irrational and incapable of being fully responsible for her actions and crimes due to her biology and sex. In similar fashion to that of Klein and Kress in the mid 1970's Carlen's work also makes occasional reference to women offenders acting rationally. Carlen has identified four major characteristics belonging to female offenders. The first characteristic identified is economic rationality.

Carlen however, does little more than state the possibility that women are acting rationally and where her argument is more fully developed she concentrates on rationality as a form of escape from economic dependency and economic hardship. More importantly, Carlen's own analysis of rationality is one that is restricted to rationality born of a need to escape from poverty not one borne out of a vision of prosperity or the attraction and pull of material possessions.

Yet one of her most renowned co-authors of Criminal Women, Jenny Hicks suggests she established her own criminal firm, defrauded a post office out of a quarter of a million pounds and used the profits from this to finance a lifestyle which included drugs. Similarly Chris Tchaikovsky '....my criminality was the result of a rational choice - nobody had coerced or cajoled me into it'. Daly has identified several pathways into criminality.

There are street women and those who enter through a relationship with a violent man and those whose friends/ partners are involved in selling drugs. As suggested by Hicks and Tchaikovsky, it can be argued however, economic gain, the attraction of money and economic reward as a pull factor, is another. Shoplifting for example, may hold out the attraction of money and economic reward and is just one type of outlawed economic activity that may be an attractive earner to women.

Carlen does occasionally suggest that escaping from poverty and abuse is not a generic and comprehensive explanation for women's involvement in crime. Similarly Klein and Kress acknowledge that rationality may not be an entirely male preserve. Although none of the develop this theme, they reiterate and acknowledge the possibility, that for some women who commit property crimes a different explanation may be appropriate. Clearly I suggest this could be an explanation that sees some forms of offending as a more purposely rational activity.

DOING GENDER–DOING DIFFERENCE

In line with a recent observation and recommendation offered by Steffensmeier and Allan, I would argue that it is productive to proceed following a gendered paradigm that 'acknowledges both the utility of traditional theory and the need to describe how the organization of gender specifies the impact of social forces suggested by traditional theory'. Some recently emerging literature is beginning to focus on the gendered nature of crime. This work is illuminating both gender difference, for example in the area of youth street gangs and gender similarity in crime.

Gender can now be viewed as a situated accomplishment; girls and boys 'do' masculinity and femininity. Crime is used as a resource for 'doing' gender, male youth crime is a resource used for accomplishing masculinity. Precisely what this means for women and girls is not yet clearly theorized but implies that women who 'do crimes for economic gain' would 'do' prostitution, shoplifting, cheque frauds and so on. To develop the idea of 'doing femininity', if we assume the 'doing gender - doing difference' approach, one consequence of this is that we never need to consider the 'generalisability problem' because of the separateness of the gendered explanations, women would simply be emphasizing their femininity.

On the other hand we may choose to take on board the generalisability problem first which could reformulate the theorizing as follows, Generalisability and 'doing gender - doing difference':

- Take the rational choice perspective from mainstream criminology,
- Consider this perspective adopting a gendered position, with specific reference to women,
- Subject the outcome to the 'doing gender - doing difference' test

These are some of the complex and searching questions that can now begin to be addressed following developments within mainstream and feminist criminology's in the late 1980's.

RATIONAL CHOICE

The rational choice perspective was used as an example of a development within mainstream criminology that emerged in the 1980's. Cornish and Clarke provide the most developed explanation for the viability of the rational choice perspective in the introduction to The Reasoning Criminal. Rational, Choice Perspectives on Offending.

John Carroll and Frances Weaver: 'Shoplifter's Perceptions of Crime Opportunities: A Process-Tracing Study', to this edited volume. This empirical study of shoplifting, uses verbal protocol procedure to find out what criminals 'really' think about when they are considering actual crime opportunities. The study, whilst it has limitations, is useful in two respects. First, it emphasizes the value of empirical and crime-specific analyses i.e. shoplifting.

Second, the findings suggest a fairly high degree of rationality in the decisions of both expert and novice shoplifters. Retrospective accounts through interviews were not carried out. In addition and significantly for the purposes of this stage, gender differences/similarities were not discussed in any depth although it is apparent that the data could have been further exploited on this subject.

In the early 1980's Steffensmeier also broached the question of rationality, but through a gendered lens. He looked at an organizations criminal enterprise in the context of 'sexsegregation in the underworld'. He suggested, 'rationality refers to the link of means to ends or the extent to which expeditious means are used to achieve goals' and with specific regards to women: if women are less into crime and are relatively less successful at it, this is less a result of single-mindedness in the rational pursuit of crime than because they lack access to organizations and social contacts that would enable them to pursue criminal enterprise more safely and profitably. It seems that the rational choice perspective may be called upon and further developed in respect of specific offences such as shoplifting, that the methods used to investigate this should be more pluralistic, and that the whole inquiry might usefully be conducted on women offenders. The concept of rationality needs to be subjected to the generalisability test.

In this context 'rational choice' requires deconstructing in order to evaluate the extent to which rationality may be a concept peculiar to masculinity, an entrenched male attribute. A different understanding of rationality may need to be constructed suitable for analysing women who 'do' their own types of crime for gain.

SHOPLIFTING

It is often claimed that women's crimes tend to reflect their place in society. It is nothing new to suggest that traditional women's crimes are linked to domestic life such as shoplifting and social security fraud. This apparent link is difficult to deny although a simplistic link between expressions of women's role and their offence choice is inappropriate. Take for example the crime of shoplifting.

As Allison Morris points out all women shop but only some shoplift. In this example the generalisability problem comes into effect when theories used to explain female crime are grafted on to explain male crime although this is not an exercise that is ever carried out, and would result, if the doing gender doing difference perspective were also taken on board, in male shoplifters being labelled homosexual. Several authors have focused upon the offence of shoplifting and these works can be divided into various categories.

Some for example have focused upon who shoplifts, others have been more interested in shoplifting as a vehicle for examining differential sentencing patterns between men and women. Others have focused upon the prevention aspects of shoplifting. Some have made use of observational data, others have used the survey method to elicit information. In other areas of crime authors have developed the so-called offenders perspective by listening to known offenders about their habits, targets and so on. In 1964 Cameron wrote that 'every town, has its little old kleptomaniac lady who steals at will...'.Over 30 years later such impressions are still typical. Gibbens and Price's survey in 1960 found two and a half times as many women as men were accused of shoplifting. Twenty five years later Munday found the balance had swung so that more than one and a half times as many men as women were accused of shoplifting.

The stereotypical images of the shoplifter that persist continue to be overwhelmingly female and also now include; the menopausal housewife, the confused foreign tourist, the mother striving to feed and clothe her young children, women and girls tempted by glitzy bright jewelry and clothes. When it comes to further analysis and theories concerned about explaining crime, criminology has generally been gender blind, assuming that crime is a masculine preserve. In addition, explanations in respect of why men and boys might be engaged in property crime have changed several times during the course of the twentieth century.

Men and boys actions have moved from being explained by innate biological impulses through to psychiatric explanations, though to explanations that show shoplifting to be an essentially social activity where peer group pressure and sub-cultures are important influences through to socio-environmental explanations including poverty and need, greed and excitement. The classic explanations throughout criminology; anomie, sub-culture, differential association, rational choice all draw upon examples using men and/or boys either explicitly or implicitly as illustrations.

In contrast women and girls who shoplift can be much more easily explained. It is their sexuality rooted in their biological make up and psychiatric characteristics that are the root cause of their criminal tendencies. As in any other area of crime or social life women have never been deemed to act rationally, not even when in dire material need.

Explanations when it comes to women and girls have ignored the fact that like men and boys they may also be badly or even worse off, have little or no money or earning capacity or legitimate opportunity to earn a decent living now or in the future. Traditional explanations never recognized the economic motivation or the fact that money might be equally a motivating factor for women as for men. The possibility of rationality being a female criminals attribute has never been systematically explored. Such a history of female offending and its explanation is typical and shoplifting in particular serves to show forcefully that studies have not challenged these images and explanations. Even criminological examinations of the offence-specific variety have served only to reinforce the stereotypes that have been typically showed in other areas.

An article published in a psychiatry journal has as recently as 1995 shown continuing emphasis on psychopathological explanations for shoplifting in adult female offenders. Although a variety of research methodologies and techniques have been employed in the various studies mentioned, none adopt a plurality of research techniques or a qualitative approach that investigates the day-to-day business of the female shoplifter by in depth interviewing from the female offenders perspective.

To conclude on the explanations of women as shoplifters, the overwhelming feeling of being stuck in time - due to a form of ahistoricsm and a lack of incorporation of the developments that have taken place in criminology - persists. Although some recent work has begun to emphasize how rational and purposive are women offenders, women engaged in property crime, shoplifting and cheque frauds, drug use and prostitution just as to these views, have all chosen these options albeit in the face of constrained choices due to poverty. It seems that there has been little examination of the links between types of crimes committed, particularly the attractions offered by some crimes for economic gain, and female offending.

RATIONAL OR WILLFUL WOMEN

Rather than focusing upon theories which seek to explain all forms of criminality amongst women this document requires a particular concentration and focus upon those crimes which are more likely to contribute to the informal and illegal marketplace and have been referred to as crime for gain.

The crimes of interest here are those committed directly or indirectly for economic benefit such as property crimes where the property can be sold on for cash or bartered, theft of money and cheque frauds, shoplifting, dealing in illegal drugs, welfare and social security frauds. These crimes are also those that are amongst the highest arrest categories for women namely shoplifting, prostitution, fraud and forgery and drugs related offending. Field usefully differentiated between crime for gain and crime not for gain.

The commission of directly economically beneficial crimes, such as those previously referred to in Carlen's work and those listed directly above, together with prostitution - a clear example of deviance as work - might be subjected to both a gender and rationality test. Two authors writing about women sex workers have recently advocated a 'presumption of wilful rationality' to capture the idea that the background of prostitutes cannot be denied as unimportant when considering recruitment into the sex industry but the idea of free and informed choice might be important too.

Such an approach recognizes 'doing crime' is one's own free will and choice, however, at the same time it can be regarded as exercising one's reason. The notion of 'willful rationality' might be appropriate for considering other forms of crime for gain that women 'do'. It might also be considered alongside Carlen's 'optional', 'incidental' and 'professional law breaking' categories.

THE INFORMAL AND CRIMINAL ECONOMIES

This whole area would appear to be dominated by an assumption of rationality. Twenty seven years ago Mary McIntosh, analysed how crime can be seen 'as a rational economic activity, geared towards making money and minimizing risks,' and as having parallels with legal forms of work in the context of organized and professional crime.

At the time McIntosh did not draw out the gendered nature of that activity. The work of Henry begins to touch upon a criminal economy. He suggests it includes both recorded and unrecorded or undetected crime. Chambliss, Klockars and

Block and Chambliss have showed how the criminal economy is comparable to the regular economy analysing organized crime, fencing, and the Mafia respectively. Chambliss notes that the profits of organized crime and their business is an important part of the gross national product.

His is a portrayal of illegal networks and corruption, illegal business on a typically American and grandiose scale. More recently Auld, Dorn and South on heroin use and Hobbs on professional forms of crime, provide useful insights into the motivations and lifestyles of criminal men and youth and deviant entrepreneurial activities. The informal economy has been variously defined with a variety of disciplines doing the defining.

Many attempts to show the informal economy have been made by economists in the UK , US and elsewhere including analysis of the 'unofficial economy', the 'Underground Economy', where crime is seen as distinct from the underground economy, the 'Shadow Economy' which includes the 'black economy' but is much wider than simply illegal activity, the 'Subterranean Economy' which encompasses the whole unmeasured economy of open society. Although many examples of illegal activities are provided, there is little in the way of analysis and the work belongs to the 1980's and earlier. Even more recent work has concentrated exclusively on the fiscal economy.

Others have distinguished between the informal and formal sectors in the tradition of Hart whose work was associated with the development process and urban economies. None of this collection offers a developed definition of a criminal economy. Others have approached the informal economy from a criminological framework. Such work includes Mars' typology of work and its rewards and much earlier work belonging to Henry, Ditton.

More detailed studies of those who take part in crime within the informal economy in the UK is now dated. The literature review of forms of economic activity by Harding and Jenkins, in some respects bridges the gap between these two frameworks; the economic and the criminological. These authors usefully show economic activities and their location on a map of formality/informality and work/employment. They suggest that the connections between these elements is best achieved by subscribing to the idea of continuums. Criminal activities range on a continuum from crime to fiddles and outright corruption. In a similar vein MacDonald has recently focussed attention on the elusive distinctions between work and employment, raising questions about different allegiances to work including the options of alternative ways of working in the face of restricted avenues for legitimate employment, notably 'fiddly work'.

Debates are ongoing in respect of the contested definitions of organized and professional crimes, lines between formality and informality, between work and employment, legality and illegality, all adding to the complexity and problems of boundaries. Current work on the informal economy in a European context argues in favour of making these 'fuzzy lines' between the formal and informal, and boundaries between the informal and criminal economy, problematic.

Further, Shapland argues that this complexity is 'liberating'. From the bottom up perspective of those women who are committing crimes for economic gain, as advocated in this document, this complex view of the informal and criminal economies can indeed be regarded as a useful and liberating starting point.

6

Violence against Girl Child in India

INTRODUCTION

Violence against women is partly a result of gender relations that assumes men to be superior to women. Given the subordinate status of women, much of gender violence is considered normal and enjoys social sanction. Manifestations of violence include physical aggression, such as blows of varying intensity, burns, attempted hanging, sexual abuse and rape, psychological violence through insults, humiliation, coercion, blackmail, economic or emotional threats, and control over speech and actions.

In extreme, but not unknown cases, death is the result. These expressions of violence take place in a man-woman relationship within the family, state and society. Usually, domestic aggression towards women and girls, due to various reasons remain hidden. Cultural and social factors are interlinked with the development and propagation of violent behaviour.

With different processes of socialisation that men and women undergo, men take up stereotyped gender roles of domination and control, whereas women take up that of submission, dependence and respect for authority. A female child grows up with a constant sense of being weak and in need of protection, whether physical social or economic. This helplessness has led to her exploitation at almost every stage of life. The family socialises its members to accept hierarchical relations expressed in unequal division of labour between the sexes and power over the allocation of resources. The family and its operational unit is where the child is exposed to gender differences since birth, and in recent times even before birth, in the form of sex-determination tests leading to foeticide and female infanticide.

The home, which is supposed to be the most secure place, is where women are most exposed to violence. Violence against women has been clearly defined as a form of discrimination in numerous documents. The World Human Rights Conference in Vienna, first recognised gender- based violence as a human rights violation in 1993.

In the same year, United Nations declaration, 1993, defined violence against women as "any act of gender-based violence that results in, or is likely to result in, physical, sexual or psychological harm or suffering to a woman, including threats of such acts, coercion or arbitrary deprivations of liberty, whether occurring in public or private life". Radhika Coomaraswamy identifies different kinds of violence against women, in the United Nation's special report, 1995, on Violence Against Women;

- Physical, sexual and psychological violence occurring in the family, including battering, sexual abuse of female children in the household, dowry related violence, marital rape, female genital mutilation and other traditional practices harmful to women, non spousal violence and violence related to exploitation.
- Physical sexual and psychological violence occurring within the general community, including rape, sexual abuse, sexual harassment and intimidation at work, in educational institutions and elsewhere, trafficking in women and forced prostitution.
- Physical, sexual and psychological violence perpetrated or condoned by the state, wherever it occurs.

This definition added 'violence perpetrated or condoned by the State', to the definition by United Nations in 1993. Coomaraswamy points out that women are vulnerable to various forms of violent treatment for several reasons, all based on gender.

- Because of being female, a woman is subject to rape, female circumcision/genital mutilation, female infanticide and sex related crimes. This reason relates to society's construction of female sexuality and its role in social hierarchy.
- Because of her relationship to a man, a woman is vulnerable to domestic violence, dowry murder, sati. This reason relates to society's concept of a woman as a property and dependent of the male protector, father, husband, son, etc.
- Because of the social group to which she belongs, in times of war, riots. Or ethnic, caste, or class violence, a woman may be raped and brutalised as a means of humiliating the community to which she belongs. This also relates to male perception of female sexuality and women as the property of men.

Combining these types of abuse with the concept of hierarchical gender relations, a useful way to view gender violence is by identifying where the violence towards women occurs.

Essentially, violence happens in three contexts - the family, the community and the state and at each point key social institutions fulfil critical and interactive functions in defining legitimating and maintaining the violence.

- The family socialises its members to accept hierarchical relations expressed in unequal division of labour between the sexes and power over the allocation of resources.
- The community provides the mechanisms for perpetuating male control over women's sexuality, mobility and labour.
- The state legitimises the proprietary rights of men over women, providing a legal basis to the family and the community to perpetuate these relations. The state does this through the enactment of discriminatory application of the law.

Margaret Schuler has divided gender violence into four major categories;

- Overt physical abuse Psychological abuse Deprivation of resources for physical and psychological well being
- Commodification of women

Adriana Gomez has also talked about two basic forms of violence, that is; structural and direct. Structural violence arises from the dominant political, economic and social systems, in so far as they block access to the means of survival for large number of people; for example, economic models based on the super-exploitation of thousands for the benefit of a few, extreme poverty in opposition to ostentatious wealth, and repression and discrimination against those who diverge from given norms. Structural violence just as to her is the basis of direct violence, because it influences the socialisation which causes individuals to accept or inflict suffering, just as to the social function they fulfil.

Open or direct violence is exercised through aggression, arms or physical force. The Fourth Conference of Women, 1995 has defined violence against women as a physical act of aggression of one individual or group against another or others. Violence against women is any act of gender-based violence which result in, physical, sexual or arbitrary deprivation of liberty in public or private life and violation of human rights of women in violation of human rights of women in situations of armed conflicts. Violence is an act carried out with the intention or perceived intention of physically hurting another person.

Gender Violence is defined as "any act involving use of force or coercion with an intent of perpetuating promoting hierarchical gender relations". Adding gender dimension to that definition amplifies it to include violent acts perpetrated on women because they are women. With this addition, the definition is no longer simple or obvious. Understanding the phenomenon of gender violence requires an analysis of the patterns of violence directed towards women and the underlying mechanisms that permit the emergence and perpetuation of these patterns. Liz Kelly, Surviving Sexual Polity has defined violence as "any physical, visual, verbal or sexual act that is experienced by the woman or girl at the time or later as a threat, invasion or assault, that has the effect of hurting her or degrading her and/or takes away her ability to contest an intimate contact".

Dr Joanne Liddle modified this definition as "any physical, visual, verbal or sexual act that is experienced by the person at the time or later as a threat, invasion or assault, that has the effect of hurting or disregarding or removing the ability to control one's own behaviour or an interaction, whether this be within the workplace, the home, on the streets or in any other area of the community".

FEMALE FOETICIDE AND INFANTICIDE

Technologies like amniocentesis and ultrasound used in most parts of the world, largely for detecting foetal abnormalities, has been used in large parts of the Indian subcontinent for determining the sex of the foetus so that it can be aborted, if it happens to be a female. The information of the sex of the unborn was being extensively misused. To prevent female foeticide and to restrict this misuse, the Prenatal Diagnostic Techniques Act was passed on 20th September 1994.

The Act forbids the communication of the sex of the foetus, but the enforcement of this act is not easy. Medical Termination of Pregnancy Act 1971 allows abortion if the doctor is of the opinion that the continuance of the pregnancy would endanger the life of the pregnant woman or involve grave injury to her physical or mental health; or there is substantial risk that the child would suffer from disabling physical or mental abnormalities.

The anguish caused by pregnancy as a result of rape, or as a result of failure of any device or method used by a married couple for the purpose of limiting the number of children, may be presumed to constitute a grave injury to the woman's mental health. If the pregnancy is twelve weeks old, the opinion of one registered medical practitioner is sufficient; for pregnancy of between twelve and twenty four weeks, the opinion of two registered medical practitioner is required. The matter is thus purely between her and the medical practitioner and even the husbands' consent becomes unnecessary. In reality, however, a woman's' right to abortion is very restricted and mostly it turns out to be a family decision. Various court judgements have held that aborting a foetus without the husbands' consent would amount to cruelty under the Hindu Marriage Act and hence a ground for divorce.

The procedure gets rampantly misused with the collaboration of the medical fraternity, as an alternative in the case of couples who do not opt to practise family planning methods and who want to do away with the unwanted child. The earliest known legislation against female infanticide was enacted by the British Government in 1870.

Prior to this, there were regional regulations established by the British, such as the Bengal Regulation of XXI 1795 and Regulation III of 1807, that declared that infanticide amounted to murder. The Infanticide Regulation Act of 1870 was passed nearly a hundred years after the British discovered it officially. This Act acquired the compulsory registration of births and deaths to enable verification of female children a few years after birth. Since Independence, the Constitution of India contains certain provisions that guarantee the welfare and development of children.

The Indian Penal Code also has defined infanticide as murder. While the deliberate act of causing a miscarriage or injury to the new born child, exposure of the infant and concealment of births are covered under Sections 312 to 318 of the I.P.C, the intention of preventing a child being born and causing bodily harm to the infant are covered under I.P.C Section 315. Section 317 makes the concealment of the birth and secret disposal of the dead body an offence.

Miller categorises infanticide as a fatal form of child abuse. There are more passive forms of infanticide like neglect, sustained nutritional deprivation, delayed health care for female infants or, in other words, an unequal allocation of household resources detrimental to the health of the girl child.

In fact, the passive forms of infanticide remain unrecorded as infanticide by health workers and sociologists. Female infanticide and foeticide has occurred not only in several cultures across history, but is known to occur in contemporary societies as well. Several scholars have documented female infanticide for the period of British Colonial rule. In the period since independence, the practice has been reported as occurring in many parts of the country including Tamil Nadu where the practice was not known to exist before independence.

The first recorded instance in India, dates to 1789 when Jonathan Duncan, a British Resident at Benares, Uttar Pradesh State, North India, detected the practice among a Rajput clan. The British passed the Infanticide Regulation Act in 1870 and subsequently, a special Census was taken in 1881 in the Western Provinces and Oudh to detect female infanticide. Evidence from the British records and other historical sources shows that the practice was confined to Northern and Western regions of the country including present day Rajasthan, Punjab, Uttar Pradesh and Bihar.

By contrast, female infanticide in Tamil Nadu is essentially a post independence phenomenon. In South India, the practise of female infanticide existed among the Toda tribe of Tamil Nadu. The only factual evidence to prove that it still exists among them, is the sex ratio data in the Nilgiri District of Tamil Nadu. The data that Chunkath and others analysed confirmed that, the practise of female infanticide is widespread in Dharmapuri, Salem and Madurai Districts.

They arrived at this conclusion after preparing a table on, distribution of Blocks by number of female infanticide deaths, as per PHC records. They observed that there is a contiguous cluster of blocks where female infanticide occurs and what should be a cause for particular concern is that the phenomenon is spreading from the core area to a much wider neighbouring periphery area and beyond. In 1986, when the practice of female infanticide in Madurai District of Tamil Nadu first received major media attention, the focus was on the caste group known as 'Piramalai Kallars' and it was held that the practice was confined to this caste. Over the past two decades, the region has attracted wide attention due to the prevalence of the practice of female infanticide in Usilampatti taluka. This region has a predominant large population of Kallars. In 1992, when female infanticide was found to be widespread in Salem District and the Gounder community was considered to be the one practising it. In a survey done by Chunkath and Athreya, it was found that this practice has spread to many castes.

The data they collected from one district alone - Dindugal, Tamil Nadu, show occurrence of female infanticide in 35 caste groups. They conclude that while the Piramalai Kallars and Gounders in their respective areas of numerical and social dominance may have initiated the practice of female infanticide, it now appears to cut across all castes. They say that, probably the practice of female infanticide by the dominant peasant/landlord caste of the local community served to legitimate and provide social sanction to the practice and contribute substantially to its spread among all castes. The value system and norms of ritual expenditure pattern of the dominant peasant/landlord caste of the region raise the perceived cost of bringing up female infants, for poorer members of the dominant caste in particular, and for all castes in general.

Although this may be true in some areas, it cannot be generalised. Chunkath and Athreya in their study, also found that the practice is widespread among the scheduled castes and tribes. The study done by George and others in 1992, out of the 18 cases of female infanticide that they came across, 17 were among the Gounders. The remaining one case occurred among the Arunthatis a scheduled caste.

In Bihar, according to a study done by Adithi, a local NGO in Katihar District, of 35 Dais, this practise originally began among Rajputs but spread to many castes including the Bumihars, Brahmins, Kayasthas, Yadavas and some scheduled castes. This, they say, is similar to the case in Tamil Nadu, where it originally began with Gounder caste and has now spread to almost all castes. What makes the practice important in the contemporary society is that there are indications of its increase in occurrence. It is difficult to obtain carefully confirmed first hand data on infanticide cases and social variables related to infanticide. There is also a problem of gathering data on direct or indirect infanticide through any brief field work. It makes it even more difficult to obtain data when people remain tight lipped about the situation. Now that the practice has been recognised as a crime by law and the increase in awareness among the people, they have become cautious about revealing facts to investigators.

There are few clear indicators to identify the extent of female infanticide. However it is known that in any genetic group, the proportion of males to females is fairly equal. Studies based on hospital birth records show that boys outnumber girls at birth under natural circumstances. Initially the mortality rate among boys is higher than among girls, so the ratio balances out in the long run. Hence an adverse sex ratio especially in the first few years of life, and gender differences in Infant Mortality Rate are significant pointers towards the possibility of female infanticide. Agnihotri has worked out a statistical formula for disaggregating the 'missing females' in the overall population of the country and has computed the missing females in a demographic analysis based on sex ratio.

He has used the census data for this purpose. Sex ratio data would undoubtedly include those who are victims of malnutrition, delayed health care and other forms of childhood abuse, including infanticide, and in recent years foeticide. His estimation is based on the total number of females required to be added on to reach the level of the male population over a period of years. This disaggregation can be done for the whole country, for any caste, class, age, or regional sub group to show which part is contributing largely to the 'missing females' in the population.

Chunkath and others in their report say that PHC provide information on pregnancies, deliveries, births, still births, early neo natal deaths, other neo natal deaths and post natal deaths gender-wise. The field staff of the public health network also obtains information on causes of infant deaths and one of the cause is 'death due to social causes'. This category refers to male/female infanticide. The most significant indicator would be the neo natal mortality rate and it is here that the gender differences assume significance especially if the analysis is based on PHC records. What also needs to be found is the accuracy of this data. It may be possible that the registering of a neo natal death is done in the post natal period, in which case the data will be distorted.

Tamil Nadu, in 1996, had decided to conduct the survey of 24 revenue districts divided into 41 health unit districts. The data that is easily accessible and available in Tamil Nadu, may not be in some other states. The National Family Health Survey found that the post neonatal mortality is 13% higher for females than males, and child mortality is 43% higher for female than for males. But these are all India figures, which do not convey the regional differences.

What is required is data on gender - neo natal, post natal and infant mortality rates for all India, State and District level. The experience of Chunkath and others in their survey has been that, reliable data on vital rates is available through Sample Registration Survey but only for the State as a whole. Hospital records are a major source by which, one can speculate that female infanticide has occurred. Negi states, in a number of cases, especially in hospitalised delivery, the female infants are sent home in good health.

Subsequently, within a few hours after reaching home, the family claims that the child has died due to various causes. This leads to speculate that, a case of infanticide has occurred. Even the ritual, that is normally observed on death in the family is never followed in cases of female infanticide. There are also survey findings to prove that the babies and mothers vanish from hospitals on knowing that a girl child has been born.

George and others in their study recorded nearly 600 girls born into the Kallar caste in the Usilampatti government hospital every year. Out of these an estimated 570 babies vanish from the hospital, with their mothers. Hospital sources estimate that nearly 80 per cent of these vanishing babies become victims of infanticide. The Registrar General of India, Mr Vijay Unnikrishnan says that each year there are 25 million births and 9 million deaths in the country, but only 40% of these events are registered. These non-registered births and deaths are untraceable by any secondary data. The hospital records can only report the births that take place in hospitals. It is a common practice in rural India that the delivery is done by the midwives and at home. It is also known through various surveys that midwives are pressurised to kill the children. Women may migrate to their paternal home for delivery.

All these factors make it difficult to record the death of female babies. The people who actually kill the child are the dais, fathers, mothers or elder female members of the family. Adithi, a local NGO in Katihar District, Bihar conducted a survey in four districts in Bihar. According to their findings, Katihar District alone accounts for over 1000 infanticides cases per year. The survey, based on interviews with the 35 midwives in the district reveals that each of them kill at least three to four babies every month.

A similar situation was found in Sitamarhi, Gumla and Purnia districts. In Bihar, the new born girls are killed primarily by the dais, at the behest of the parents. They receive an amount of Rs 25 to 30/- for the deed. The child is normally killed within the first three days or the first week of its birth, after which the chances of its survival increases. It is only in rare instances that the child is killed after the first week. 17 of the 19 female infanticides occurred within seven days of birth, one on the ninth day after birth, and the remaining one on the 16th day. In the entire study population, there were a total of 18 female infant deaths during the first seven days after birth. One of the key points that emerged from the findings of Chunkath and others, is that, there is hardly any gender differential in post-natal infant death rates in most of the districts surveyed in Tamil Nadu.

On the other hand, mortality rates are considerably higher for female as against male infants in the entire neo-natal phase. This means that the babies are killed at a neo natal stage, which makes it more important to find out when the reporting of death is done in the PHCs. Modernisation has been cited by Negi as a reason for female infanticide, as there was a shift from growing traditional crops to cash crops. Madurai District was rainfed zone and both women and men used to be jointly involved in the process of cultivation. Women had the knowledge of how to cultivate seeds in the traditional way, when to start collecting them, when to sow them and how to store them. They also had the knowledge of, what kinds of fertilizers are necessary and should be used and so on.

With the construction of Vaigai dam in 1950, Madurai District came to be irrigated and with it came the introduction of cash crops. The local traditional pattern vanished and the knowledge of women were no more needed or required. The skills and resources were external. The seeds, pesticides, loans, electricity and skills of management came from outside. The men started going out to government offices to get loans, to bring seed and pesticides, to sell the crops and overlook the irrigation and started making decisions. Over the period of time the land lost its fertility, the ground water has gone down. Women became mere liabilities with her knowledge having become redundant and men aspired to marry only those women whose family can afford to offer more dowry.

Sergent et al, 1996 has mentioned that, in the landless classes, the presence of sons ensures a higher labour participation and correspondingly a high financial support to the family, as a consequence, the family is likely to favour a male child, increasing the probability of female infanticide. Modernisation has brought about changes in the traditional systems and thereby lowering the status of women in the society. The sharp decline in Juvenile sex ratios is relatively a recent phenomenon.

Dowry, given at the time of the daughter's marriage, has influenced the status of women. The daughter is considered to be a liability as her contribution to the family is temporary upto the time she is married and sent to another family. Dowry is not the only transaction as far as the daughter's marriage is concerned. Krishnaswamy, 1988 has mentioned about a series of ceremonies in South India, Tamil Nadu, associated with the girls in the family. Gifts in cash and kind to the husband's family during ceremonies connected with pregnancy, childbirth and ceremonies for piercing the ear of the girl child and so on. It is the inability to meet the dowry-related demands from the in-law's family, that is a major cause for female infanticide. The fear of sexual abuse of the girl child is also a cause for female infanticide. The husbands' inability to do anything against the practice of sexual abuse of his wife by his father is due to the fear that he would lose his share of the property from his father.

The father-in-law due to his own child marriage loses interest in his wife and finds it more convenient to find a bride for his son and to have his "sexual fulfilment" through her. Mothers, sometimes, kill their babies as an act of 'mercy' that they may be saved from future excesses by husbands in the form of domestic violence. They feel justified in killing their girl child so that she is saved from all the suffering she may have to undergo all her life. Harris-White has cited poverty as one of the reasons for female infanticide.

According to the survey done by Chunkath and others, the occurrence of female infanticide is widespread among the poorer and socially disadvantaged community including the thevars, vaniyars and scheduled castes. In contrast, Adithi and Community Services Guild has mentioned several communities, including the wealthy Gounder community, the landed caste in Salem District, Tamil Nadu, also practice female infanticide. George and others in their study point out although the Gounders, live in remote villages, they own a significant proportion of land and are in the upper social stratum of their villages, in the North and South Arcot Districts in Tamil Nadu.

It has been proved through various studies that the practise cuts across all classes and caste. Negi in her report has mentioned, the society and families having used coercive tactics to ensure that female infanticide continues, limiting the scope for outside influences in arresting the problem. Experiences of Negi, 1997 and others who have researched on this issue, is that, there is a social sanction to the deed. The familial and social situations seem to outweigh personal reactions and therefore women opt to kill their new born girl children. Indian Council for Child Welfare, Tamil Nadu has mentioned that the feeling of guilt and trauma is almost absent in the community that perpetrates the practise, although there is grief among the mothers. Social pressures play a vital role in bringing about changes in society for the better or worse situations.

George and others have also observed maternal motivation in their study as a factor affecting infanticide. They also came across one case of male infanticide just before the beginning of their study period where the mother lost her husband and killed the male child soon after birth, after which the mother remarried. In case of the unwed mother, she tried to abort the pregnancy, which was unsuccessful and committed infanticide when it was born.

Maternal motivations for infanticide may be said, therefore, to vary on the basis of marital status. According to one of the dai interviewed, in the survey conducted by Adithi, Bihar, "mothers are never willing, it is the men who force them". The same study holds that the male mainly take the decision to carry out the killing of the newborn babies with females being reluctant participants.

One mother justifies her action by saying that they have hardly any access to medical care. All deliveries take place at home and often the mother is left to bleed after a particularly difficult child birth. They categorically state that they do not wish to expose their girls to such harsh conditions. A question that arises with regard to female infanticide is whether birth order influences the chance of survival of the female infant. According to the study by Chunkath and Athreya in Tamil Nadu, the first female infant is, in a majority of cases, not a victim of female infanticide even in the high female infanticide Health Unit Districts, although there are instances when it is. The second female infant has a much greater chance of escaping infanticide in Madurai HUD than she does in Periyakulam and Dharmapuri HUDs. While the third female is at much greater risk than the first in all three HUDs, both the second and third seem to be equally at risk in Periyakulam. The survey finding by George and others mentions 19 female infanticides and 18 of the victims had birth orders greater than one and one involved a first born daughter. Each of these families had at least one surviving female child at the time and usually they had two. In their study they also found that no twin died as a result of direct infanticide, however, they also say that they are subject to more neglect than a male twin and a female infant born after a set of twins is very likely to be killed.

The studies prove that birth order does influence the chances of child's survival. Negi after conducting interviews and discussions with people and NGOs closely working in Madurai District point out to the prevalence of a superstition that, killing a new born girl child increases the probability of a male child being born in the family. Some of the other findings in the survey conducted by George and others in 1989 is that, the villages in which female infanticide occurs tend to be even more remote and have less educated people than the villages with no cases of infanticide. Lack of scanning centres has also been cited as reason for infanticide. As people do not have this facility, they kill the child after it is born. According to Soma Wadhwa, every year 50,000 female foetuses are aborted in India.

These people are not very different from those who kill the baby after she is born. The latter, she says, simply do not have enough money or facility to kill her in the womb Observation made by Kumarbabu, 1996, is that even in the so-called remote, less-developed areas, "scanning centres exist. Although it may be true in some cases, one cannot generalise whether remoteness of the village, education of the people, or lack of scanning centres have any correlation with the occurrence of female infanticide. Psychopathologists have also tried to analyse why people kill new born girl children. Sabu George, Rajaratnam Abel and B.D.Meller have carried out research in 12 villages of K.V.Kuppam block, North Arcot Ambedkar District in Tamil Nadu State for four years beginning in April 1987 to September 1989. After creating a good rapport with the people, the father or other family members would tell the village worker that if the current pregnancy resulted in the birth of a female, it would be killed. They found that each village had an assigned village level worker whose primary function was to provide education about child care to village mothers. The worker in all cases was a local resident of the village. The main findings of the survey conducted by George and others, was that in the study population of 13,000 there were a total of 773 birth outcomes recorded, involving 759 live births of which 378 were male and 381 were female.

Among the cohort of live births, 56 died in the period of two and a half years and of these 23 were males and 33 females. Thus the female male ratio was about 3:4. Of the 23 male deaths, there was no infanticide. Among the 33 female deaths, there were 19 infanticides. Thus more than half the female deaths in the 12 study villages were due to direct or indirect infanticide. In the six villages in which all infanticides occurred, infanticide constitute 72 per cent of female deaths. In the 12 village study population, the overall sex ratio at the time of the study was 977.5. In the village where female infanticide was practised, the sex ratio was 939.8, while in the other villages, it was 1018.6.

CHILD MARRIAGE

A girl child is twice vulnerable for being a child and a girl. Discrimination against them begins even before their birth and continues as they grow. Their psychological, physical and economic dependence on the family makes them vulnerable to violence and child abuse within or outside the family. Since 1872, the following efforts have been made to legalise the minimum age of marriage.

The Civil Marriage Act of 1872 was passed as a result of the efforts made by Raja Ram Mohan Roy, before which, a provision of the Indian Penal Code rendered the consummation of marriage before the girl attained the age of 10, punishable with life imprisonment. Social reformers of 19th and 20th century tried to counteract child marriage as they felt it was marring child's educational, physical and economic progress. Noted social reformer Har Bilas Sarda, from Ajmer District, Rajasthan authored and piloted a Bill in British Legislature to stop child marriage, which, in course of time became law. The Child Marriage Restrain Act of 1929 which fixed the minimum age for boys at 18 and girls at 15, extended only to British India. The Act did not prohibit marriages nor did it declare these marriages invalid or illegal.

With the codification of the Hindu Law, the Hindu Marriage Act passed in 1955 made the minimum age of marriage for girls at 15. In 1978, a further revision was made in the minimum legal age. With this last amendment, the law was finally brought nearer in line with the accumulated scientific medical evidence showing that the adolescent girl is at grave risk of her health, as also that of her children, until she has reached the age of 18 at least. Alongside, the minimum age of marriage for boys also underwent an upward revision to 21 years.

However, it did not empower the police to prevent the marriage by arresting a person without warrant or magisterial order. Under the amended provision of this Act the jurisdiction was given to metropolitan magistrates or to judicial magistrates. They have been empowered to try any case related to child marriage. Anybody including social organisations, the police or the any person can make a complaint to the police or to the magistrate directly. Acting on a complaint, any court can itself make inquiries.

However in practice this whole process is so complicated and so time consuming that by the time these authorities are in a position to take preventive action the marriage is already over and all proof of such a ceremony obliterated. Further, Section 12 of the amended Child Marriage Restraint Act empower the magistrate to issue injunctions prohibiting marriages in contravention of this Act, but before issuing injunction the affected parties have to be given a notice to enable them to present defence. An injunction issued without this notice is not valid. This procedure is so time-consuming that marriages in contravention of this Act are completed before the court can pass an order preventing them. The court cannot even issue a general direction that marriage of a child shall not be solemnised within some particular time limit, say eight months or two years. The punishment under the amended Child Marriage Restraint Act remains mild, i.e. only simple imprisonment extended to three months and a fine of Rs 1000. According to the provisions of Section 5 of the Act whoever performs, conduct or direct child marriages shall be punishable.

Ancient Hindu religious manuals like the Manu Smriti and Grihayastra set the age of life partners at 13 for girls and 16 for boys. In the Vedic period early marriage of girls began to gain approval and it became obligatory to have a girl married before she attained puberty. The age was lowered still further in the Brahminical period, resulting in the abuse of children. The phenomenon of child marriage prevails all over the country.

According to Chattopadhyay, 1986, the phenomenon of marrying off minors persists in almost every caste and community of Rajasthan. This practice prevails in Gaduliya Lohars of Central, Western and South Eastern Rajasthan. It also exists among the Muslim converts and among higher castes of Pushkaran Brahmins. According to Saxena, 1999, during the Akha Teej or Akshaya Trithiya, the most auspicious day for marriages, practically everywhere in Western Rajasthan - Bikaner, Tonk, Jhalwar, Jodhpur and Jaisalmer, marriages are performed en masse.

Every street, house, tractor and even buses seem to reverberate with music and marriage guests. But in all marriages the bride and the groom are children, some just two or three years old and some babies barely able to walk. These brides and grooms are carried by their parents or are perched on a thali and taken around the holy fire for performing the most important ceremony of their life. In communities like Dakot, Dhobi, Jatava, Kasai, girls are married between the age group of 11 to 13, and in case of boys it ranges from 14 to 16 years of age. The number of minor children married in a mass marriage, in Rajasthan was reported to be 25000 in 1984 and 30,000 in 1983, 40,000 in 1985 and unofficial sources confirmed no decline in 1986. On 29th April, 1998 the day of Akshay Trithiya, National Human Rights Commission deputed a senior officer to Bikaner and Jodhpur to report on the actual state of affairs. According to a Senior Superintendent of Police from the Commissioner's Investigation Division, who was witness to the event, says several marriages were solemnised with great celebration and gaiety and without any obstruction from the authorities or members of the public.

Nair sites an example of Dumma Village in Deogarh District, Uttar Pradesh where almost all girls become brides before attaining the age of 10. There is not a single girl unmarried above 12 years of age in the village. The child-brides or grooms do not understand the solemnity of these ceremonies, but for elders it is the safest and most tested way of keeping property and money within the family and innocent children become pawns in family business. According to Nair, the phenomenon of child marriage is linked to poverty, illiteracy, dowry, landlessness and other such social evils. There are several social factors that have contributed to the prevalence of child marriage.

The girl is considered to be a burden of the household and thereby she is married in an early age. Marriages between cousins is common in South India. Sometimes marriages are settled even before the birth of the child. In Rajasthan communities like Balai, Bhangi, Bolal, Chamar, Dholi, Gujars, Malis and Meenas believe, that marriage can be performed in childhood days irrespective of their age and maturity. Sometimes betrothal takes place before the pair is born, commonly known as 'kotha tharpana'.

This custom ensures that the girl is secure as she has been married within the clan. Parents believe that, it is easy for the child-bride to adapt to a new environment as well as it is easy for others to mould the child to suit their family environment and practices. Child marriage is also done to maintain pre-marriage chastity among the girls. Sex within or outside families, as a result of a chance encounter - willing or otherwise

- happens oftener than one can predict. After having spoken to a number of parents of such girls, Kuala is convinced that this apprehension of their unmarried daughters getting pregnant is the single largest cause of parents being so eager to marry off their girls at a young age - 'lest they bring shame and scandal to the family'. According to Ahuja's findings, among the 94 rape victims he studied, unmarried girls constituted 63 per cent, married girls 33 per cent and widows 4 per cent.

Some parents believe that, it is easier to impose their will on their children while they are still infants. They believe that, once married, boys do not flirt around with village girls and the girls learn to take responsibilities. There is also a conviction that it is easier for the couple to adapt themselves to each other as the children stay with each other since childhood. Despite growing up together, the boys are not completely connected or committed to their wives and some even seek relationships outside marriage.

The girl is considered to be an additional labour as she is involved in unpaid jobs within or outside the house in the rural as well as urban scenario. This is another reason why the parents are worried about the girl's chastity before marriage. There are various economic factors that lead to the prevalence of child marriage. In some parts of rural India, mass marriages are conducted and the marriage celebrations become less expensive if the girls are married on this occasion. Elders are convinced that child marriages, since they are solemnised in groups are cheaper and easier to perform. In the month of April, Rajasthan celebrates the Akha Teej festival, the day of Akshay Trithiya, by solemnising thousands of child marriages. The prevalent ritual of the childhood ceremony in Rajasthan, according to Kabra, is based on social financial considerations. Firstly, there is no system of dowry in this agreement.

Secondly, since the marriages are conducted for a number of children in the family simultaneously, it works out as group marriage, thereby cutting down the expenditure drastically. Finally, its seasonal, one time community occurrence operates as very convenient social logistics for the rural folk. The main arguments of the parents are that if a girl is married off early they will have to pay only Rs 500 or less as dowry. After girls attain puberty, the cost of marriage could go upto Rs 15,000. However, a large amount is paid when the girl is sent to the groom's house. According to Nair, elders hold their poverty responsible for the prevalence of this phenomenon. In case of those who have landed property, irrespective of any caste, the preference to marry the son/daughter to the brother's/sister's children or maternal uncle was largely based on the economic principle that, the landed property would remain undivided and would not go out of the clan.

To save the cost incurred, marriages are conducted at times when there is finance available with the people. It is also conducted jointly with other events which require feast to be given to all relatives. On the eldest daughter reaching puberty, all the daughters are married at a time, regardless of their age. In the event of a death in the family, marriage of the girl, regardless of her age, is performed, so that the feast to be given during the marriage can be jointly given. Marriages are also conducted immediately after the harvesting since the finances would be available with the farmer.

In case of the joint families, the parents would want to perform the marriage of their daughter before the division of the property among the sons. Marriages within the clan is also arranged as the monetary adjustments are easier within the clan than an outside alliance where else, the socio, psychological and economic security is unpredictable. The impact of child marriage over the young bride's future is enforced widowhood, inadequate socialisation, education deprivation, lack of independence to select the life partner, lack of economic independence, psychological as well as marital adjustment, low health/Nutritional status as a result of early/frequent pregnancies in an unprepared psychological state of the young bride. Thousands of adolescent girls are at risk from child marriage and the implications are not only on their health but also on the right to fulfil their human potential unhampered by the premature assumption of adult roles and responsibilities. Boys suffer less in this male dominated society.

Most grooms, once educated and grown up, migrate to urban areas and get better jobs. Many abandon their village brides for city women. Some continue to keep two wives. In some cases the grown up boys, don't even bother to acknowledge their child marriage and the brides are forced to go back to their parent's house.

The argument that it is easier for the couple to adapt themselves to each other may not always be true in reality. In case the husband dies before even the consummation of the marriage, these child brides are treated like widows and cannot remarry. The deserted and widows are invariably given in nata to some widower in the family. Nata is an obnoxious custom. Officially, the child is the wife of some widower but in fact she becomes the common property of all the male members of the family.

Roopa Shaha, who has stopped several child marriages says that child marriages are the root cause for many personality disorders and sexual problems later in life. Girls get a mental shock when their husbands force them to have sex and they develop a feeling of hatred because they cannot emotionally understand the changes in their body and feelings during pregnancy. There have been arguments that child marriage does not lead to early pregnancies and child abuse. It has been argued that, the girl does not go to the in law's house immediately after marriage and she is sent only after she attains puberty.

On the other hand there have been arguments that the norms and customs are highly flexible. According to Singh, since women work outside the home, the girl is an economic asset, and therefore her parental family tries to keep her with them for as long as possible. According to Kabra, the ceremony practised in the rural areas of India is only for social authentication of an agreement between two families to marry their wards at an opportune age much later.

He adds that, child marriages do not result in early pregnancies or more children as child bride never goes to the husband's house after the marriage. The real age at which the marriage is consummated is 17 to 19 years. While there is a widespread recognition that girls should begin regular cohabitation only after they attained puberty, the custom was customarily violated. Once the marriage had been performed, a lot of domestic, especially feminine pressures pull the wife into the husbands family much earlier than puberty. In many cases, gauna is also done before the permitted age. The girl becomes a mother early.

Herself a child, she is unable to look after another child. She is pressurised with multiple responsibilities of being a wife, mother and daughter-in-law. After marriage, in case of there being no daughter in the in-laws house, she is taken there to work, or to facilitate the work during the harvest season. Early child bearing that is, under the age of 20 years has serious consequences on the health of both mothers and children. Age differentials of risk are further sharpened in a society with poor health, low income, inadequate medical care and nutrition. Ravindran, 1995 says child marriage is one of the indirect causes of infant and maternal mortality.

An adolescent conceiving and giving birth to a child when her body is not fully developed and that too without adequate prenatal care, puts the lives of her child and herself in jeopardy. A study conducted by Family Planning Foundation, 1991, reported that mortality rates were higher among babies born to women under 18 and the rate two to three times higher among women suffering from malnutrition. The study covered 800 villages of 33 districts in Uttar Pradesh, Madhya Pradesh, Orissa, Karnataka and Maharashtra.

According to the study, nearly 29 to 58 per cent girls from poorer parts married under age and also became mothers. There are other socio-economic factors that determine absolute levels of risk at any age, but it is the biological processes that determine the age pattern of risks. Medical research from all over the world shows that maternal age has an independent influence on relative risks and that childbirth is much more hazardous for mothers under 20 years than for those in their twenties. In addition to those who die, many women suffer from serious illnesses related to pregnancy, abortion or childbirth. Maternal age also influences infant mortality.

Almost everyone is equally guilty, whether it is local MLA or the school teacher. They have either themselves married their children very young or have enthusiastically participated in such marriages. Besides administrative laxity, it is the rigidity and callousness of the local people, which has led to widespread and open practise of child marriages. Despite the administration being fully aware of the custom, and sometimes even having advance knowledge about it, the crime against innocent children continues. As the administration has turned a blind eye to the problem, local people have no fear for law. Caste affinity and social pressure is so great that no one reports such cases or comes forward to give evidence. Past experiences have taught a session to many of that authorities don't respond in time of such crisis. Bhanwari Devi, a Saathin of the Women's Development Programme in rural Rajasthan, was gang raped as a punishment for her efforts to prevent child marriages in her village in 1992.

Joseph writes, "all she got for trying to implement the existing laws was harassment, humiliation and violation, not only from hostile parts of the local community but also, subsequently, from members of the official law enforcing agencies, including the police and the judiciary". A few years ago a cop who tried to stop a child marriage in Bharatpur, Rajasthan, was murdered and his body tossed into a nearby well. Of course, every year routine appeals for not performing child marriages are issued by the government and non-government organisations. Sathins, anganwadi workers, social organisations and the police are alerted and asked to take preventive measures. Yet the baraat with the baby groom arrives for the toddler bride. Festivities take place in the open. The tractor trolleys with the festive people even drive past the local police station but no action is taken by anyone. How can any person of the community or authority raise the issue, when everyone is guilty?

CHILD SEXUAL ABUSE

Sexual abuse is defined as "all sexually oriented conduct, commentary or gestures, intentional and repeated, not desired or accepted freely by their object, for whom it is an imposition, a humiliation or attack on their dignity". The term abuse includes physical as well as non-physical acts. There is enough evidence to suggest that it often receives wider familial sanction. It is institutionalised in various forms, ranging from long hours of labour, often within and outside the home, denial of food, neglect of ailments and verbal abuse to physical violence by the husband and sometimes other family members. Far more difficult to acknowledge are problems caused by the narrow definition of sexuality as a means of perpetuating control over their minds and bodies in a conjugal relationship. Legally child sexual abuse is interpreted as 'rape' of a child who is below 16 years of age and rape as defined in Indian Penal Code is penetration without her consent.

However, in Indian law has interpreted and defined rape as penile-vaginal penetration. This definition is inadequate as in most of the child sexual abuse cases, Sakshi has worked with, there has been no sexual penetration. Child sexual abuse is the physical or mental violation of a child with sexual intent. Thus Narang, 1998 defines child sexual abuse as follows:

- An adult exposing his/her genitals to a child or persuading the child to do the same.
- Adult touching a child's genitals or making the child touch the adult's genitalia
- An adult involving a child in pornography which includes exposing a child to pornographic material.
- An adult having oral, vaginal or anal intercourse with a child
- Any verbal or other sexual suggestion made to a child by an adult
- An adult persuading children to engage in sexual activity

According to Kemps sexual abuse is defined as "the involvement of dependent, developmentally immature children and adolescents in sexual activities they do not really comprehend, to which they are unable to give informed consent, or that violate the social taboos of family roles. According to Schmit, Sexual abuse is defined as any sexual misuse of the child by a care-taking adult. Sexual abuse includes incest, oral-genital contact; sodomy, molestation, digital manipulation and so on. RAHI includes exploitative sexual activity, whether or not they involve physical contact, between a child and another person, who by virtue of his power over the child due to age, strength, position, or relationship uses the child to meet his or her own sexual and emotional needs to the definition of child sexual abuse.

The act though sexual in nature is also about the abuse of power and the betrayal of trust. A child's dependency needs for nurturance, touch, caring, caressing, and the like are not the same as adult sexual desires. The adult or older person completely disregards the child's own developmental immaturity and inability to understand sexual behaviours. The act, therefore, is not only a gross violation of the child's body but also of the trust implicit in a care giving relationship. Child sexual abuse, according to the report is any sexual contact between a child and an adult.

The contact covers a wide range of behaviours. It may or may not involve physical contact, force or violence, but always involves coercion. It can also include fondling of the breast or genitals, rape, oral sex, and/or sodomy. It can also include an adult demanding that a child touch his/her genitals either directly or through clothing. Non-physical sexual contact also includes exhibitionism, obscene talk or pornography. Child sexual abuse takes place in all cultures, races and in every strata of the society.

Both males and females are sexually abused. Girls however, are abused more frequently and over a longer period of time. Findings based on research done at Sakshi as well as international statistics on child sexual abuse indicate that at least 2 out of 4 girls and 1 out of 6 boys are victims of sexual abuse. A study carried out by a Bangalore based NGO, Samvada, in 1994 of 348 girls from Karnataka, revealed that 83% of the respondents had experienced some form of child sexual abuse. The preliminary report of an ongoing survey of Sakshi with about 650 girl students indicates that about 60% of the girls had experienced some form of abuse till the age of

15 years. Out of these 60%, about 20% had suffered abuse by close relatives. DCP S. B. K. Singh reported in a daily newspaper, 'The Pioneer', that 85% of the rape cases registered in the District during 1997, involved persons known to the victims.

According to the World Health Organisation, one in every ten child is sexually abused. In a 1980 study of 1000 victims of child abuse, A.B.Dave, et al found that 81 per cent could be classified as victims of physical abuse, 7 per cent of what the authors call neglect, 9.3 per cent of sexual abuse and 2.7 per cent of emotional abuse. None of these categories can be treated as exclusive and it is important to note that studies of this kind are extremely difficult to undertake. This particularly so in the area of sexual relations where the overall attitude of secrecy and suppression which governs any discussion or reference to sex making it difficult to come to any definite conclusion on the extent of sexual abuse of children.

Yet of available figures, of almost 10,000 reported rapes in 1990, an alarming 25 per cent are of girl children below the age of 16 and about a fifth are those under ten. A recent analysis done by the Crimes Against Women Cell, Delhi Police, points out that of the 143 rape cases registered between January and June 1992, 107 or almost 75 per cent were in the age range 7 - 18 years. Forty of the rapists were immediate neighbours and seven were relatives. Conversations with those in charge of the cell indicate that such cases are on the increase. According to a survey done by Sakshi, sixty per cent of 650 school girls questioned in a survey said they had suffered abuse, close relatives having abused twenty per cent of them. The word perpetrator is used in relation to the person or people who are directly abusing a child or children.

Although this can be applied to the person responsible for any other form of mistreatment, it tends to relate to those committing child sexual abuse. It is not used to refer to other adults who may have played a role but were not directly involved, such as a non-abusing parent who might have been aware of the abuse but unable to intervene. In most cases, the abuser is known to the child family friend, sibling, relative, servant, teacher and so on. There have also been cases where the abusers have been very close relatives - father, grandfather, brother and uncle. The abuser is usually an older person who is in some position of trust and/or power vis-avis the child. Even though both men and women can sexually abuse a child, most abusers are male.

The abuser violates a relationship of trust with the child. They may use tricks or threats to persuade the child to take part in a sexual activity. The abuse generally takes place in the child's home or the abuser's home. Given that the abuser is often known to the child and usually has both access to as well as authority over the child, the abuse does not commonly involve physical violence and generally continues over a long period of time. The abuser uses threats or blackmail to warn the child against telling any one about the abuse.

This may be the primary cause for the child's silence. Child sexual abuse is on the increase because of the responses to it and towards the victims. One of the response being denial of its existence and disbelief: Many people with whom Sakshi has interacted, deny any existence of child sexual abuse especially within a family. The concept of Indian families is perhaps the most sensitive and revered. Therefore, it is difficult to believe that sexual abuse in the families really happens. For them, if at all the concept of child sexual abuse exists, it is limited to a particular class.

The popular belief is that it is very rare and happens only in low class families. Even if some people believe that child sexual abuse exists, there is denial publicly as it is difficult for them to deal with the fact that it is prevalent in our traditional Indian families. Due to ignorance, denial of its existence, and inability of adults to deal with the subject, the child is met with disbelief when he/she finally summons up the courage to confide in someone about the experience and trauma of being sexually abused. Thus the child is forced to suffer in silence giving the abuser greater power over the child. Sexual abuse is shrouded in shame and secrecy. Sexual organs or any reference to sex is considered to be shameful. Children are not given proper answers when they ask questions about sexual organs. They get the messages that certain body parts are dirty and they should never be talked about. So, when a child is abused, there is total silence. The child knows that there is something wrong going on, yet the child does not have the language or the words to express it.

There is loneliness because the child cannot talk about it to anybody and does not know whom to approach. This hampers disclosure and thus the abuse continues. In families where parents/relatives accept and realise that a child has suffered sexual abuse, the child is forced into silence given the culture of privacy, family prestige and family unity. The child generally does not receive much support from the family as they do not want the matter to be disclosed and the family name exposed. Thus the abuser is not confronted and the child is encouraged to 'forget' the traumatic experience. The child and her future are sacrificed for the image of the family. A healthy environment is a family situation where family communication is clear, direct and specific and rules are flexible. Children can freely approach elders or adults with questions or concerns about sexual experiences in the full knowledge that the adults concerned will address these issues with the child's welfare in mind.

In this situation no trusted older individual violates the child's person and the child feels the freedom to say no to potential abusers and report the incident with full confidence that he or she will be protected. Families in which incest occurs often appear to be like any other family. However, they are riddled with secrets and psychological stress. Incestuous families tend to be closed, inward families lacking in any real emotional connection to people outside the family.

These families often have a history of problems for several generations, which increase the potential for incest. Frequently the mothers of abused children were themselves molested as children. Many victims assume that being dominated and treated poorly by the offender is just a fact of life and not something to be challenged. However it is vital to note that, while family influences may contribute to incest, the dysfunction itself cannot cause an individual to become sexually abusive. However, the situation makes it easier for the symptoms to play themselves out. The offender is the sole person responsible for the abuse. In some cases, the mothers do not want to take action against the abused as they are constrained by the status of the abuser within the family, for example; a father.

Economic dependence, low self esteem, lack of power within the family, incapacity to accept the responsibility of single parent and moral shame of the act keep the mother quite Members of voluntary organisations says that a mother would often suppress and wish away the event, not only because of a sense of shame and outrage, but also out of fear of reprisals from her husband, son, or other relatives. According to Wadhwa 1993, in 1992 - 93, there were eight cases of rape and molestation reported by mothers to Crime Against Women Cell in Delhi. Officials at the cell pointed out that this was a significant development as hardly any such instances were reported earlier.

At the same time, wives expected the police to merely caution their husbands; filing a case against them would be unheard of. Society constantly judges women including young girls and children. They are made to feel responsible, guilty or persecuted. Girls are very scared of this judgement, and of being exposed, which forces them into silence. Abusers are aware of this societal attitude towards women and this becomes their power.

Society's attitude enables them to go scott-free. Child sexual abuse is usually dismissed because in most cases it is not 'rape' as defined by law. It is met with disbelief and girls are accused of being destructive when the complaint is against a family member. In cases where there is no penile penetration or when rape cannot be proved due to inadequate evidence, the accused is charged for 'outraging the modesty of a woman' where they may be sentenced only for a period of six months of two years. In most cases, the accused are acquitted in absence of adequate laws on child sexual abuse and inadequate interpretation of existing laws. The court room environment is hostile and girls are humiliated over and over again. This poses to be a major obstacle for girls who want to file a complaint against their abuser. The effects of child abuse are long lasting and are carried into adulthood leaving deep scars on the personality of the abused. Healing is an important process and must begin as early as possible. Singh has pointed out that child sexual abuse triggers a host of complexities in the child's psyche.

Periodic bouts of low self esteem, sexual dysfunctioning, guilt are some of the problems that arise out of child sexual abuse and which continue to haunt the individual well into adulthood. Sexual abuse is not the only childhood experience that causes difficulty for people as they mature. Long term effects are often identical to those of other early developmental setbacks. The difference however is that most of them can be talked about freely and without involving embarrassment. The person who is sexually abused in childhood is faced with the taboo of talking about it. Most former victims keep their experiences a secret for many years.

Consequently their emotions are likely to run very deep and when they eventually surface the effects can be devastating. The abuser conveys the message that the abuser's needs come first and so it destroys the basis for child-adult trust. Victims of sexual abuse grow up without a sense of protection and security, something that is essential for them to build inner strength and venture into new experiences. As a result, they also have difficulty in trusting others and forming relationships.

Survivor's sexual activity as children were dominated by perpetrators emotional needs and selfish orientation towards sexuality. Tension, fear, betrayal, pain and mistrust coloured the victim's sexual awakening. Consequently, as adults, the sexual behaviour of survivors is severely impacted. They face issues such as sexual maladjustment, abstaining from sex or compulsively seeking it out. Adult women victimised as children are also more likely to manifest depression, self destructive behaviour, anxiety, feelings of isolation, low self esteem, a tendency towards substance abuse, over-eating and various other addictions. The most disturbing effect of child sexual abuse is that the worst scars are on the emotional and mental health, which may show up as unidentifiable symptoms. Children are prone to a variety of psychological and behavioural disturbances caused by the trauma of abuse. These include bed wetting, nightmares, sleep disorders, depression, anxiety, running away from home, multiple personality disorders, low self esteem caused by guilt and shame.

Many children also develop a negative attitude towards their body as they blame themselves for the abuse. Renu, victim of sexual abuse began hating herself and her body. She started eating constantly, as she wanted to look ugly and so that she would not fall prey to abuse again. Thus it can lead to disturbing the child's relationship with her sexual identity/ sexuality and she can fall anywhere in the spectrum, which extends from promiscuity to frigid. It effects her self worth and the future interactions that she will have, especially with men. Shobha Srinath NIMHANS, points out to a fact that a young child below ten may not always be aware that her sexual violation is in fact qualitatively different from thrashing and abuse; it is only with the onset of puberty that she becomes aware of her sexuality.

In fact in an environment where physical contact, both affectionate and abusive, by relatives of both sexes is not uncommon, child rape needs to be viewed a little differently from the rape of a post-pubertal girl. Not unexpectedly, the families rarely talk about the rape of their young daughter: when the rapist is a father or brother, the chances of reporting is even lower.

According to Prasad, a victim of incest may attempt suicide, may have bouts of panic attack and depression. The child may not even confide in the parents. He adds that, the wide prevalence of the crime can be gauged by the fact that according to a study, 16 per cent of the patients being treated for genito-urinary symptoms in the dermatology and sexually transmitted diseases department of a public hospital in New Delhi, were below 14 years of age. The child feels three Ds according to him - dirty, damaged and different. There is a lot of anger, shame and guilt involved. There are suicidal tendencies, drug addiction and alcoholism. They also exhibit self-mutilating behaviour and have panic attacks and depression.

According to Dr. Khetrapal, at times the impact plays itself out in certain compulsive behaviour like over-eating, bulimia, anorexia nervosa generally seen in abused girls. According to Ms Seema Prakash a counsellor at RAHI, there would be a slump in academic performance, increased temper tantrums, "different" conduct with some members, exhibition of sexual awareness in crude manner which are indicators of abuse. According to Singh Dhiraj, most often children do not have the language to describe sexual activity.

It is difficult for a child to articulate his or her experience. Moreover, they are extremely traumatised as they try to make sense of what has happened to them. Hurt and fear of disclosure or punishment are the initial responses that prevent a child from speaking out. Hence it is very important to cultivate openness within the immediate family where the children can confide in their parents without the fear of ridicule or reproach. Parents can look for certain telltale signs and reactions to find out how safe their children are, says Singh,

- The child tries to stay away from friends and people he was close to earlier. This could be due to guilt that has flooded his little conscience.
- He or she may seem depressed. Depression itself may not be easy to gauge in children but it is translated into more expressible emotions such as being irritable, withdrawn and listless
- The child may resume bed-wetting if he or she has stopped it. Sometimes he or she can get incontinent while awake.
- He or she may avoid a particular individual and show fear when forcibly made to come face to face with this person. This person could be abuser or someone who looks like him.
- Difficulty in concentrating or failing tests at school
- Sudden use of sexual language and swear words.

- Sexual exploitation or exploration of other children.
- Irritation in throat and bladder infections.
- Sexually transmitted infections.

CHILD PROSTITUTION AND TRAFFICKING

The UN Special Rapporteur on the sale of Children, Child Prostitution and Child Pornography defines Child Prostitution as the sexual exploitation of a child for remuneration in cash or in kind, usually but not always organised by an intermediary. Thus the violence against the girl child acquires a new dimension in the sale of young girls below the age of 18 for prostitution and trafficking. To curb this, the Suppression of Immoral Trafficking Act, later modified to the Prevention of Immoral Trafficking Act has been passed.

Prostitution in India is a Rs 40,000 crore annual business. It has been estimated that 30% of the sex workers are children, who earn Rs.11,000 crore. This has been reported by a study by the Centre of Concern for Child Labour. At present the number of child prostitutes in India is between 270,000 and 400,000, with the number of children in "commercial prostitution" increasing at the rate of 8-10% per annum.

The practice of child prostitution is in blatant contravention of the UN Declaration on the Rights of the Child, endorsed by the "National Policy for Children" of the Ministry of Social Welfare, Government of India. Principle 9 of the Declaration states: The child shall be protected against all forms of neglect, cruelty and exploitation. These shall not be the subject of traffic in any form."

Poverty and deprivation, coupled with a low status in society for girls is a primary factor for child prostitution. It is well known that prostitution exists in the Third World because of poverty. According to a UNICEF Report, children are often required to work to supplement their meagre incomes. Thus in a country like India, child prostitution in most cases stems from child labour. Prostitution is often viewed as an avenue providing easy money, which seems attractive for families steeped in poverty. Dr. K.K.Mukhpadhyay from Delhi School of Social Work, University of Delhi, in his presentation based on surveys he conducted for the Government of India, said that young girls in India were taken away from their parents in poor backward and drought affected districts of the country for purposes of trafficking. These were also states with gender inequality and low literacy rates.

The trafficking network was well organised in these areas. He found in his survey that about eighty per cent of the girls who were in this profession entered it as children and due to difficult circumstances, such as poverty, illiteracy, ignorance, and deception. The increasingly consumerist society only further complicated the situation. Children are often hired out or sold by their families to agents who may or may not reveal the true nature of the work offered.

The agent may promise a job as a domestic servant or factory worker at a wage many times higher than is customary in rural areas. A sum which is large in the eyes of the family, may be handed over to them, and the child is obligated to work to pay off the debt. Some young girls are deceived by young urban boys who go to villages. The biys conduct fake marriages with these girls, bring them to the cities and sell them to the brothels.

On the economic front, it must be noted that development policies and patterns of development promoting tourism, industrialisation, rural to urban migration particularly of males generate a demand for commercial sex. In such a situation, the developing countries bear the brunt of the problem. Economic disparities within countries, and between countries and regions fuels the demand for trafficking from low income to high income areas.

In addition, population mobility has been facilitated by globalization and liberalization as they have opened borders and relaxed controls. Such a scenario gives a spurt to tourism which leads to 'sex tourists' from the West journeying East with the purpose of exploiting children. Goa has become one such haven for paedophiles and people indulging in child prostitution. According to unofficial estimates, there are at least 400 minors in the locality involved in the trade. Further, there is no respite in the situation as the existence of minors is often hidden on receiving a tip off about the raids. There are also instances of the arrest of 25 odd girls and their being summarily released subsequently, once their ages have been found to be above 18. The exploitation is shown in the fact that a girl below the age of 16 is available for Rs 300- Rs 500, justifying for Goa the name of 'India's Bangkok'.

Men who travel to the Third World for 'sex with children', argue that there is nothing new in going abroad to escape the moral strictures at home. This phenomenon is further enhanced by the growing demand for very young girls with a premium on virgins. According to Ms. Prasanna, a research scholar with the Department of Criminology at Madras University, the fear of AIDS often makes the Western 'sex tourist' to seek virgins.

Such a demand is catered to by large markets in Bombay and Hyderabad also. Child prostitution in India is further aggravated by the presence of social conventions and myths prevailing in society. It is popularly believed that sex with a virgin is a cure for venereal and other diseases. Moreover, a reason for the rise in child trafficking can be attributed to the myth that having sexual intercourse with a child would protect the client from AIDS. This was stated at a workshop organised by UNICEF on "The Rights of the Child". With the low levels of education and literacy, such myths are only perpetuated. It is well known that the female sex is further disadvantaged due to the inadequate educational and employment opportunities, gender disparities in access to opportunities and the lack of social safety nets.

Social conventions play an important role in the continuance of the phenomenon of child prostitution. These include child marriages, polygamy, dowry and social stigma against single, unwed, divorced women and girls who have been sexually abused. Children, especially young girls, in these circumstances are especially vulnerable to the prostitution racket. There have been instances of girls being driven into the sex trade following traumatic sexual experiences during childhood, including rape. If, in the case of Shahida of Kozhikode , it was the violence inflicted by her father's younger brother followed by molestation by her cousin and then rape, Lakshmi's tale of woe began when she was raped by her step father at age 8 and her further sexual exploitation for food when she left home.

Prostitution thus becomes a viable option for children who have been abandoned, for those from disrupted families and for those who are financially supporting their families. The prevalence of traditional and religious practices in some communities that consist of dedicating girls to gods and goddesses serve to encourage child prostitution. The evolution of the Devadasi cult can be traced to a period earlier than the entry of Aryans in India. The cult appears to be a relic of the Dravidian matriarchal society. It exists today in India with many regional variations.

This social convention condemns nearly 5 to 10 thousand girls every year to a life of sexual servitude and subsequently into prostitution. The devadasi girls form 15% of the total women in prostitution in India. In the border districts of Maharashtra and Karnataka states, their percentage in prostitution is nearly 80%. The striking fact is that all of them have entered prostitution in an extremely organised manner. This process involves first making the girl a devadasi and then legitimising her entry into prostitution with the help of 'religion'. The practice receives sanction from mythology and was once supported by feudal land owning systems. Social backwardness is the most closely linked factors to both devadasis and prostitutes.

It is known that ethnic minority, "scheduled castes" and "other backward classes", indigenous people, hill tribes, refugees and illegal immigrants are particularly susceptible to the racket. Interestingly, the "signs" used to identify the chosen child are those of ill health - white patches of eczema, leprosy and even mental retardation. Researchers now speculate whether prostitution was one lucrative way of making use of such otherwise "worthless children". Among those involved in child prostitution, it is the street children who are most vulnerable to it. According to Dr. A.B.Bose, advisor in the Planning Commission, the problem of street children is primarily the outcome of four circumstances - poverty, nonexistence of a supportive social and economic structure, rapid urbanisation leading to chronic housing shortage and the growth of slums and an oppressive home environment.

The prevailing situation is aggravated by the lack of awareness of legal rights, the exploited situation of the victims and the absence of a channel for seeking redress. In the presence of the growth of trans-national crime and expansion of drug trafficking networks, weak law enforcement mechanisms, exploitation by corrupt law enforcers and officials are the order of the day. On paper, prostitution per se is not illegal and hence there are loopholes in the law that ensure a person goes scot-free even if he sells a minor girl to a brothel, provided there is a stamped receipt. The erosion of traditional family systems and values and the pursuit of consumerism encourages sale of children.

The National Commission for Women identifies sexual glorification by the electronic media as one of the prime reasons for minors in prostitution. In 1991, the Central Social Welfare Board conducted a study on Child Prostitution. Among the causes of entry to prostitution, economic distress accounted for 41%; desertion by spouse = 24.5%; deception = 11.9%; social customs = 5.35%; family tradition = 5%; kidnapping and abduction = 2.25%. The study also indicates that many of the young girls join, emulating the example of girls who have joined the trade and as a consequence are living well. It has also been shown that most prostitutes are forced to remain in their professions due to police highhandedness and the clout of local henchmen.

This makes chances of rescue and rehabilitation very slight. It has been found in 1994 that India has four lakh child prostitutes. According to Mr. K.T. Suresh of the Bangalore based NGO "Equations", about 20% of India's 2 million prostitutes are below the age of 15. Bombay city alone is believed to have 40,000 child prostitutes. The flesh trade in India is liberally replenished from Nepal, which is believed to contribute an estimated 20,000 young girls every year. The survey conducted by the Central Social Welfare Board in 1991-92 in the cities of Bombay, Calcutta, Delhi, Madras, Hyderabad and Bangalore shows that 15% are below the age of 15 at the time of entry and 25% are minors in the age group of 16-18 years. However, among the various studies conducted, there does appear to be some discrepancy in their findings.

A study on prostitution in Delhi has challenged the findings of a report by the National Commission for Women on child prostitution. While the NCW says that children form 60% of the prostitutes in the Capital's main sex market at G.B. Road, the study by Jan Shakti Vahini figures it as low as 7%. On a similar note, very few cases of child sex workers have been reported in the state of Kerala. However, according to the study conducted by Loyola College of Social Sciences on "Girl Children in Prostitution", this does not imply their total absence; it merely indicates that locating them is difficult. Violence against prostitutes is of two kinds, argued Mr Dasgupta, and relates to violence at the workplace.

Girls are sold by their parents or procured by abductors. A good number, about 25% to 30% are known as chukris in Calcutta. These women who are sold by their parents or husbands are severely beaten and tortured into submission. As a rule they have to pass on all their earnings to the keepers and any deviation from this norm is also countered with violence. Lack of space accounts for the presence of keepers in a big way. However those with a place of their own face yet another problem: Goondas forcefully seek entry into the women's houses and assume the role of the pimps.

They live off their earnings and, in case of resistance, get violent. Data revealed that clients were the least prone to use violence. Mr Dasgupta's study showed that 75% of women in the prostitution industry are from West Bengal, of whom a third are from Murshidabad, Birbhum and Burdwan or the Radh area. The Radh are a has traditionally sent girls to Calcutta for prostitution. What is important here is the prevalence of child marriage and child widows. When they returned to their parent's home, as they were considered burdens, they were sent off to Calcutta to work as housemaids or prostitutes. Earlier, these women came from Kulin Brahmin and Kayastha families, nowadays they are from all castes. Micro studies conducted by Prerana, Mumbai, conducted 10 focus group interviews of five children in each group reveals that the age of becoming a prostitute was under 18 for 90.3 per cent of the girls, the average age being 16 years. When dealing with child prostitution, the best possible available indicator as to its prevalence is the incidence of AIDS and sexually transmitted diseases in the age group below 18. According to UNAID, one in every two women in Mumbai's brothels was infected by 1993 and one in every three attend STD clinics.

Nationally, it estimates that the incidence of HIV was 25% among women in prostitution and 10% among clients. Sudden increases in the number of kidnappings and abduction of young girls and their subsequent adoptions could possibly be indicators of the practice of child prostitution. The National Crime Records Bureau reported a 100% increase in kidnappings in the last two years. Often, young girls are kidnapped from their homes. 60% of these children are forcibly "married", and then hidden by the brothel owner until they reach the "profitable" ages of 9-13 years.

CHILD LABOUR

Patil B.R has defined child labour in two dimensions. If the purpose is to prevent child labour and to provide compulsory education, child labour would mean and include, all those who are below the age fourteen and who are neither in school nor in employment. If the concern is to withdraw children from all kinds of jobs and employment - whether hazardous or non-hazardous - and to bring them into main stream of the human society through education, training and rehabilitation we need to define child labour in a very different manner.

One such definition is: the children, who have not completed the age of fourteen, employed for wages or no wages in occupations and employment, whether carried on by the employer or by the family or by self, that interfere with their childhood and education and are injurious to their health and physical, intellectual, spiritual, moral and social development. Neera Burra has divided child labour into four categories - those who work in factories, workshops and mines, those who are bonded, street children and children who form part of the familial labour force areas. Gupta has classified the child labour into five types, Child workers with their family; those working in home or cottage industry; those working in a factory or factory type production unit, commuting daily to the work site; Child workers not staying with their families; children sent by parents to work away from home; children who run away from home; destitute children, who have no home or parents.

Children engaged in begging and prostitution are part of organised criminal exploitation of children. Although the estimation of the recorded child labour by census of India 1991, this is only a tip of the ice-berg, as several micro studies have proved the figures to be much higher. Child abuse includes sexual aggression, beatings as well as extracting hours of labour from children who should be in school or at play. According to Laskar, 1999, child abuse can be economic, physical or psychosocial. The most vulnerable children in the society, according to him are the child labourers, street children, bonded children, child prostitutes, child refugees, child soldiers, jailed children, unaccompanied children, orphans or beggars.

In the domestic scenario many children are exploited and this generally does not get focused. A large number of children are forced to work in hazardous workshops or factories and are exposed to multiple health hazards. Since schooling is not compulsory for any age group in India, there are no restrictions on when children can enter the labour force. Traditional Hindu notions of social rank and hierarchy are subtly incorporated into the ways educated Indians distinguish between education for children of those who do manual work than those who are in services, that is, middle class employment. The National Human Rights Commission has itself felt revolted that officers consider it necessary to permit a 'small justice' in the form of child labour to promote the interests of earning foreign exchange in the export market. In fact the Government policy seems to promote the employment of children. Small scale industries are legally permitted to use child labour directly or to subcontract with the so called family owned workshops. There is no statutory protection for children in factories which employ not more than 10 workers.

The government's support to cottage industries and the small sector promotes the employment of children in unregulated hazardous work. And through its centres for training children as weavers in the carpet industry, the government competes with schools to attract children. Government officials are frank in saying child labour helps sustain the otherwise uneconomic small industries by keeping the cost down so that the carpet, gems and brass-ware industries can expand their exports. The child labourers are exposed to several kinds of physical hazards and even sexual harassment.

In the absence of any stricter laws or any provisions for compulsory primary school education, less than half of India's children in the age group of 6 to 14 do not attend school. Either they are found at home caring for the cattle, collecting firewood, working in fields or engaged in cottage industries, tea stalls, restaurants. Some even work in factories doing extremely hazardous jobs. Some find employment as household workers in middle class homes. Some even end up as prostitutes or bonded labourers.

Unfortunately nothing worthwhile is being done to improve the conditions of these children. The Centre for Concern for Child Labour, a Delhi Based NGO, in a study has divided the girl child in the domestic sector into two categories - one who did household tasks and the other who was engaged in outdoor economic work. The study revealed that middle or upper middle class families with small children preferred to employ young girls because, the help from them, in that case not only came 'cheap' but was also considered safe. The study observed that like all other women workers in the informal sector, the child domestic workers are subjected to sword of false allegations. Working in inhuman conditions, often for a pittance, children are abused at work and within homes where their earnings become the property of the parents. Not unexpectedly, child labour has become an emotive issue resulting in a sense of moral outrage in the international community and the boycott of products using any form of labour.

However banning child labour is a simplistic response to a much deeper problem, which lies embedded in structures of power, availability of alternatives and schooling as well as the overall immiseration of at least a third of the population. For those children who do not work for wage but contribute to the family workforce, leisure, education and anything remotely regarded as the rights of the child need to be defined keeping in mind the cultural specifications of notions of childhood, play, learning and consequently exploitation and abuse.

Dr Neera Burra argues that the general argument favouring child labour gets justified by poverty or that children are put to work at a young age to learn the required skill or the traditional craft. Further Dr Burra mentions that child labour gets justified in less hazardous workplaces but the question is, what is the definition of hazardous? She quotes the example of a domestic servant in Hyderabad who was beaten up mercilessly by his employers. A child may be working in a non-hazardous environment, but might be subject to violence.

The neighbour who saved him with the help of a women's organisation later got him enrolled in a school. Studies from Bidi industry show that children are mortgaged for money; the Supreme Court Commission of 1983-84 on children rescued from the carpet industry documented atrocities such as not allowing them to urinate and being hung upside down and beaten for making errors in weaving.

State Development Corporation had come up with a scheme for young women who would be taught weaving. However what has actually happened is that young girls instead of women were employed under this State-funded programme, and that too at the cost of having left school. These young girls are so young that they balance on their toes so as to reach the thread. They would be on their toes for hours together. Possibility of sexual abuse also could not be ruled out. According to Choudhary, it is the poor life situations in families that bring children into labour force. Studies show that child labour is on the increase, particularly for those who work as marginal workers.

According to Choudhary, the increase of girls has been dramatic in both rural and urban areas. According to Maxim Gorky, traditional factors may be a cause for child labour. Schoolbased education was meant for the privileged class. This tradition prevails even today among some segments of the have-nots. Many are not aware of the disadvantages of nonschooling. The children first join their parents to work and slowly get absorbed in the labour force. Stronger than tradition, he says is the factor of chronic poverty which is responsible for the prevalence and perpetuation of child labour.

When disease, other forms of disability or unemployment upset the balance of the family budget, there may not be an alternative except to send the child to work. Poverty and child labour thus beget each other and tend to reinforce themselves in families and communities. The most important cause ,according to Chandra, is widespread of absolute poverty due to which they are forced by the parents to seek employment. Disease and other contingencies may need extra money and the employment of children is resorted to an easily accessible method to earn money.

The problem of child labour is inter-related to the problem of the inadequate wage of adult worker, which compels children to work, in return for compensation and the employer takes advantage of this weakness by providing work to them on low wages. Associated with poverty is the existence of large families. Large families with comparatively less income cannot give protected and encouraging childhood to their children. If a family is limited and well planned, there would be no scope for sending their children to the labour market and the children could be educated. Illiterate and innocent parents think just contrary to this. Thus, if parents have a small family size, they can provide all facilities to their children which are necessary for their mental, physical and social growth. According to Maxim Gorky, child labour and non-schooling has a significant linkage among the poorer parts of population.

According to him a child is willingly sent to school in the age group 6 to 9 because at this stage he/she is more a nuisance at home than an asset, but as he/she crosses this age limit, the positions reverse. The child can now work at home or earn something outside. This is especially true of girls who have to assist the over-worked mother at home. In many far-flung areas of the countryside, schooling facilities are scarce and inaccessible and parents do not feel motivated to avail them for their children. Many children are forced to stay at home as their parents cannot afford the prescribed minima of uniform, books and stationery. Schooling is perceived as something that would deprive them of the income.

Against the backdrop of schooling, child labour thus has a double appeal; it saves the parents from spending on child's education, and is a reckonable source of income to the family. Educated unemployment highlights the futility of education. Gupta has mentioned disintegration of family as a cause of child labour. This could occur due to separation, divorce or death. He also mentions the low status of women in the house as a key factor of child labour. This is because she does not get the job or income she deserves, she is under paid and badly exploited. A mother or elder sister will not like the child to work if she earns enough to support the family or to supplement the family income.

According to Raj, the most common explanation for child labour is that parents are very poor and cannot afford to send their child to school. In places where schooling is free, the explanation given is that the family is so poor that they need the money every family member, including the child, can earn. If child labour is stopped the family will become poorer. Many factory owners who employ children argue, "why blame us? We do not force the children to come. It is the parents who send their children willingly to work rather than to school since they need money". Child labour exists primarily because there are people willing to use children for a profit. A child is paid much less than an adult worker and so is cheaper to the employer. Children are more likely to be obedient and less likely to organise themselves into labour unions and create trouble for the management.

A child's' mind and body can be moulded for performing repetitive tasks. According to Chandra, with the advent of industrialisation, the tendency among the employers to have quick and more profits at low costs has increased. Hence, in every country there is employment of children in large numbers in factories, who are paid very low wages, are subjected to excessive hours to work, and are made to work in terrible conditions. Some of the other reasons for child labour mentioned by Chandra is the absence of scheme for family allowance.

He says there is conspicuous absence of schemes for family allowance, as can be given to family so that people may maintain an adequate standard and may not be forced to send their children to the labour market. This type of scheme comes under the social security measures which is in practice in many developed countries. In addition to the above causes, Chandra has also mentioned bleak employment opportunities, lack of physical and mental fitness, sheer encouragement to take up jobs instead of going to school, inadequate inspection mechanism to check child labour and slow process of protective legislation as reasons of child labour.

Lal has also mentioned migration as a cause for child labour. In search of job poor rural parents migrate, which leave no scope for education of their children. In this process parents face various problems like unemployment, under employment, lack of shelter, and so on, which force the parents to send their children to work.

7

Crime against Women in India

DOMESTIC VIOLENCE

Physical violence as well as explicit forms of aggression are used by the more powerful in the household as methods to ensure obedience of the less powerful and therefore related to power dynamics in a household. At every stage in the life cycle, the female body is both the objects of desire and of control. Domestic violence includes not only inter-spousal violence, but also violence perpetrated by other family members.

Generally, an important part of the power relationship between spouses and their families relates to dowry and its ramifications. There is a wide societal tolerance for wife-abuse, which is very often even considered justifiable under certain circumstance: Disputes over dowries, a wife's sexual infidelities, her neglect of household duties, and her disobedience of her husband's dictates are all considered legitimate causes for wife-beating. It is only when the torture becomes unbearable or death appeared imminent that most women appeared willing to speak out.

Glass defines domestic violence as "anything that is experienced as fearful, controlling and threatening when used by those with power against those without power. Domestic violence includes, harassment, maltreatment, brutality or cruelty and even the threat of assault - intimidation. It includes physical injury, as well as "wilfully or knowingly placing or attempting to place a spouse in fear of injury and compelling the spouse by force or threat to engage in any conduct or act, sexual or otherwise, from which the spouse has a right to abstain". Confining or detaining the spouse against one's will or damaging property are also considered as acts of violence.

DOMESTIC VIOLENCE IN MARITAL RELATIONSHIP

Ahuja and Visaria have recently conducted studies on 'domestic violence' within marital relationship. Domestic violence has been defined as " all actions by the family against one of its members that threaten the life, body, psychological integrity or liberty of the member. In identifying factors leading to wife beating, both Visaria and Ahuja, in their survey, have tested the co-relationship between wife beating and education. According to Visaria's survey in Gujarat, illiterate women face more violence than literate women.

Relationship between abusive behaviour and level of education has been found to be statistically significant. Illiterate women and those with education up to primary level tend to be more subjected to violence as compared to those who had received education beyond the primary level. However, one has to keep in mind that the percentage of literate women in Gujarat is overall only between 20% to 50%. In one district, Banas Kantha in Kutch, the total percentage of literate women is even lesser than 20%.

In contrast a study by Ahuja shows that there is no significant relationship between beating and educational level of the couple. Educated women are beaten as much by their husbands as those who are illiterate or less educated. About one-fourth of the batterers in Ahuja's study were those who were moderately educated and about one-fourth were highly educated. However, he added that men whose educational attainment is low, are more likely to beat their wife than men who are better educated.

Study findings of Ahuja shows that although women of all ages are victims of wife-battering, a larger number of victims are among those with an age difference of unto 10 years between spouses. According to the survey findings of Visaria, women who experience domestic violence early in their marriage, continue to be subjected to it even with increase in age. His findings point out that family structure, the presence or absence of children, and the size of the family have little co-relation with wife battering. The study also points out that family income, husband's occupation and employment of women are not co-related with wifebattering. According to survey findings of Visaria joint family tends to offer women some protection or acts as a deterrent to husbands using physical force to subdue them.

The forms of violence commonly found by Ahuja were slapping, kicking, tearing hair, pushing and pulling, hitting with an object, attempting to strangulate and threatening. Forms of psychological abuse were also found to exist, for instance, verbal abuse, sarcastic remarks in the presence of outsiders, imposing severe restrictions on freedom of movement, totally ignoring the wife in decision-making processes, making frequent complaints against her to her parents, friends, neighbours, and kin much to the embarrassment of the wife.

Some of the reasons given by the women were financial matters, behaviour with in-laws, back-biting, talking to any male without the liking of the husband, asking for money, preventing him from drinking and husbands personality traits. Some of the worse forms of violence has been reported by Visaria in her study for instance, beating with sticks or iron rod, knives, utensils, blades and ladles, throwing women against objects or bashing their heads against the walls, burning of breasts and vagina. In addition, sexual assaults in the form of both hitting women in the vagina by kicking or forcing her into sexual intercourse were reported by nearly 10% of the women.

Some of the women who had become victim of this form of violence indicated that injury in their private parts cannot be noticed by anyone and they would be too ashamed to talk about it to others. A couple of women also hinted that men know that their wives cannot report such punishment even to their own parents or seek medical treatment due to a sense of shame. Some of the reasons given by women, in the survey done by Visaria is, meals not served properly, economic constraints, financial matters, men wasting money at tea stalls, drinking of alcohol, men feeling that women are paying less attention to the children and vis-à-vis, men feel women have a lot of free time and so on. One of the main cause why domestic violence prevails and continues is the lack of alternatives among the victims.

Women and children may be economically dependent on abusers. Elderly people and children may feel too powerless to escape. Language or cultural barriers may isolate victims from seeking help. Victims generally feel, it is better to suffer in silence than to be separated from loved ones. They keep hoping for improvement, but it is normally observed that, without help, violence gets worse. Victims may also feel helpless, guilty or worthless.

They may feel ashamed of the poor quality of the relationship. Abusers may fear the consequences of seeking help, unaware that continuing as before may be even more dangerous. Family members may be unaware of the help that is available from the local agencies. They may also be unaware of their legal rights.

In India we have no provision for protection of a complainant, not even under the Prevention of Dowry Act. A woman who has complained of harassment goes back to the very people against whom she has complained. What security can she possibly feel in such a situation, and how can she continue to act on her complaint?

She obviously continues to be victimised often paying the ultimate price. Many complainants are faced with eviction from the family home, are cut off without maintenance, and are unable to follow the complaint precisely because they have no means to do so.

Frequent, unexplained injuries, reluctance to seek medical treatment for injuries or denial of their existence, fear in the presence of certain family member/s, social isolation, disorientation or grogginess, especially in elders indicating misuse of medication and decline in physical appearance and personal hygiene indicating increased isolation and a lack of desire to continue living are some of the indicators of violence.

DOWRY HARASSMENT AND BRIDE BURNING

Dowry is a transfer of property from the bride's family to that of the bridegroom, at the time of marriage. According to the present practice, dowry usually subsumes material gifts and cash paid to the bridegroom and his kin. This practise continues even after marriage. The dowry given at the time of marriage is not the only transaction as far as the daughters marriage is concerned. There is a series of ceremonies associated with the girls in the family.

The practice of giving gifts to the husband's family in cash and kind and rituals connected with pregnancy, childbirth and ceremonies for piercing the ear of the girl and so on. The gifts are no longer a token of affection from parents to the daughter, but instead an elaborate demand from the marital family. The commonest elements of dowry in India include gifts for the bride such as clothes, jewels and other house-hold and luxury goods like a refrigerator and kitchen utensils and so on. These are ideally treated as the bride's streedan and form the nucleus of the conjugal estate.

Dowry also includes gifts for the son-in-law and other luxury items like scooter, VCR, VCP, and such other gifts for the bridegrooms' parents and other relatives. Over and above, it includes hard cash paid as contribution towards the marriage expenses. In some cases, dowry is also paid as compensation for the expenditure incurred on the education and other training of the groom. The bridegroom's parents usually keep this money. Some state that this is kept by the parents as security against the bridegroom staying separately after marriage.

According to Chatterji, the practice was a means of giving gifts to the daughter during the marriage, so that the couple can start a life on their own and to compensate her share of the property, as she is otherwise excluded from inheriting parental property. The Dowry Prohibition Act 1961 was amended in 1984, 1985 and 1986. Dowry deaths constitute a special category of death that was for the first time defined in a part introduced into the Indian Penal Code In 1986, Section 304(B) stipulates that death of a woman within seven years of her marriage by burns or bodily injury with evidence of cruelty or harassment by her husband or his relatives in connection with a demand for dowry is 'dowry death' and punishable with imprisonment for not less than seven years. Three years prior to this, Section 498(A) was introduced in the IPC.

This states that 'any form of cruelty, whether it is from a husband or the relative of a husband, to a woman is an offence that is punishable with imprisonment up to three years'. Cruelty, as defined in this part, includes 'any wilful conduct that could cause mental torture, physical injury, or drive the woman to commit suicide, whether in connection with any unlawful demand for property or not'. The first part of also be invoked in case of dowry death or suicide. Under sections 299, 300, 301 and 304(A), culpable homicide, murder and death by negligence are crimes.

Section 302 lays down punishment for murder: death sentence or imprisonment for life. Sections 113(A) and 113(B) were added to the Indian Evidence Act and can be invoked in cases of dowry murder or suicide. The Code of Criminal Procedure lays down the procedure and principles of investigation into a crime. Despite a list of legislation protecting the rights of women, most importantly the prohibition of giving and taking of dowry under the Dowry Prohibition Act 1961, women in India are tortured physically and mentally and even killed or driven to suicide by their husbands and in-laws for not bringing sufficient dowry. Dowry related violence against married women by the families they marry into is a phenomenon that is on the increase in the country.

An indication of the increase in dowry related violence against women. However this data is only a tip of the iceberg, as most of these cases do not get reported unless it reaches an extreme case of death In an investigation done by Vimochana, the category of dowry deaths in a technical sense only include those cases that had been booked by the police under the relevant sections of law. The accident cases that have been closed for want of evidence, however are largely due to stove-bursts or kitchen accidents. There are rarely any eyewitnesses who are prepared to give evidence against the murderers as the crime is committed within the four walls of a home and those who are present inside are those who are committing the crime. According to Menon, the large number of these deaths is an indication that the law is not a sufficient deterrent for those who commit these crimes. The following are some of the reasons why these gruesome murders are registered under accidents.

There are pressures on the woman to conceal the truth about the reality even if they are on the verge of dying. Her husband's family often threatens to harm her natal family or her children if she does not declare that it was an accident. Relatives and family members of her natal family also sometimes remain silent, as they fear the husband's family. The victim's dying declaration, which is supposed to be taken in private by the policeman in the presence of a doctor, is invariably a public procedure.

While on one hand the family does not want to get involved in the time-staking and laborious process of legal proceedings, on the other hand the police do not take interest to penetrate this community resistance to look for evidence of what really could have happened. According to Damodaran, exposure to the media has resulted in an increasing trend towards consumerism. People cannot afford the luxuries that are thrust upon them through advertisements targeted at the urban population.

They see dowry as an avenue to fulfil their otherwise impossible dreams. The interplay of pre-capitalist values and modern forces with the accentuation of the free market economy and the consumer culture in the era of unequal development have thus become a part of the complex and contradictory fabric of our present-day society. The traditional values of the necessity of marrying a girl for spiritual merit and the modern system of calculation and other considerations of the groom's family in a milieu of inequality and insecurity have brought to the surface a sense of competition and manipulation to the advantage of the bridegroom. According to Paul the treatment of a daughter-in-law depends very much upon the quantum of dowry she brings along with her before, during and after the marriage ceremony. However there have been cases when the status of the girl's parents has reduced after the marriage, or there is a loss in the business and the girl is illtreated in the husband's house thereafter. The dowry normally continues for many years after the marriage. Often, the dowry brought by her is taken away after marriage. In times of financial problems in the husband's house, her jewellery and dowry items are normally the first to be sold. For some people, paying dowry at their daughter's marriage is an investment for fetching high dowry through their son's marriage.

Some others, including women discuss on 'marriage with high dowry', with pride. Generally, marriages with pomp and show is preferred. The girls too think it is their right to take dowry with them when they go to the husband's house. People believe that the effective way of equipping women is to resort to dowry in arranging a marital alliance. Another feeling among the mothers-in-law is that when she herself brought dowry from her house at the time of her marriage, why shouldn't she take dowry for her son. According to Menon, dowry related crime is motivated mainly by greed.

SEXUAL HARASSMENT AT WORK

According to Mac Kinnons sexual harassment of working women is primarily a problem faced by women, that men rarely face this problem and therefore it should be considered a form of sex discrimination. Sexual harassment as defined by the court stipulates:

- "Such unwelcome sexually determined behaviour as physical contact and advances,
- A demand or request for sexual favours, sexually coloured remarks,
- Showing pornography and any other unwelcome physical, verbal or non verbal conduct of sexual nature".

Burt says "unwanted sexual overtures", has the virtue of parsimony but necessarily concerns intentions and motivation, not just overt behaviour. Defining sexual harassment as unwanted sexual overtures has the same problem inherent in defining rape as unwanted sexual relations. In practise the woman has to prove that the sexual relations or the sexual overtures were unwanted. The male colleague will go out of the way to prove that the woman is of loose character. According to Quinn defining sexual harassment means setting boundaries on the term and differentiating sexual harassment from expressions of sexual interest.

Not all expressions of sexuality in the workplace could possibly be called sexual harassment. Men and women do meet dating partners and future spouses at work. Some people may even enjoy sexual jokes and flirting that can be ego enhancing and enrich their fantasy life. National Commission for Women has laid down the code of conduct at work place to prevent sexual harassment of women, which has been sent to all Government offices, Ministries, and Universities with the hope that employers would become more sensitive towards women.

The guidelines highlight that it shall be the duty of the employer to prevent or deter the commission of any act of sexual harassment at workplace would include unwelcome sexually determined behaviour by any person either individually or in association with other persons such as eve teasing, unsavoury remarks, jokes causing embarrassment, innuendo and taunts, gender based insults or sexist remarks and unwelcome sexual overtones in any manner, touching or brushing against any part of the body, molestation or displaying pornographic or other derogatory pictures or sayings.

Recommendations to the National Commission for Women based on the view that the definition of sexual harassment is deficient and that "sexual favours……sought by homosexual or lesbian employers of the same sex" also be included. The Court places an obligation on employers in both the public and private sector to "take appropriate steps to prevent sexual harassment" and "provide appropriate penalties" against the offender. The criminal law should be resorted to where the behaviour amounts to a specific offence under the Indian Penal Code. The Court also recommends that a complaint made by the victim and that such a committee should be headed by a woman, and not less than half its members should be women. However this guidelines does not specify any time limit for drafting the code.

The Court provides that the employer is responsible for drafting codes to prevent sexual harassment in the workplace. If the power to evolve these codes is to be in the hands of the employer, then given the conservative sexual climate in which we live, what is to prevent the employer from producing a code that encourages gender segregation in the workplace. The codes could be formulated so as to discourage gender interaction in the workplace, or encourage the establishment of same sex schools and universities instead of co-educational institutions. Perhaps more specific guidelines are required which provide that such sex segregation is not an appropriate response for dealing with sexual harassment.

In many cases, it has been found that the committees within the organisations were set up only when there were serious allegations of sexual harassment. Many working women point out that, even if there is an enquiry committee, does anyone really bother to find out what happens to the victim when the enquiry is going on? She is an object of curiosity, sympathy, disdainful glances or simply isolated by her colleagues.

The situation at home is worse. Instead of sympathising with her plight or standing by her, the attitude is one of distrust and suspicion or often humiliation and shame. The work environment where sexual harassment occurs has hierarchy, norms, rules and constraints that profoundly affect the way people behave in that setting. In particular, the formal rules and informal norms of managers affect both the managers and their subordinates.

The top management has the power to influence the employee's work habits, style of dress, recreational interests and social behaviour. When the top management tolerates or condones sexual harassment of employees, the standard reverberates throughout the organization. Certain individuals use their positions of relative power to engage in sexual interactions. This type of behaviour clearly constitutes sex discrimination. Male ego problems, sexual perversion, sexual obsession, widow-hood, pornographic materials and media portrayal is said to be some of the reasons for their harassment.

LAWYERS FACING SEXUAL HARASSMENT AT WORK

A survey conducted by Sakshi, a Delhi based NGO, in a few major cities reported that 65 per cent of women lawyers interviewed were always or often subjected to, or had observed, verbal or physical sexual harassment from other lawyers.

The harassment would take various forms according to the survey. They include use of stereo-typed role characterisation, sexual innuendo, devaluation of women's work, use of obscene or vulgar language, and comments on appearances and character. The bar report narrates two incidents. In one case, a woman lawyer was openly punched by a male colleague in the High Court premises for refusing to join him for a cup of coffee.

When she tried to report the incident, a senior member of the bar dissuaded the police from registering it, on the ground that "it would tarnish the reputation of the Bar". Forty-eight per cent of the women lawyers surveyed also stated that they had heard or experienced remarks or jokes that were demeaning to women. In a survey done by National Commission for Women of 1200 women, nearly 50 per cent complained of gender discrimination and physical and mental harassment at work.

While 40 per cent of the women said they "usually ignored" such provocation, 3.54 per cent said they reported these to their supervisors, 7.8 per cent to their colleagues and 1.24 per cent to the police. About 10 per cent said that they protested against such behaviour while 9 per cent said they warned the offenders. At least 20.17 per cent of the respondents said that no investigation was done on their complaints while 1.5 per cent said police harassed them again instead of making the enquiry. A majority of the respondents 84.97% were not aware of the supreme court judgement given in August 1997, for specific protection of women from sexual harassment at work.

SALE OF WIFE

In traditional farming communities, women helped in farming and bridegrooms paid a bride price to her parents. In the past this used to be a token amount. If a widow or a married woman chose to enter into a live-in relationship with another man, the latter in turn paid the first husband the amount he had spent at the time of the marriage.

This system has, in the last decade become completely distorted with women being sold and resold for astronomical sums and the panchayats and police turning a blind eye to these goings on. With the bride price sometimes running into a lakh or more, 'nata' brokers have mushroomed around Kotah, Bundi, Deoli, Ajmer and Tonk districts of Rajasthan, whose only job is to keep an eye on prospective women and force them to enter into a nata because the local brokers earned a hefty commission out of this deal.

The kind of money at stake can be gauged from the fact that one of the fathers admits to having spent Rs 62,000 in bringing her back. Realising the selling and reselling of girls had reached rampant proportions, a Deoli based NGO, 'Women's Rights Committee Against Atrocity' conducted a survey in Sandla and Bhanvarthala villages in Tonk District of Rajasthan and came up with some disturbing conclusions. Of the 517 households surveyed, the survival rate of marriages in the backward classes during the last five years was less than 50 per cent and in some cases as high as 70 per cent.

Nata exits also in Rajgarh district of Madhya Pradesh. It is the practise of the sale of the women to men in return for a handsome price. The largest beneficiary is the father of the girl who uses her to gain a neat sum. Closely connected to the issue of sale and resale of women is the custom of child marriage. Unless a boy is committed to child marriage, he cannot indulge in nata. Men are prepared to pawn their goats, cows and buffaloes and in well-to-do households, even gold and silver to get a woman. In all these transactions the woman is never in the picture - she accepts the deal as part of her womanhood. Indira Pancholi, the Co-ordinator of the committee believes, "no household has remained unaffected, there is an unsuccessful marriage in every household here."

The Panchayats have turned a blind eye to this jostling around. They are accused more often than not, of siding with the husbands and are blamed for pushing up the nata rates. The jhagda money is decided upon in presence of the Panchayat with the amount being written on a document called Kagli. "Husbands are selling their wives to get more money and the Panchayats are doing nothing to protect these women", points out the Jaipur based women's rights activist, Kavita Srivastava.

She cites an instance of Lalibai, an anganwadi worker, who was harassed to enter into a nata after her husband's death. She refused and had to seek intervention of social activists to escape harassment. According to a Jaipur based DIG, Sudhir Pratap Singh " lack of education and total ignorance of inheritance rights amongst women are the reasons why this practice has continued." Indira Pancholi, the Co-ordinator of the committee believes, "the inability of a bride to return to her marital home would be a triggering factor, especially in cases of atta satta agreement where two families exchange children in marriage when they are quite young. After marriage, the boy's family reciprocate by not sending their son to bring the bride.

Entire villages are at war with each other." For instance, Simla Ram, from the village Nappa Ke Kheda of Rajasthan is facing rejection from her college going husband who does not want an illiterate wife. Village custom demands that the husband either comes down himself or sends someone to fetch her. Four years into the marriage, Simla is still waiting to be escorted to her husband's home. Simla is completely against nata.

She says she would like to settle down only with her husband. Marriages in villages have come under pressure for other reasons as well. Dowry and modern lifestyle demands, including incompatibility, are reasons cited for marital breakdowns and consequently the sale of women.

EVE TEASING

Eve teasing is an act of terror that violates a woman's body, space and self-respect. It is one of the many ways through which a woman is systematically made to feel inferior, weak and afraid. Whether it is an obscene word whispered into a woman's ear; offensive remarks on her appearance; an intrusive way of touching any part of a woman's body; a gesture which is perceived and intended to be vulgar: all these acts represent a violation of a woman's person, her bodily integrity. Eve teasing denies a woman's fundamental right to move freely and carry herself with dignity, solely on the basis of her sex.

Some acts of eve-teasing mentioned by girl students interviewed are; indecent remarks, singing obscene songs, hitting, touching or pinching in crowded places, snatching dupatta and in some cases even forced kissing, mailing anonymous love letters and exhibiting male genital in front of women. Eve teasing by itself is not an offence under any law, but Sections 294 and 349 of the Indian Penal Code cover substance of eve teasing. Sections 294 punishes "whoever, to the annoyance of others does any obscene act in any public place, or sings, recites or utters any obscene song, ballads or words in or near any public place" is liable to be punished with imprisonment or with fine.

The part is very wide in nature and a person can be hauled up even if the acts forming part of the substance of the offence are addressed to the public at large, provided this cause annoyance. Clearly a girl or a woman who feels annoyed by any obscene song or words can take recourse to the provision of the part and put up a complaint before a police station. The offence is cognisable, i.e. a police officer can arrest the offender without a warrant but it is bailable. A graver form of eve teasing is accompanied by the use of gesture indicating threat or use of force. 'Criminal force' has been defined under Section 349 of Indian Penal Code. According to this part 'a person is said to use force to another if he causes motion, change or cessation of motion to that other person'. In such a case also, action can be taken against the person using it. The punishment is such cases are imprisonment for two years or fine or both. The offence is cognisable.

Thus, simple eve teasing accompanied with gesture to use force are punishable under the existing provisions of the Indian Penal Code. A graver form of eve teasing is accompanied by the use of gesture indicating threat or use of force. In such a case also, action can be taken against the person using it Stereotypically, men are conceived of as natural prey to uncontrollable lust. Women therefore have to protect themselves at any costs. In an ironic twist of responsibility, women then bear the burden of guilt for an act of violence against themselves. This is the basis for the second typical response to a violation of women's bodily integrity: to exhort women to censor their movements and appearance. Another misconception believes that men who abuse women are rowdy lower class elements.

In fact, men who violate a woman's space and body do not belong to any particular social group or class. Eve teasers are there in the family, the neighbourhood, in one's classroom and place of work. What is perceived as male lust in our culture represents a desperate and frantic inability to communicate with women. This inability often translates into acts that hurt and terrorise. Consider the fact that popular representations of romance, as in film, clearly link up eve teasing to love. This not only naturalises abuse as love, but also legitimises male power over women.

In the larger cultural context the man - woman relationships is simply not open to free, unfettered discussions of romance and sexuality. In such a context, communication between the sexes necessarily suffers. There is an influence of the cinema and cheap literature in which sex permeates. The current advertisements trying to promote sale of under garments, towels bed-sheets, etc. by indecently exposing the female anatomy also lead to degeneration of women as a commercial commodity in the mind of man. There is a rush to the urban area in search of adventure and employment. Away from the restraining influence of the families, the youngsters look for excitement and thrills which they seem to get in acts of eve teasing. Infliction of pain on the eve acts as a stimulant to their sex desires.

There is also a lack of fear of punishment or adverse publicity or social disgrace. The police with its insufficient strength and preoccupation with other problems of law and order and courts with their proverbial delays and intricate legal procedures fail to bring most of the perpetrators to book. There are no particular places where eve teasers congregate. In this sense, no place is really "safe" and inviolate for women. Roads, buses, train, cinema halls, parks, beaches, even a woman's home and neighbourhood may be sites where her self-worth is abused. It does not matter if a woman is alone, with a friend, in a group, or sometimes even with another man. Segregating the spaces that men and women occupy only compounds, not solves the problem.

8

Crime against Old Women

The elder abuse as 'harm to an elder person caused by someone in a position of trust, who may have control over the victim. This includes material abuse such as financial exploitation, physical abuse, such as pushing, physical assault, psychological abuse, such as chronically threatening, swearing at or insulting the older person, and neglect or failing to provide necessary help such as meal preparation, housework or personal care.

In the past few years, the aged have frequently been the target of gang robberies or brutal killing by servants or outsiders. Old are attacked frequently due to their inability to put up a fight. Elders normally have to face up to the facts that, their energy and authority is eroding. To add to their woe is the death of any one of the spouse. Widows have to be dealt with specifically, as the death of a spouse for a woman in any age is a tragedy in itself, because of the norms and tradition and the manner in which she is treated after the death of her husband.

VIOLENCE AGAINST WIDOWS

Closely linked with Sati and harassment of widows, is the custom of child marriage producing number of child widows, but not child widowers. Widow remarriage is not common and not sanctioned by society, however men were allowed to remarry. Sati idealised as sitting on the funeral pyre of the deceased husband; and those widows who did not go through this had to make themselves physically unattractive and absent from public functions. Widows are called inauspicious and are avoided, whenever possible. Sati according to Giri was recommended after 500 AD in the dharmashastras and spread across the country around 1000 AD. There are three kinds of widows. One is a young girl with no children, a woman who becomes a widow after some years of marital span and has children. The third is case of a woman who is widow of 50 years and above of age. Giri mentions three options for a widow woman according to orthodox tradition; sati, ascetic widowhood or remarriage. Widows are expected to lead an ascetic life by the society with restrictive codes of dress, diet and demeanour and of social ostracism from the religious and social life of the community.

She is expected to remain in perpetual mourning, and give up eating 'spicy food', in order to cool her sexual energy, and remain celibate, devout and loyal to her husband's memory. According to Dreze J. the well being of widow is not just a question of economic security, but also one of dignity, self-respect and participation in society. Many widows in the Chen sample suffered from different forms of social isolation, psychological abuse or emotional distress.

According to Dreze J., the social marginalised of widows was frequently found to take one or more of the following forms: Rumours and accusations: Widows are often accused of being responsible for their husband's deaths, regarded as sexually threatening, and generally considered as inauspicious by the society. Widows are also accused often of immoral realtions Enforced dress and behaviour codes: Many widows are under strong pressure to observe restriction in codes of dress, appearance and behaviour.

Some of the traditional restrictions have become quite rare, even among the upper castes, but others remain widespread. Social ostracism: A widow is often excluded from the religious and social life of the community, due to her perceived in auspiciousness. Physical violence: violence against widows primarily takes the form of sexual harassment or property related violence. Emotional harassment: Sarcastic remarks in the presence of others, verbal abuse, beating and illtreatment of her children are some of the forms of emotional harassment. There have also been reports of houseowners sexually abusing widows who are living alone and cannot pay rent. Not all widows, according to Dreze J. face these type of mistreatment. Many older widows who live with their sons enjoy their respect and love.

Some older widows are happily integrated in their daughters households. If is young widows who are most vulnerable to mistreatment, unless they have the support of their parents or brother. Percentage of total widows to total female population is 6.5 for women and 1.94 for men. The percentage of women widows is much more than men from age group 40 onwards to 80+. The highest male female difference is in the age group 70 to 74, where the percentage of female widows is 66.51 and male widows is 18.70%.

Some of the essential factors that account for high levels of deprivation among Indian widows include limited freedom to remarry, insecure property rights, social restrictions, on living arrangements, restricted employment opportunities and lack of social support. Patrilocal Residence: The system of patrilocal residence, which has the effect of isolating women, is a fundamental source of gender inequalities in many parts of rural India and also plays a crucial part in the deprivation of widows. Patrilocality in the narrow sense refers to the norm, prevalent in most Hindu communities of India, according to which a woman has to leave her parents home at the time of marriage to join her husband in his home.

In a broader sense, especially in most Hindu communities of North India where marriage rules dictate marriage outside the clan and village. If could also result in drastic alienation from her parental family. In North India, widows are expected to remain in their husband's village, and most of them do so. At the same time they are unlikely to receive much support from their inlaws. On the contrary, the relationship between a widow and her in-laws is typically quite tense. Widows are thus denied both the freedom to leave their husband's village, and the support they need to live there happily. Limited freedom to remarry, in some communities, particularly in northwest India, ascriptive leviratic unions remain quite common. Elsewhere, the standard pattern is that most childless widows remarry, but only a small proportion of widowed mothers does so. Out of 562 respondents in the Chen sample of widows. 510 women had lost their husbands and did not remarry; 35 women, who had lost their husbands, remarried and then became widowed again by losing their second husbands, and 17 women who had lost their husbands, remarried, and were still married at the time of the survey.

In the Chen sample of 562 ever-widowed women, 13% in North India had remarried compared with only 6% in South India. The lower probability of remarriage in South is due in part to the practice of levirate in the North. The issue of remarriage, according to Srivastava is linked to property issue. Widow remarriage is not allowed so that part of the property does not pass into another family's hands. Some part of the population encourage leviratic relationships to ensure that the property stays with the family.

In cases where she gets into a 'nata', the relationship is formalised by the village community and she loses right to her first husband's property. She has a lower status in a 'nata' than a remarriage. Employment restrictions: Aside from these general restrictions, widows face specific difficulties in seeking gainful employment opportunities. These include: lack of access to indivisible productive assets owned by the deceased husband's family: weak bargaining power vis-à-vis male partners in economic transactions, frequent absence of a literate member in the household: limited access to institutional credit, and, particularly in the case of widows with young children, the burden of domestic work.

Social restriction of living arrangements: One of the clearest and most important findings of Chen's and other studies is the overwhelming dependence of widows on themselves and their own sons. The proportion of widows who live in households headed either themselves or by one of their sons are well over 85% in the Chen sample. The proportion of widows who live in a household headed by a brother-in-law or parent-in-law is below 3% and the number of widows who live in a household headed by a brother of the father is also below 3%. Legal inheritance rights: Formally according to contemporary Indian law, a widow has an unequivocal right to a share of her husband's property, including his land. This is in addition to the legal rights she has irrespective of her marital status to a share of her parents' property.

Field studies, however, indicate that these legal rights are comprehensively violated, and that a large majority of widows have very limited and insecure property rights. This deprivation of property rights not only represents the loss of a potential source of independent income, but also diminishes the bargaining power of a widow vis-à-vis her in-laws, sons and other potential supporters. Modernisation: Singh has mentioned urbanisation and modernisation and consequently the erosion of the traditional form of care of the elderly people, which was prevalent in India like joint family. There is an emotional estrangement between the young and the old in nuclear family.

Lack of loyal servants: Even if the old has money to fend for themselves, many are unable to do so due to the lack of loyal domestic servants. Indicators: Some of the other indicators of violence against the old and widow could be symptoms of withdrawal. Mental deterioration, cessation of activities, felling of inferiority, inadequacy and frustration. Old and widows are victimised by relatives, informal care providers, house-owners, friends or formal care-givers in institutional settings. They are abused almost by anybody who has power over them.

9

Prison Visiting System in India

AN INTRODUCTION

One of the main objectives of incarceration, right from the inception of this concept in a sovereign state, was to curtail the liberty of movement and the freedom of initiative of a person, if he was found to have violated the established law of the land. Prisons took shape as institutions of state retribution as a natural outcome of the materialization of this objective.

Resultant segregation of offenders. from the society, and the obligation of prison guards to restraint their movement against escape from lawful custody, constrained the architects of prison buildings to burden them with high walls, narrow galleries, labyrinths, shutters, locks, chains, fetters, cells and places of solitary confinement.

This physical structure of prisons and the archaic rules of management of these punitive. institutions endowed them with a cover of obscurity in which fundamental human rights could be unofficially violated and officially denied. Prisons grew to be places of low visibility where inhuman and even cruel conditions could prevail. The possibility of inflicting injury and injustice on inmates always lurked in these closed institutions.

State supervision over day-to-day happenings within such institutions became a mere formality and the surveillance of the society was conspicuous by its absence. In spite of the fact that prison system has, during the past some decades, undergone a massive change both in its objectives and in its physical structure, the basic character of prisons — as closed institutions with little public scrutiny — continues to this day. The need for non-government intervention in prisons was recognized as early as 1894 when the Prisons Act accepted that a system of visitors would be of value in providing humanitarian aid to prison inmates secluded from the society. The Cardew Committee appointed by the British Government in that year devoted a whole stage to making this system more effective and efficacious.

As a result the concept of non-government intervention in the management of prisons was for the first time conceived in The Prisons Act of 1894. Although this concept did not find place in the body of main provisions of the Act, but in Section 59, which speaks of powers to frame rules consistent with this Act, the State Governments were empowered to make rules for the appointment and guidance of visitors of prisons. in sub-section (25). The present provisions for official and nonofficial visitors in Prison Manuals of various states are the result of this sub-section (25) of section 59 of The Prisons Act of 1894. The first comprehensive work of studying prison conditions and of making remarkably suitable recommendations for the reformation of both prisons and prisoners was done by the Indian Jails Committee, 1919-20 appointed on the 28th day of April, 1919 under the chairmanship of Sir Alexander G. Cardew, ICS, Member of the Executive Council, Madras, with six distinguished members.

Quite a large number of recommendations made by this committee still hold good after the expiry of 80 long years. This Committee devoted a whole stage to the improvement in the system of Visitors. of prisons. Addressing the need for external supervision on prisons the Committee wrote:

- The plan of appointing persons, official and non-official, to serve as visitors to jails seems to us to form a very valuable part of the Indian system of jail administration. In the first place, it insures the existence of a body of free and unbiased observers, whose visits serve as a guarantee to the Government and to the public, that the rules of the Prisons Act and Prison Manuals are duly observed, and that abuses, if they were to spring up, would be speedily brought to light. In this respect the Indian system is, we think, superior to that followed in other countries where the visitors become a part of the prison organization, with definite powers and duties, and so become more or less identified with the prison administration. In India, they remain impartial and independent. In the second place, the existence of non-official visitors is specially valuable as supplying a training ground where members of the public can obtain an insight into jail problems and learn to take an interest in prisons and prisoners. It is of great importance to create such an interest in the public mind and the appointment of non-officials is one of the best methods of promoting this end. Although, therefore, some of our witnesses have criticized the system, we think it has only to be extended and improved in order to be productive of even greater advantages in the future than in the past.

LEGAL PROVISIONS

Sub-section (25) of section 59 of The Prisons Act, 1894, the current basic law for the management of prisons in the country provides for the framing of rules forthe appointment and guidance of visitors of prisons. The Indian Jail Committee, 1919- 20, had laid down guidelines for the appointment of prison visitors stating that:

- The person selected for the position of a non-official visitor of a jail should be chosen on the ground of definite qualifications, such as an interest in prison matters or other social work, or ability and willingness to assist in finding work for prisoners on release. Selection should not be made solely on the ground of social position, wealth or political influence, but on the basis of special fitness..

Only a few states of independent India incorporated these guidelines as legal provisions for the appointment of non-official visitors. One such state was Maharashtra. The Prison Manual of Maharashtra dealing withAppointment of Non-official Visitors. says:

- The appointment of non-official visitors shall, subject to the provisions of sub-rule, be made by the State Government from amongst persons who in its opinion, are interested in the administration of prisons and are likely to take interest in the prisoners and their welfare both while they are in prison and after their release.

These guidelines and some of the other rules governing the operation of prison visiting system in Maharashtra need to be emulated by other states. Rules in most of the other states of the country do not specify any qualification for a person to be eligible for appointment as non-official visitor of a prison. They empower the State Government to appoint non-official visitors, six for each Central Prison, three for each district prison and two for each lock-up jail, on the recommendations of the Divisional Commissioner or Collector and District Magistrate of the district in which the jail or lock-up is situated. Inter alia these rules provide for the duties of visitors, procedure for the removal of a non-official visitor and the powers of the District Magistrate to cause the preparation of Roster for monthly visits and to form a Board of Visitors for each prison in the concerned district.

A visitor, so long as he retains his official connections with the jail, is precluded from giving publicity in the press or otherwise to matters connected with its administration. The rules also provide detailed guidelines on the points to be noticed by visitors during their visit to prisons, but, unlike the rules of Maharashtra, there is no mandate about giving a copy of these rules to non-official visitors at the time of their appointment.

DUTIES AND FUNCTIONS OF PRISON VISITORS

Prison Rules of various states prescribe what the prison visitors should do and what they should not. Generally speaking these duties and restrictions are as follows:

Do's:

- It is the duty of a visitor to satisfy himself that the law and rules regulating the management of prisons and prisoners are duly carried out in the prison;
- To visit all part of the prison and to see all prisoners;
- To hear and inquire into any complaint(s) that any prisoner may make; he may for this purpose talk to any prisoner out of the hearing but in the full sight of the officer accompanying him;
- To see, if necessary, any book, paper or record connected with the administration of the prison;

Don'ts:

- No visitor may issue any order or instruction to any subordinate jail officer;
- No visitor shall touch prisoners. rations in the kitchen, but he can taste the food if he so desires.
- Non-official visitors may not visit prisoners on hunger strike or prisoners who are ill and are not allowed to be interviewed on medical grounds or those detained under the Preventive Detention Act.
- Non-official lady visitors shall not visit men's portion of the prison and shall confine themselves only to the women's part;
- Non-official or official visitors shall not, without the previous sanction of the Superintendent, hold conversation with any under-trial who may happen to be their client or relation.

Now, there are some provisions which are out-dated and do not fit in the present democratic system. Why should an NOV be debarred from visiting a prisoner on hunger strike? May be that this prisoner has taken resort to hunger strike as a last option for seeking redress to some unresolved complaint, and a non-official visitor has a right to listen to such complaint. Similarly, the restriction on non-official visitors to meet prisoners kept under the Preventive Detention Act is also an archaic provision that suited the British rule in India, and should now be lifted. Even the ban on visitors to touch rations in the kitchen, or on lady non-official visitors to visit the men's part are uncalled for. If a visitor properly washes his hands, why should he not be allowed to touch and feel the quality of rations.

And, in an age when there are women superintendents at men's jail, why should lady visitors be not allowed to visit the entire prison with appropriate security arrangements. There is yet another controversial provision in rules which says that a visitor, so long as he retains his official connections with the jail, is precluded from giving publicity in the press or otherwise to matters connected with prison administration. There is a strong argument that this provision is a violation of the fundamental right of speech and expression that every citizen enjoys under the Constitution and it cannot be withdrawn from a person only because he has been appointed a visitor of prison.

Such restriction could perhaps be permissible or even justifiable a hundred years ago when it served the interests of British Rule because the visitors provided a cross check on prison administration and the government did not want any criticism to pass to the media without proper censor. Democratic principles had not come into play then, and the government wanted all infirmities to be kept within the system created by it.

But, in a democratic set-up, any flaw in administration or neglect on the part of concerned authorities that deserves public notice for an accelerated remedial measure, should be brought to light through media, particularly when we have accepted the principles of transparency in administration through citizens charters and the right to information. And, if the institution of prison visitors that has been introduced to break the obscurity of prisons, is forced under law to conserve the same obscurity, the very purpose of its institution shall be defeated.

Matters in this respect shall automatically improve if the qualifications, antecedents, experience and social status of persons appointed as prison visitors are duly considered at appropriate levels and nominations are made strictly according to the procedure laid down in the rules.

BOARD OF VISITORS

Obscurity to society has perhaps been the main reason why it has been so difficult and sluggish to bring about improvement in prison conditions. This obscurity results partly from the basic nature of prison institutions and partly from the predisposition of management combined with the complete disinterest of society in general.

This was perhaps foreseen by the framers of the Prisons Act a hundred years ago and therefore they slid a provision in the Prisons Act to bring about the institution of prison visitors. It is also for this reason that some kind of extra-departmental and social intervention has been sought through the appointment of visitors of prison from out side the prison set-up.

The formation and involvement of a board of visitors by the state is the only area where the prison bumps into society. The way, state provided for the formation and functioning of the board of visitors tells us something about the nature of the role it expected society to play in the process of the management of prisons. Rules provide for the constitution of Board of Visitors. through the office of the District Magistrate/ Divisional Commissioner.

The purpose of the constitution of these Boards is:

- To regulate prison visits by official and non-official visitors through the roster of visitors,
- To ensure at least one visit of the prison per month by an agency other than the officials of the department,
- To involve all persons nominated as official or non-official visitors and to give each one of them some occasions of visiting prison, and
- To provide a forum for discussing problems of prisons and prisoners outside the intervention of the prison department.

All non-official visitors of a jail except those debarred by the Government are eligible to be on the Board of Visitors. Rules provide that a Board of Visitors shall be selected biennially by the Collector and District Magistrate of the concerned district from amongst the official and non-official visitors of each prison and this Board shall inspect the prison twice a year on dates to be fixed by the superintendent in consultation with the President and members of the Board. The Board shall consist of two official and two non-official members, one of whom shall be nominated Chairman by the Collector and District Magistrate.

At the District level, the Collector himself is the chairperson of this Board but at lock-ups the Sub-divisional Officer, City Magistrate, Extra-Magistrate or Judicial Magistrate is the Chairperson. A meeting of the Board of Visitors is required to be held once in a quarter. In Sunil Batra case the Supreme Court expressed that the Board of Visitors comes in handy for the protection of the rights of prisoners. It thought that the board, which includes judicial officers and people from varied social backgrounds and is vested with visitorial powers, could be instant administrative grievance mechanism to protect the rights of prisoners. It specifically cautioned visitors that the pressure of warders or officials were inhibitive and must be avoided.

It also suspected that open inquiry of prisoners in the presence of the prison official would lead to reprisal. Whatever have been the directions of the court, the prison department has been following only the colonial document of prison manual in the manner it conceived and has structured the role and scope for intervention of society and judiciary in its own way.

The prison manual explicitly and in unambiguous terms subjects all possible means of communication between the prisoners and the outside society to restrictions. It conferred unbridled and unguided powers to the level of absurdity in the hands of prison superintendent. These rules fail to stand the test of articles 14, 19 and 21, of the Constitution, which subject the actions of state to non-arbitrariness, reasonableness and principles of natural justice.

This draconian document based on the notions of 19th century criminality, is yet be revised. It continues to be applicable as it still serves the purpose of present state. A look into the kind of social arrangement made in the prison by the law gives us a hint about the true nature of its functioning in the society.

COURT RULINGS ON THE ROLE OF PRISON VISITORS

The role of prison visitors as independent observers of the functioning of prisons has been repeatedly recognized by the higher and apex judiciary. It came into sharp focus in Ranchod Vs. State of M.P. in which the callous behaviour of jail doctors, maltreatment by jail staff and tampering of jail records came up for judicial scrutiny.

All this went on for years with the Prison Visitors and Visiting Boards apparently oblivious of it all. According to the facts of the case an inmate of the Central Prison of Indore had died of utter negligence on the part of prison administration and the medical staff posted there. A letter written by two coinmates of the deceased was admitted by the High Court of Madhya Pradesh as a writ petition and was decided by Hon'ble Justice V.D.Gyani and Justice B.B.L Shrivastava. Reacting sharply to the facts on record Justice V.D. Gyani, Judge of M.P. High Court observed:

- The petition has many facets exposing the negligence of authorities, callous disregard to duty by all concerned, including the jail staff, the Executive Magistrate, the Visitors to jail appointed by the State Government, the District Judge, the police and the unethical conduct of doctors..
- This letter petition brings into sharp focus and throws light on many other ills besetting the system. Do our District and Sessions Judges, who are exofficio visitors to the jail within their respective jurisdiction, the Director of Health Services, the Civil Surgeon or Medical Officers, the representatives of people representing particular urban or rural constituency in the State Legislature and the non-official visitors, as appointed do they satisfy themselves that the law, rules regulating the management of prisons and

> prisoners are duly carried out? Their duties are enumerated in.. the Jail Manual. They can call for and inspect any book or other record in the jail. Have they regularly visited the jail so as to apprise themselves of the genuine problems the prisoners are facing and their grievances. The non-official visitors to the jail, appointed by the State Government, have they justified their appointment by getting themselves acquainted with the prisoners. problems and making efforts for amelioration of their lot, within the framework of the Jail Manual itself; if all this had been going on smoothly, as is expected and sought to be, possibly there was no need for. this letter petition. The question looms large, who bothers..

In spite of such eye opening judgments and judicial aspersions, prison conditions in the country continue to be appalling. The system of prison visitors is still considered by prison staff as an un-necessary intrusion in their work, and non-official visitors reduce their functions to mere clerical formality in the absence of any accountability. In order to shun the rejective attitude of prison staff NOVs prefer not to visit the prison at all.

After all what do they lose if they knowingly evade uncomfortable situations that could arise in confronting a non-cooperative prison staff. If they have to wait for long to meet a prison superintendent who thinks it a waste of time to cause his jailor to take them round the prison on a lawful visit, it is better to avoid visiting such jail.

Even the visits of ex-officio visitors of prison are not as regular and purposeful as intended in the rules. Hon'ble Justice J.S. Verma, former Chief Justice of India and later Chairperson of the National Human Rights Commission, addressing a letter to the Chief Justices of all High Courts with regard to human rights in prisons, wrote on January 1, 2000:

- The state Prison Manuals contain provisions for District and Sessions Judges to function as ex-officio visitors to jail within their jurisdiction so as to ensure that prison inmates are not denied certain basic minimum standards of health, hygiene and institutional treatment. The prisoners are in judicial custody and hence it is incumbent upon the Sessions Judges to monitor their living conditions and ensure that humane conditions prevail within the prison walls also. Justice Krishna Iyer has aptly remarked that the prison gates are not an iron curtain between the prisoner and human rights. In addition the Supreme Court specifically directed that the District and Sessions Judges must visit prisons for this purpose and consider this part of duty as an essential function attached to their office. They should make expeditious enquiries into the grievances of the prisoners and take suitable corrective measures.

- During visits to various district prisons, the Commission has been informed that the Sessions Judges are not regular in visiting prisons and the District Committee headed by Sessions Judge/District Magistrate and comprised of senior Superintendent of Police is not meeting at regular intervals to review the conditions of the prisoners..

He implored Chief Justices to consider giving appropriate instructions to the District and Sessions Judges to take necessary steps to resolve this acute problem as it has the impact of violating a human right which is given the status of constitutional guarantee.

THE NEGATIVE VIEWPOINT

Even today one could find a significant number of persons working in the criminal justice system, or in the open society, who hold the view that the image of a prison must inspire awe and fear in the minds of offenders. They try to convince that the life in prisons should be demonstrably torturous to deter a prospective criminal.

Reformation of a criminal, they say, is impossible and that rehabilitation is a hollow imagination of some non-practical persons. In order to generalize their perception they have a few examples to quote. They forget that their views are more sentimental than scientific. Studies in social science have proved beyond doubt that harshness of punishment has never been a deterrent to a prospective law breaker.

While the continuance of death penalty for murder has not been a curb on the rate of the incidence of homicides, the abolition of this harsh punishment in a large number of federating states in the U.S.A has not increased the number of murders there.

The loss of liberty by itself is sufficient to prevent a common man from indulging into violation of rules of the society. We all know that the society itself plays an important role in inducing some people into deviant behaviour, and that a large number of prisoners do not commit the second crime after their release because they have had the session of their life in a single incarceration.

According to the statistics gathered by the National Crime Records Bureau, MHA, the number of inmates in prisons who had two or more previous convictions at the end of the year 2002 was only 2.7% of the total prison population in the country. To those who do not believe in improving prison conditions or in the conservation of basic human rights in custody, Pandit Jawaharlal Nehru wrote in India and the World Prison Land.:

- Another error which people indulge in is the fear that if jail conditions are improved people will flock in ! This shows a singular ignorance of human nature. No one wants to go to prison however good the prison might be. To be deprived of liberty and family life and friends and home surroundings is a terrible thing. It is well known that the Indian peasant will prefer to stick to his ancestral soil and starve rather than go elsewhere to better his condition. To improve prison conditions does not mean that prison life should be made soft; it means that it should be made human and sensible..

Cruelty does generate cruelty. It undoubtedly has the tendency to squeeze all compassion out of a person and to make him unsocial. Prison conditions must therefore adhere to certain norms in which an inmate could be prevented from being dehumanized. It is for restoring prisons to these basic minimum norms that the institution of Prison Visitors is so necessary and useful.

HOW THE DECAY HAS SET IN

In spite of all meticulousness in the procedural details of prison rules, transparency in the management of these impermeable institutions has always been lacking. Since secure custody of inmates is the basic function of prisons, anything that is a threat to security is laid off. How can prison management be transparent, it is argued, when secrecy is the keyword of security.

High walls and wards and cells and locks and keys and stringent rules are all for keeping inmates out of the reach of their kin and the society. Easy access to public eye could infringe upon this age-old system of segregation and obliterate the very purpose for which prisons were conceived. Secure management has thus slowly but consciously slipped into obscure management and, once transparency is shadowed, accountability becomes a farce. Prison management could, if it so preferred, become repressive and yet pass unnoticed. No inmate could complain of repression for fear of more repression.

How can one dare to harness enmity with the system in which one has to live a substantial period of life in seclusion from the society. It is common knowledge that this obscurity becomes the breeding ground of several evils. If atrocities, corruption and irregularities go un-noticed, they flourish. Misuse of authority for unlawful gain becomes the order of the day.

One can create discomfiture and charge for ease. Cliques are formed in which old-time inmates become party with the staff and run an unholy business., the gains of which are distributed among stakeholders., who, in fact, have nothing at stake except their conscience. The network spreads. The higher it goes, the more it is necessary to extract, and therefore new methodologies are evolved to keep the game plan going. Those few who prefer to keep away from this degradation, are ridiculed. They are disdained, isolated, rejected, placed in unimportant positions and sometimes punished on false grounds. But atrocities in prisons are not all of the making of prison staff. A substantially large number of them result from the system itself and the neglect to which it is subjected by all concerned—the courts, the police, the probation system, district administration, the PWD and so on.

Physical and psychological torture resulting from overcrowding, lack of space for segregation of sick, stinking toilets for want of proper supply of water, lack of proper bedding, restrictions on movement resulting form shortage of staff, parading of women through men's wards for lack of proper separation, non-production of undertrial prisoners in courts, inadequate medical facilities, neglect in the grant of parole, rejection of pre-mature release on flimsy grounds, and several such afflictions result not from any malfeasance of the prison staff but from the collective neglect of the whole system. Those who can deliver goods do not know. Those who know have no means to remedy the ills.

There is lack of effective communication. Those who communicate lack perseverance. There is no accountability for non-performance. There is no linkage, no monitoring, no deadlines, no evaluation and therefore no result.

REFORMATION—THE CHANGE IS SLOW BUT OBVIOUS

In spite of the fact that there are several maladies in the prison system in the country, it would not be appropriate to totally condemn the whole set-up. Obviously, there are difficulties of man-power, funds, training and right kind of attitude to deal with socially handicapped inmates, but all these ills need to be corrected with the joint effort of the government, the people and the staff manning prison institutions. Some prisons are an example of the best utilization of the resources available, and it is educative to see them. Prison visitors of different states should be given an opportunity to visit such prisons to see how they function and how those conditions can be emulated in other prisons. Housed in comparatively new buildings constructed on the principles laid down with regard to minimum space per person, and having appropriately provided facilities of sanitation, medical care, hygienic kitchens, play grounds, separate entrance for women part, space for vocational training and prison factories, adequate staff quarters, and suitable dormitories for single-person security staff, these prisons present an image of a scientifically built custodial institution. Reformative programmes are regularly conducted in these prisons with the help of local non-government agencies and philanthropic organizations.

Preksha-dhyan, Vipasyana, spritual discourses, lectures and preaching on issues of healthy social life, literacy classes and de-addiction programmes, adult education classes, plantation, horticulture and environment improvement with the material assistance provided by government and non-government agencies, are some of the regular features of the prison.

Services of educated prisoners are availed to promote literacy and to hold regular education classes for those who wish to appear at Board or University examinations as private candidates. All fees and other expenses on the education of these inmates is borne by voluntary organizations such as Rotary Club, Lions Club or by public welfare part of established banking institutions. All these activities are geared and monitored by prison management with the personal efforts of some wellintentioned prison personnel supported by active and effective prison visitors.

Such correctional programmes not only break the monotony of prison setting but charge the atmosphere with an urge for betterment. These prisons do not present a dismal picture of human beings languishing in idle confinement, but are places buzzing with activity, both administrative and correctional. There appears to be a horizontal coordination of prison officials with the officers of other departments and with functionaries of other organs of the criminal justice system.

The jail Superintendents and other staff have amiable informal relations with other district level local officers. This facilitates their official functioning. They leave no occasion, official or informal, to meet these district level officials and invite them to all functions held at the prison. Problems of prison are introduced to concerned officials during courtesy meetings to draw their appropriate attention and an early solution.

Such congenial ambiance prevents unnecessary delay of bureaucratic procedures in getting things done for the prison and prisoners. One can visualize here that a purposeful and constructive local cooperation of officials of prison, police and the judiciary can go a long way in ameliorating the sufferings of prison inmates. And, if some well-meaning non-government social organizations are involved in the corrective process of prisons, it can make the rehabilitation of offenders after their release, much smooth.

It is in the creation of this congenial atmosphere that the role of Prison Visitors both official and non- official—can be best appreciated and obtained. It is they who can best bring to the notice of the government, the deficiencies of the system at appropriate time so that they do not accumulate or grow to unmanageable proportions.

It is they who can help prison administration in securing the cooperation of non-government agencies engaged in philanthropic work for extending their activities within prison walls where a neglected mass of human beings waits for the support of society. It is they, again, who can prepare the society in shedding off their rejective prejudices for casual offenders who make mistakes in haste and repent at leisure. The institution of Prison Visitors is, thus, not only desirable but essential for the development of a correctional atmosphere in prisons.

It has to be retained and reinforced, if we want to open a casement on prisons for involving the society in general to improve prison conditions and help our less fortunate brothers and sisters in captivity to make their period of incarceration less dehumanizing and more productive.

10

Women Prisoners

INTRODUCTION

Development in the recent past has led to conflict, violence, chaos and disparities. Unplanned and unconcerned pursuits of development have caused chaos and disorders in the society. Much of the crime in the country can be attributed to the issues and problems thrown up by the implications of development. Deprivations of the benefits and fruits of development pursuits generally led to disparities, resulting in the criminality and unrestness.

Moreover, the denial of the justice to the poor led to the growth of agrarian agitation in Bihar and Uttar Pradesh. The politicization in agrarian regions has exacerbated conflicts. Crime has implications on development too. Crime ridden areas lag behind in development. Violence and terrorism obstruct the industrial and business development. Several regions of the country like north east, Jammu and Kashmir, Punjab, Bihar etc. are experiencing the brunt. They are loosing a lot of foreign investment and cooperation. Thus, the peace is the prime condition for development.

SOCIAL CHANGE AND CRIME

At the beginning of the 1990s' the average number of offences per lakh population was five times higher than in the 1950's. According to Garland, there is a normality of higher crime rates in late modern society and a new collective experience of crime and insecurity, an experience which is itself structured by the distinctive social, economic and cultural arrangements of late twentieth century capitalism. Changes in crime rates link primarily to political change and the resulting consequences for the affected societies. Social factors cause delinquency and deviant behaviour. In addition, different patterns of the recording and registering offences and criminal behaviour contributed to varying crime rates. Equally, almost all criminological theories refer to the relations between crime and social conditions.

For the last fifty years, for instance, economic and social changes in industrial countries led to an extended range of behaviour defined as criminal. Computer crimes, environmental crimes, credit card fraud or offences in connection with internet have only been made possible by the technical and economic development of last years. In addition, the public sensitivity for deviant behaviour has risen as well, fundamentally influenced by increasing sensational and aggressive media coverage.

Equally important, the women's movement contributed to bringing offences and behaviour to the public attention that comprise women's and children's right. For the last decades there have been further fundamental societal changes contributing to an increasing crime load.

Taylor holds following social changes responsible for the increase in both crime rates and the fear of victimization:

- Job crisis,
- Crisis of material poverty and social inequality,
- Fear of falling and fear of others,
- Crisis of nation state,
- Crisis of inclusion and exclusion
- Crisis in the culture,
- Crisis of masculinity and gender order,
- Crisis of family and parenting and
- The size of market society.

Unemployment, inequality and poverty cause the breakdown of the everyday order, perspectives, and social relations which further more may lead to the considerable feelings of insecurity, deprivation and apathy. Unemployment may lead to financed problems and thereby poverty, but also to social isolation. Unemployed people are in danger of sinking into poverty and therefore, becoming socially marginal. Relevant studies proved again and again that unemployment fosters intra family conflicts and tensions and even violent behaviour.

Significantly, the globalization process with its concomitant integration at the economic, technological and cultural levels contributes to the globalization of crime as well which appear in the form of terrorism, drug trafficking, money laundering and organized crime with international dimensions.

Development also brings about change in forms of and patterns of crime and also their cause and conditions. When development process reaches a certain stage at which the economic security and social well being of a majority of population is assured the pattern of crime begin to change from crime typical of poverty to crime is typical of affluence.

In the changed scenario, the traditional agrarian castes at the middle and lower middle levels were able not only to enhance their economic standards, but also acquired considerable political power. In cultural and educational domain they are still deprived in relation to the upper castes. They are not only to competitive rivalry with the upper castes, but the lower level debits. They now have exploitative and conflictual relationships.

The ascendance of this new middle class in rural areas have several important implications for the emerging patters of caste related crimes and violence in rural areas. Importantly, lack of social responsibility and accountability, erosion of social values and austerity, an enormous amount of money goes into the black market resulting in the parallel black money which has a destabilizing and crippling effect on the economy.

In urban areas, enormous growth of population, unplanned development, lack of civic amenities, increasing urban problems, growing, unemployment etc. has all contributed to the urban unrest, violence and crime. The pressures on urban infrastructure and the perception of privatizations of urban areas in comparison to rural areas gives rise to rural urban tensions and conflicts. Privatization, liberalization and market friendly policies have lead to the growth of economic crimes. There are social and cultural consequences of liberalization and globalization with implications for social tensions and crimes. Moreover, there has been a qualitative change in the political leadership and processes.

Politicization of the crimes is the main characteristics of today's political leadership. Political goals are increasingly sought to be achieved by violent means. Political mobilization on easer, communal and regional grounds often takes place employing violent means. This has necessitated the assistance and inclusions of criminals and mafia in politics.

FEMALE CRIMINALITY

In the wake of industrialization, westernization and urbanization, Indian society has been passing through drastic and fundamental changes both in the structures, socio-economic and cultural spheres which not only produced a changed physical environment and a new form of economic organization but also affected the social order, solidarity, human conduct and thought. Traditionall· women, whose role was mainly confined to the domestic area has now switched over to productively job sector. She is found to be actively participating in area sphere of professional life along with the male counterparts.

The urbanization, industrialization, liberalization, globalization, and market friendly policies have resulted in increased opportunities for employment to women. Moreover, women centred policies; programmes and projects accelerated the process of women empowerment. Women are participation in economic activities, political insulations and a social sphere has increased to the greater extent.

However, because of family disorganization, marital discord, high aspiration level and frustration due to non fulfillment, stress and failure in coping process and alteration women are found to getting involved in criminal activities more in number in the present day society. Statistics on female criminality reveals that female criminals contribute a numerically smaller proportion than that of male offenders. But at present, there is upward trend in the number of crimes committed by women. According to crime in India Report, the female percentage for arrested persons at all India level was at 4.7. An increasing trend in the female criminality has been found considering their involvement in total cognizable crimes from 3.1 per cent in 1990 to 4.1 per cent in 1995 and finally to 4.7 per cent in 1996.

At the same time 10 states and 3 Union Territories recorded more than 5 per cent female arrests in total arrested persons during 1996. Again, report reveals that Manipur and Himanchal Pradesh recorded higher female arrested percentage.

During 1995, 2.29 taken females were arrested while in 1996 the figure slightly dropped to 2.05 lakh. Most of the females were arrested against prohibition Act. However, women were also arrested against serious crimes. Women are arrested mainly under the different kinds of crimes i.e. riots, murder, cruelty by husband, dowry death, hurt/serious hurt etc. A significant number of women arrested are below 16 years and 16-18 years.

Majority of the arrested women are belonging to age groups of 18-30 years and 30-50 years. While women belonging to age group of 50 years and above constituted just 10.15 per cent in 1996. The states of Kerala and Tamil Nadu registered higher female convicts inmates in their prison in 1995. In percentage term Manipur, Mizoram and Karnataka, recorded higher percentage of female convicts to the convicts held in prison. So far as the women under trial in jails are concerned, their number was highest in the state of Tamil Nadu followed by Kerala and Karnataka.

In percentage terms, the share of women undertrial prisoners was high in Mizoram, Tamil Nadu, Kerala and Meghalaya. During June, 1997, 7268 females were reported in jails and out of total women prisoners, 5658 were under trials. In the state of Uttar Pradesh, 902 women prisoners were reported and most of them were undertrial. Again, 885 children were reported in jails and most of the children were living in jails of Uttar Pradesh, Madhya Pradesh, Andhra Pradesh, Maharastra, Bihar, Delhi, West Bengal and Rajasthan. In nine states no child was reported living in jail. The number of women prisoners is fluctuating since most of the women prisoners are under trials. However, number of children living with their mothers in jails is still high in some of the jails of Uttar Pradesh.

STATE OF JAIL ADMINISTRATION

The Indian correctional system is one of the oldest and one of the largest in comparison with many other countries of the world. It comprises of vast paraphernalia of infrastructure, through out the country, in terms of many institutions such as central jails district jail, sub jail etc; land and buildings etc. About 8.6 million people are held in penal institutions through out the world and about 3.81 lakh prisoners are incarcerated in India.

The prison population rate i.e. defined as the number of prisoners per lakh of the total to population of that country. This rates is far behind to USA, UK, Australia, Russian Federation, China, Singapore, Srilanka, and Pakistan. Of the 3.81 lakhs of the prisoners incarcerated in Indian prisons, majority of them are undertrials, and convict prisoners only forms a small minority.

In an average Indian prison, a typical prisoner is likely to be a male, a first offenders, and will be mostly an under trial. The rate of increase of prison population in India is up by a factor of 2.83. If this trend continues, there will be about 12 lakh prisoners by the end of this decade. Though, the prison infrastructure available in India is huge but the main problem of the prisons is overcrowding due to under trial prisoners. The occupancy rate has been reported to be 128.5 per cent during 2000 which demands the need for additional capacity of 60359 persons in Indian jails.

The occupancy rate has been recorded highest in Madhya Pradesh followed by Uttar Pradesh. Most of the revenue expenditure by states on different agencies on criminal system goes to police and courts and hardly funds are available for jails reforms and correctional systems. The national average of overcrowding in jails is 20 per cent in 1998 as against 9.33 per cent in 1996. The problem of over crowding is not uniformly prevailing in all the states. Delhi topped the list in overcrowding, followed by Haryana, Bihar, Madhya Pradesh, Orissa, Andman and Nikobar Islands, Goa, Andhra Pradesh, Karnataka. Over crowding is not big problem in Tamil Nadu, Kerala and West Bengal.

In the state of Uttar Pradesh, there are 82 jails. Out of total jails, most of the jails are district jails. Besides there are 5 central jails and one model jail in Lucknow. There has been 5.5 per cent compound annual growth rate of population increase in jails of U.P. during 1996 to 2001. During 1991 to 2001, average number of prisoners grew by 96.49 per cent. There has been increasing trend in the rates of convicted and under trials. During the year 2001, there were 54436 persons in jails against the effective capacity of 33802 prisoners. There are about 18 districts without jails.

More than 6170 prisoners were reported living in adjoining district jails. The occupancy rate in 2002 was recorded highest in Ballia, followed by Barabanki, Azamgarh, Varanasi, Lucknow and Sultanpur. While it was reported low in Lucknow Model Jail and Naini Central Jail. In U.P. Jails, 7889 posts are sanctioned while only 7069 persons were found employed and 820 posts are still vacant. Even the vacant Posts are mainly related to class one and class two. Studies demonstrate that prison personnel operate in an all round atmosphere of inefficiency, slackness, disinterest, poor discipline and lack of motivation. This causes demoralization and frustration among the prison staff.

This is attributed to low priority by government, poor pay scales, non payment of essential allowances, poor training, stagnation and poor promotional prospects, long hours of duty, restriction by courts in adequate resources etc. The jails also lack proper planning for human resources development and rehabilitation of prisoners due to lack of financial resources and political will.

RATIONALE, OBJECTIVES AND METHODOLOGY OF STUDY

RATIONALE OF THE STUDY

The development studies of Indian Children are affected by some key social and economic factors. Prominent among these are the massive population and its high rate of growth, wide spread illiteracy, poverty of large segments of the population, backwardness of rural areas, unsatisfactory level of development of infrastructure and the poor state of public social services and civic amenities.

The population of India rose to 1027 million in 2001 and is expected to reach 1264 million in 2016. A positive development is the evidence of slowing down of the population growth rate since 1981. In 2001 India was expected to provide immunization services to 22 million infants, pre-school services to 66 million children and middle/upper primary schools to 74 million children. In view of the backwardness of the rural population on social development indicators and generally poor state of social services in rural areas, the state of children is affected by the development status of rural areas. Even in urban areas, the tremendous increase in population living in slums, which have an unhealthy environment and are very poorly served by civic and social services, adversely affects the development of the children.

Poverty and massive illiteracy are major factors affecting the development of the country and of children. Housing in both rural and urban areas inherited by low-income groups is of poor quality with basic civic amenities in an unsatisfactory state. Only 9 per cent rural households in 1991 had toilet facilities, 30 per cent had electricity, and 50 per cent safe drinking water.

Only 4 per cent rural households had all the three facilities while 31 per cent had none. The National Family Health Survey 1998-99 showed some improvement but the availability of these basic amenities are still lacking for large segment of the poor in rural areas and urban slums. India has achieved some success in addressing child health issues. Infant deaths in India in 1998 constituted 21 per cent of the total deaths. In some States like Rajasthan, Madhya Pradesh and Uttar Pradesh, the percentage is higher. In 1998 early neonatal deaths constituted 47 per cent of infant deaths. Neonatal mortality and still births have to be specifically addressed through improved ante-natal and postnatal services to bring down mortality rate. The poor health and nutrition status of pregnant women is a major contributory factor to child mortality.

Maternal malnutrition continues to be an area of concern. Low birth weight is a major problem area, with a prevalence rate estimated to be 20 to 35 per cent. Importantly, health care facilities do not function satisfactorily. The reach of maternal health services is feeble. The population segments worst affected are the rural and urban poor who suffer the most when the public health systems are malfunctioned. Some progress towards universalization of elementary education has been achieved since independence but the attainment of this goal even after nearly five decades of independence is still a long way off.

Nearly one-third children aged 10-14 years were illiterate in 1991. Uttar Pradesh and Bihar together had 40 per cent of the total number of illiterate children's aged 10-14 years in India. Low quality of education, poor physical infrastructure, low retention rate, high drop out rate and low completion rate are some of the issues for policy concern. Child labour, though virtually been eradicated from the organized sector of production, is still continued to enjoy unregulated status, despite the provision in 1986 Act.

The failure of the public sector elementary education system in enrolling and retaining the child in school, and helping the child to acquire some level of learning which will be useful, has been a major contributory factor in the perpetuation of the problem. The poor physical infrastructures of schools and their dismal functioning in large parts of the country contribute towards keeping the child away from school. A large number of children are in especially difficult circumstances and need carefully designed welfare services.

The problem of street children has acquired a high degree of visibility in urban areas. The problem needs to be given immediate attention failing which the social fall out could be serious. Current services for street children cover only a small fraction and are focused on relief and rehabilitation. Importantly, juvenile delinquency has resulted due to socio-economic factors. The implementation of the Juvenile Justice Act has not been satisfactory. States give low priority to juvenile matters.

Services, both institutional and non-institutional are grossly inadequate and provide unsatisfactory quality of care. So other categories of children in need of care and protection are emerging on social scene. Imprisonment of mothers with dependent young children is a problematic issue. A shocking survey on children of women prisoners, conducted by National Institute of Criminology and Forensic Science, Delhi between 1997-2000, documents the conditions of deprivation and criminality in which they are forced to grow up, lack of proper nutrition, inadequate medical care and little opportunity for education. These children are forced to live in the jails along with other adult criminals and a suspect in a seriously adverse situation.

In the formative years of their life, they are not only denied a normal environment of a family life but also are exposed with criminal elements all round them which make a permanent imprint on their outlook of life. Justice Iyer's Committee looked into the living conditions of children of women prisoners. The Committee observed that children of women prisoner were callously placed in prisons in general except in a few central jails for women where the child care was satisfactory.

The Committee also stated that educations and re-educational facilities for such children were most neglected. Emotional need of children was not properly cared for. Sometimes, children of 8 to 9 years also live with their mothers in the prisons in the absence of Children Homes. The Committee further observed that prevalent arrangements for looking after of these children were quite inadequate. The state of women prisoners is more distressful. Thus, living conditions are pathetic. Female wards in prisons are mostly over crowded. Adequate clothing and toilet facilities are not made available to them many a time due to over population. General health care of women prisoners in many prisons is not up to the mark. The static facilities for education, vocational training and recreational facilities are also very limited, Although the main objective of imprisonment is the rehabilitation of the prisoners in the main stream of life, due to many constraints, rehabilitation programmes have not been very successful in this country.

Moreover, majority of the women prisoners are from rural background, illiterate, shy and do not have courage to communicate their needs and grievances to the prison staff in the fails. They cannot also ventilate their sufferings and transmit the same to higher authorities. There is paucity of literature and empirical data of the problem of children of women prisoners living in jails.

Thus, the present study is an attempt to review the status of women prisoners, status of their young children living with them in jails, efforts for their rehabilitation and bringing them to the mainstream. The study may be useful in formulating of action plan for development of jailed children and rehabilitation of women prisoners'.

OBJECTIVES OF STUDY

Present study has the following main objectives;

- To ascertain the number of children living with their prisoner mothers in selected district jails of U.P.
- To study socio-economic background of the families of these children and the status of their family setup;
- To provide an in depth analysis of situation in which they live in prisons;
- To study the governmental programmes available in prisons for the care and development of these children towards socialization;
- To identify and analyse the problems, of these children and their mothers face in the jails; and

- To suggest ways and means to improve their living conditions in jails.

HYPOTHESIS

The following hypotheses have been empirically tested:

- The children living with their mothers in prisons deserve special attention because they are forced to live in such environment which is incapable to provide essential ingredients, which are absolutely necessary for their proper socialization and secondly, they are liable to be contaminated by criminogenic influences prevent in jails in their formative stage of life which is highly damaging for their proper development as a productive and useful social human beings.
- Most of these children hail from poor and uneducated families in which inter relationship in their family may not be very congenial.
- Being deprived from the normal surroundings and care and affection of their members of family like father and their siblings, they live in very difficult circumstances, where problem are many in all respect of life.
- The programmes available in prisons for their adequate care, protection and development are very inadequate and scanty.
- Their very confinement in jails without committing any off use amounts to violation of their basic human rights.

SCOPE OF THE STUDY

The study has been conducted in U.P. jails, mainly 19 districts jails and two other jails. The study is confined to under trial women since majority of the women prisoners were found to be under trials.

The study has provided data base and review of pertinent literature that is useful for formulative research as well as evolving strategies for tackling the emerging problems of women prisoners and their children living with them in prisons.

METHODOLOGY

Present study is empirical in nature and based on mainly primary data. Primary data has been collected from the field survey. The field survey has been conducted in 21 jails of U.P. one Central Jail, one Model Jail, and district jails of Azamgarh, Faizabad, Barabanki Sultanpur, Ghazipur, Jaunpur, Varanasi, Gorakhpur, Ballia, Sitapur, Rai Bareli, Banda, Mahoba, Bulandshahar, Ghaziabad, Meerut, Agra, Muzaffarnagar and Lucknow have been surveyed. In the sample 297 women prisoners were randomly selected for interview.

The women were preferred to whom young children were living with them. Importantly, a number of visits to jails provided the opportunity to interact the desired number of women prisoners because at some time the number of woman prisoners was quite low due to under trials. Besides survey of women prisoners through structured interview schedules, jail officials, staff and NGO's representatives' were also intervened in-depth.

The schedules of women prisoners have covered dimensions like identification, socioeconomical background, family relationship, criminality, delinquency, programmes and facilities available to them in jails etc., while the schedule for the prison staff and officials has contained questions relating to their general background, status and positions, details of their work and nature of duty, relationship with women prisoners, problems faced by them dealing with the children of women prisoners etc.

The secondary data and pertinent literature has been complied from published and documented sources. These include National Crime Records Bureau; National Institute of Criminology and Forensic Sciences, Delhi, UNICEF, Ministry of Home Affairs etc. The surveys and published literature has been reviewed for insight stimulation on the topic of research. Filled in schedules containing information about the women prisoners, their children and prison staffs have been processed manually for drawing out inferences, trends, patterns and conclusions. The data have been presented in tabulized form and interpreted accordingly. The policy measures are based on the analysis of research findings and critical review of pertinent literature.

THEORETICAL FRAME WORK AND REVIEW OF LITERATURE

Eminent experts in the field of criminology develop various theoretical models. Highlighting the strain theory of criminality based on tension or pressure of work, Merton states that social structures and society were equally responsible for crime causation. He said that women are prone to commit crimes when they are failed to attain 'culturally defined goals' through 'institutional means'.

Over emphasis on cultural goals at the expense of institutions means creates a tendency towards anomie. Durkheim while linking crime with social change has viewed that crime is a social fact and considered it to essential for social change. Therefore, it is functionally in evitable for the society. Fernald found that two influences are related to female delinquency i.e. poor economic background, lack of education or training and inferior mentality. While Bishop argued that due to emancipation movement more women became 'criminal minded'.

While expanding the biological and psychoscimatic condition of female criminality, Fernald states that women who turn to crime do so as a form of rebellion against their natural feminine roles and because they are maladjusted to their biological limitations. But liberation model on the other hand argues that liberation is responsible for involving women in criminal activities.

It has brought about two things. Firstly, competitive instincts, women are now more assertive, more aggressive and more masculine. Secondly, it has opened up structural opportunity for women to offend. At the same time, Simon states that the women's movement influenced female crimes in two ways. It caused an increase in property crime and introduced the violent offending of women. Again, Klein and Kress described that women turned into crime because perversion or rehabilitation against their natural feminine roles. They argued that when women move more towards equality in economic roles, the reduction in the social gap between the two sexes lead to higher rates of anti social behaviour. The study of history of female criminality can be seen to reflect the phases through which the general study of criminology has passed.

The literature reveals that the study of crime and criminals, including females, has passed through two major stages of development the pre-scientific stage and the scientific stage. Most of the literature on women was in adequate during the pre scientific period since at that time women deviants were negligible in number to draw sufficient attention. Although, they were considered corrupt, yet they were not taken or considered seriously so as to pose a danger to the society.

The few studies that dominated this stage concentrated on biological factors in the explanation of female crime. The pre-scientific stage can be further classified into two the classical works and the contemporary works. Lombroso and Ferrero, Thomas, Fernad, Davis, and Pollak emphasized on conditional factors as related to female criminology. However, Lombroso was not alone in his search for physiological and constitutional characteristics of female criminals. The Other influential writers were Makel Fernald, Spaulding and Thomas.

The biological factors explained in Lombroso were elaborated in the psychological work of Freud who viewed women as physiologically inferior. He maintained that law breaking by females represents a perversion of or rebellion against the biologically natural female role. The general feature of the psychological masculinization of female behaviour was also reiterated by Davis. He presents a functionalist explanation of one specific type of crime called prostitution, as an illegitimate extension of the female sex role. He argued that prostitution arises in circumstances where demands for sexual novelty cannot be supplied within the marriages and some men are cut off from access to being sex partners because they are unmarried, ugly or deformed in some respects. The work on criminality of women by Pollak was one of the significant works to date. Pollak analysed female criminality and maintained that offences committed by women are under estimated, under reported and under recorded, keeping the masked character of female crime, Pollak advances the theory of hidden female criminality to account for their substantially lower official strategies which according to him is a function of women's roles in society, the psychological components of femaleness, and certain physical factors.

He attributed to crimes by women to psychological and physiological characteristics in female anatomy. He recognized that social factors like the double standard' leading to frustration and envy on the part of women which can push them into false accusations against man. The biological basis of the masculinization of female behaviour was discussed by Cowie who like Lombroso and Ferreor's approach proposed that criminality is a sign of pathology and female delinquents show masculine trails. Konopka in his study on adolescent girl in conflict maintained that girls are driven to delinquency by an emotional problem loneliness and dependency.

Thus, she emphasized on female emotions as cause for delinquency among girls. The views of Vedder and Somerville regarding female's delinquency were similar to those of Konopka. Like Freud and Konopka, they viewed delinquency as blocked access or maladjustment to the normal feminine role. Ignoring the social and economic factors, they attributed the high rates of delinquency to the lack of sexual opportunities for women.

The individual theories of crime phenomenon were given by scholars like Sutherland, Freud and Dollard, W.J. Thomas. The application of Sutherland's theory to women is particularly helpful is emphasizing that criminal behaviour is learned interaction with other persons in a process of communication and is not psychologically or biologically determined. Sutherland thus emphasized on sociological factors which causes to female criminality, explaining individual's crime in terms of her past experiences rather than situations. A few criminologists have used Role Theory in explaining female crime in terms of sex roles, other than biological or psychological variables. These authors viewed women's crimes as the illegitimate expression of role expectations.

However, Smart, maintained that role theory fails to examine the social origins of sex roles and to deal with the inferior status of women in his topical and cultural terms. Similarly to Smart, Crites, advanced a new approach within criminology to the subject of women and crime. Her work indicated the increasing interest in women and crime and did not accept the stereotypical views about women. Bowker dealt extensively with statistics on women and crime and provided a new literature by discussing the criminal justice system in terms of male domination.

He also maintained that developmental, situational and macro structural variables, namely, social, education, equality, economic equality, and socio-economic status are involved in the causes of female crime and the roles women play within crime. In India, less importance has been given to women offenders. As Rao has pointed out, the lack of sociological attention to the problems presented by female offenders in India is perhaps due to the observation that smaller number of women come into contact with law enforcing agents than do men.

The phenomenon of female crime gets complicated since female offences are considered more serious as compared to make offences and this difference is believed largely due to the sociological position which the women occupy in our society. The other reason that why female criminals in India are under represented and why there are few studies on them both at the juvenile and adult levels, is considered due to cultural feature of crime in India, women in an agrarian society are in protected status with a little exposure to crime provoking situation. The fact remains that the available theories in regard to women as offenders and victims of crime are both quantitatively poor and qualitatively deficient and hence competent studies on women and crime are still lacking. We find that not many sociologists have been attracted towards criminological studies. Exclusive sociological studies had given the disruptive amount of statistical figures without discussing the nature and patterns of crime. Three decades ago Sharma was the first to attempts a sociological research on women criminals in U.P.

After her, Rao and Ahuja male attempts to study female criminality from sociological point of view. Sohoni, Bhanot and Mishra and Singh furnished a statistical account of the nature, extent and patterns of female criminality. However, little attention was paid to psychological aspects and factors contributing to criminality of women. Ahuja's study gave a new insight into the relationship between women and her criminality which prompted other researchers to undertake studies on this phenomenon.

He studied social background of female offenders and it was predominantly found that women criminals were in the age group of 20- 40 Years. Therefore, this is the problem of young women's, which are mostly married and mentally immature to cope up with the expectations of their husbands and in laws resulting in maladjustment between them and their family members.

Ahuja concluded that stressful family situation, marital maladjustment, conflict prone relationship with husband other members of the family compel women to commit serious crime like murder. In the last few years' professional interest in women criminality has considerable increased. A good number of studies have been undertaken on female criminality. Ahuja, Kawale, Rani, Nagla, Bhanot and Mishra, etc., have analysed social background of female offenders.

Ahuja observed that the incidence of crime was rather low in lower caste families whereas Rani in her study found that slightly more than 50 per cent women criminals belonged to backward classes. However, both of them found that the incidence of crime was high among women of low economic classes. It reflects that fact that the causative factor of criminality among women is economic constraint. There are several studies which correlate criminality to geographical conditions. Some of these studies reveal that urban areas have more female offenders than rural areas. This is clear that maladjustment in interpersonal relationship within the family is one of the most important causes of criminality amongst women. Rani also supported these findings in her study. She found that in more than 10 per cent of domestic factors played an important role in compelling many women to adopt criminal behaviour.

Mishra and Gautam revealed that the female criminality increases as the level of education decreases and vice versa. They endorsed the studies of Ahuja and Rani that women criminals were generally young in age, married, illiterate and who also came from very low-income groups. Prasad also maintained that illiteracy was an important factor of women criminality. His study also showed that areas of conflicts in women's life had been unhappy marital life, addiction of the husband to alcohol, drugs, gambling etc., his lack of interest in family matters and love to his wife, sexual incompatibility, discordant relationship with in laws and members in the family, family's low income and excessive expenditure etc. Nagla pointed out that growing participation of women in various fields might be one of the contributing factors for increase in the rate of crime among women.

Rao analysed the extent of increase in women's employment in organized sector. He analysed the occupational distribution of women workers in the decade of 1961- 1971, which indicated remarkable increase in the number of women workers. Kawale indicated that the offences committed by women were pick pocketing, dacoity with arms, thefts etc. These crimes were committed either singly or in combination with others.

These women belonged to such communities where they were treated equally with males. Ghosh analysed a socio psycological background and personality dynamics of family of inmates of both open and close prisons to unravel their adjustment processes and attitude structure for a comparative view point. Manju Kumari in her study on juvenile delinquency attempted answering the reasons behind juvenile delinquently on the basis of her two studies on reformatory conditions in Varanasi. Mishra also explained that poor economic condition, broken homes bad companionship and parental negligence are mainly responsible for causing delinquency Bhatta Charya discussed in detail about the pathetic condition of jails in which women were living.

Chatto Raj in his study on children of women prisoners in Indian Jails stated that hundred of small children are linguistics in different jails in the country with their jailed mothers. In the formative years of life, they are living behind the bars in such a condition, which is characterized by diverse forms of deprivations; the most important ones being loss of freedom and complete seclusion from a normal family environment.

These children belong to rural families. Their parents are mostly indigent, illiterate and marginalized. In the present study, a focused attention has been made on development of young children living with their mothers in Jails. Since no study has so far exclusively devoted on this area. The present study is expected to fill in gap of the criminological literature and criminal administration.

CHILDREN OF WOMEN PRISONERS

Prison administration is one of the main components of the criminal justice system in the country. The management of prisons is the state subjects. Several types of prisons are functioning in different states, which can be classified under seven broad categories;

- Central Jail,
- District Jail,
- Sub Jail,
- Woman Jail;
- Special Jail,
- Open Jail; and
- Brostal Jail.

These were 1306 jails of different types functioning in the country as on December, 1998. They are situated in Andhra

Pradesh, Assam, Bihar, West Bengal, Orissa, Goa, Gujarat, Haryana, Himanchal Pradesh, Jammu and Kashmir, Manipur, Karnataka, Kerala, Madhya Pradesh, Maharastra, Punjab, Rajasthan, Tamil Nadu, Uttar Pradesh including Uttaranchal, Meghalaya, Mizoram, Sikkim, Delhi, Andman and Nicobar Island, Chandigarh, Dadar and Nagar Haweli, Daman and Diu, Nagaland, Tripura, Lakshadeep and Pondicherry.

The total capacities of these jails were 2.14 lakh prisoners. About 20 per cent jails in the country were over crowded while 73 per cent of total population was undertrials. Women prisoners constituted only 3.18 per cent. In all categories of jails women prisoners are kept of total 7268 women prisoners living in jails, 5658 were under trials and the rest were convicts.

The highest numbers of woman prisoners were living in the jails of Bihar which was followed by Uttar Pradesh, Madhya Pradesh, Maharastra and Andhra Pradesh. Against this, inmate capacity of female prisoners was 1888 in central jails, 2192 in district jails, 2322 in sub jails and 1072 in women jails, thus making a total of 7747 women prisoners in 1997, 2583 were in central jails, 2574 in district jails, 1047 in sub jails, 167 in special jails and 1279 in woman jails and rest in other type of incarceratory institutions.

There are two categories of children of women prisoners; one children who are left behind in the family when their mother is imprisoned and two, children who accompany their mother when she is in prison, or those who are born in prison because the mother was imprisoned when she was pregnant. PRAYAS, a Mumbai based NGO has grouped the children of women prisoners as follows;

- Children born to mothers while in custody.
- Minors permitted to be taken into prison custody with their mothers.
- Minors taken into penal custody with this mothers who have been taken sent outside while the mother remains incarnated.
- Minors taken into custody with their mothers.
- Minors left outside when either of both parents is taken into custody.

- Minor children who grow into adulthood while their mother services her sentence.

A study under taken by Prof. B.N. Chattoraj of National Institute of Criminology and Forensic science, Delhi, 2000 came out with the following facts;

- Out of 885 children living in different prisons of the country with their prisoner mothers as on 30th June, 1997, most of the children were belonging to U.P., Madhya Pradesh, Andhra Pradesh, Maharastra, Bihar and Delhi.
- More than three fourth mothers of children were under trials of the total children living in jails with their mothers, 58.3 per cent were males and 41.8 per cent were females.
- In terms of age, ail the children were less than 6 years and mostly less than 2 years.
- In terms of period of stay in jails, it was found that 749 children out of 885 i.e. 84.63 per cent were living in jails from less than one year. The stay of about 11 per cent children was between 1 to 2 years. 10 children were also found in jails whose stay was more than 4 years.
- Out of total children in jails, 30 per cent children were from general castes while rest were belonging to backward classes and weaker parts of society. Again, about half of the children were Hindus while 21 per cent children were Muslims.
- Most of the children were belonging to married prisoners while 58.19 per cent and 83.38 per cent fathers and mothers respectively, were found to be illiterate. Out of total children, 68.11 per cent children were from rural background and mostly from joint families.
- Most of the children were belonging to low-income group families i.e. less than Rs.2000 per month only 17.8 per cent children were belonging to low middle income group.
- Children in general were living under difficult

circumstances facing diverse deprivation relating to food, health care accommodation, education and recreation.

- No suitable programmes were found to be in operation for the bio psycho-social development of children who were being looked after mostly by their mothers as no trained staff was found in any jail to take care of these children.
- In most of the jails women prisoners with children were not being provided with extra meals. Mothers' inmates generally had to share their meals with their children. In some cases occasionally extra food mostly in forms of a glass of milk was available to some children. In some jails separate food used to be provided only to growing up children, over the age of five. But the quality of food used to be same as of those, which used to be supplied to adult prisoners.
- No separate medical facilities for the children were found to be prevalence in jails. Children had to share the same medical facility as was available to the adult prisoners.
- Some kind of general education was reported to be provided to the grown up children of women inmates.
- In the name of educational facilities only playground was available in most of the jail. For the small children no arrangements were found in any jails. A few jails in some states had crèche to take care of children during day time.
- No special consideration was reported to be given to child bearing inmates of food or any other facilities.

A study conducted by PRAYAS in Maharastra during 1994-97 came out with the following main findings:

- The separation of mother from her children, on being arrested and subsequently imprisoned, leads to a series of rapid changes in the lives of both. For many women, especially first times, this is certainly one of the worst aspects of imprisonment.

- After being arrested, most women reported that they were not allowed to meet their children. Many also mentioned not being informed that rules permitted their taking into custody with their children below five years. So babies who are a few months old too were left behind.
- Where a child was present at the time of arrest, the forcible separation, in fact the suddenness with which the situation was precipitated, appeared to have left many women at a loss about what action to take for him, or her right for them.
- Women arrestees and women prisoners were deeply disturbed about what must be happening to their minor children left outside. They looked extremely worried about the health, physical security, illness about their children left behind.
- Women prisoners carried acute anxiety about the welfare of their children their underlying fear also being that children may not recognize them after her release from the prison.
- Many women prisoners completely believed that their removal from their child, life was a vacuum that could never be filled by any one else.
- Imprisoned mothers were often overwhelmed with distress about what their minor/dependent children have had to undergo as a consequence of their incarceration.
- Minor and dependent children of imprisoned mothers had to face lot of difficulties, especially in such families where there was no responsible adult person to take care of children when the father was out in the day for work.

Children should not be allowed to stay in jail. The imprisonment of mothers with dependent young children is a problematic issue. The women in jails are violent and use abusive language. This affects the psychological development of young children. During 2002, the India Council of Legal Aid and Advice filed public interest litigation in the Supreme

Court, asking that state government formulate proper guidelines for the protection and welfare of children prisoners. Though, facilities are extended to women prisoners within the limited resources. This range from medical checks ups for pregnant women and health education classes for mothers to vaccines for children. Officials state that prisons in Karnataka, Maharastra and Rajasthan have special diets for lactating mothers and babies. In Meghalaya, breastfeeding mothers are kept in a separate enclosure. In Tamil Nadu, the special prisoners for women in Vellure and Madurai have crèches, as do Presidency Central Jail in west Bengal and Nari Bandi Niketan in Lucknow. Jail conditions are deplorable in Bihar and Madhya Pradesh.

Unfortunately, prisons are not a priority for any government because inmates are typically poor, illiterate and powerless and because of the prevailing attitude that prisoners deserve what they get. All India Committee on Jail Reforms popularly known as Justice Mullah Committee had observed that; it is the small number of women in prisons, which, in our view, is responsible for their needs being neglected. The position of these women scattered in small clusters in jails, is highly vulnerable. The committee recommended that:

- A separate place with proper toilet facilities should be provided on court premises for women prisoners availing premise before presiding magistrate.
- Bail should be liberally granted to women under trial prisoners, and those not able to furnish surety might be released on personal recognizance.
- The probation of offenders act should be extensively used for the benefit of women offenders.
- Women prisoners should be lodged in separate institution meant exclusively for them.
- Enclosures for women in common prisons should be so renovated as to ensure that women prisoners do not come in view of male prisoners. Their enclosures should have a proper double lock system.
- All general duties with regard to women offenders should be performed by women staff only.

- Newly admitted women prisoners should be medically examined for pregnancy. Pregnant women prisoners should be transferred to local maternity hospital for purposes of delivery.
- While registering the birth of a child to a woman prisoner, the place of birth should not be mentioned as 'prison'. If such a birth takes place there, inside the name of locality be mentioned.
- Pregnant and nursing women prisoners should be prescribed special diet and exempted unusable types of work.
- There should be a separate women ward in prison hospitals.
- Women prisoners should be permitted to retain their Mangal Sutra, glass or plastic bangles.
- Women prisoners should be given adequate and proper clothing and facilities for personal hygiene and personal maintenance according to their customers.
- Woman prisoners should be given the facility for maintaining contracts with their families through letters, visits from relations and leave.
- Children accompanying women prisoners may be allowed to be kept with them in specially organized crèches outside the main prison building.
- State government should encourage and support voluntary woman organizations in looking after women offenders.
- Voluntary organizations should be encouraged and given financial aid to set up children institutions for such children as cannot be released on probation or on license.
- Prison superintendent should take a monthly review of children confirmed in prison and send a report to the appropriation authorities for necessary action.
- Juvenile probation and non-institutional services for children should be effectively organized.
- Each state and Union Territory should prepare

master plan for setting up a network of non-institutional and institutional services for children.

- Children, dependent on prisoners, preferable be kept with the relatives or friends of such prisoners.

The Report of National Expert Committees on Women Prisoners, popularly known as Justice Krishna Iyer Committee, 1997 extensively dealt with the problems that have risen due to women prisoners' custodian invisibility. The report observed that Jail rules developed locally under Prison Act accept the right of the prisoner mother to keep her child with her untill 5-6 years of age.

The rules also state that clothing and diet as prescribed will be given to the child in jail. One of the committee's members felt that the entity, rights and entitlements in terms of food, clothing, childcare, learning and viziting rights etc. of the child in prison need to be separately recognized in law and explicitly stated. The child must be empowered with rights per se to facilities when in prison, including physical space, and relevant provisions must be introduced in the jail manuals. The main findings of the report are as follows.

- Separate prisons for women are a more satisfactory custodial option. In the spirit of correctional justice, the smaller numbers of women prisoners, in comparison to man can not be held as a valid factor limiting the creation of separate custodian facilities.
- In existing prisons where women are in sufficient numbers, a proper classification system must operate which should include medical, criminological and social assessment of the inmate and serve as basis for specialized and segregated case, treatment, employment, training, education and rehabilitation of the inmates.
- Medical diagnostic and care facility must be available to inmates routinely and by a famous doctor, where full or part time women medical staff are ill afforded, local female doctors from government health facilities must be inducted to serve the prisoners on a visiting consultant basis.

- Diet, clothing and basic living facility are due to every prisoner. Whatever adjustments within the prison procedures are possible should be made to help remove minor irritants.
- The physical state of most prison buildings is known and recognized to be bad. In certain states and below the level of central prisons especially, the situation is accepted immediate provisions must be made for upgrading structures, adding to them and replacing them as necessary and feasible. In setting up new structures, keeping in view the lesser security risk posed by women offenders, and to suit their psychological needs better, it may be advisable to consider cottage type, medium security provision which can provide less formal and more common type custodial experience.
- On the question of women prisoners neglect the committee observed that ' women in custody are tragic testimony of judicial futility, statutory importance and implementation calamity.

The analysis simply demonstrates that state of women prisoners and their young children in jails is far behind satisfaction. Their conditions in jails are pathetic despite legal provisions and emphasis laid on ensuring fundamental rights of children of women prisoners.

There are no minimum facilities for over all development of minors in jails since very limited resources are available for correctional measures.

PROFILE OF WOMEN PRISONERS

A wide variety of factors in the socio-cultural environment are correlated with crime rates. The stage deals with an outline of some of the personal social characteristics of the prison inmates. Such description is desirable from the point of view of understanding the realities of the prisoner's social life, the cultural antecedents of the offenders as well as their social background and personal qualities such as age, caste, education, religion, occupations etc. may have an important impact on mode of their perceptions. These antecedents are equally significant is understanding and determing the offenders social attitudes and behaviour patterns or the basics of the data collected from intensive interviews of inmates, the following pattern emerged from the general characteristics of the women prisoners.

AGE

Many studies demonstrate that very young persons are more susceptible to crime. But in the present study women offenders are mainly from the middle age group i.e. 26-44 years. In some cases, women offenders were found to be belonging upper age group i. e. 46- 55. It was found more pronouncing in Azamgarh, Barabanki and Ghazipur district. Even women from the age group of above 56 years were also found offenders. It was reported highest in Ballia followed by Sultanpur. Women offenders come all the age groups and there is correlation of age with women communality. In most of the studies of this nature.

It is maintained that young women are more from to commit crimes and the incidence of their crimes describes with increasing age. While the findings of the present study indicated that the predominance of women offenders was in middle age group i.e. 31-50 years. In most of the communities, the young girl is more protected than her brothers. She is confined more within the family home both through parental control and also because of the nature of her household and family duties.

Therefore, young women get fewer opportunities to commit the crimes at a young age. But the middle aged women are more exaggerate and aggressive in deviant behaviour. It is also due to the fact that the young women and unmarried girls are protected even committing crimes by their in laws to avoid the consequences of going jail.

Their aged women and particularly middle aged women are being jailed. Most of the women offenders were found involved in dowry case. It appears the before reasonable that although the majority of offenders were found to be committed by young and middle aged, it seems difficult to give any firm explanation regarding the ages at which women show tendencies towards criminality.

CASTE AND RELIGION

It is believed that religion has been instrumental in developing and maintaining morality. It has influenced, since times immemorial, the behaviour, and the majority of life of individuals. By and large, the religion patterns and beliefs, may guide the behaviour patterns in the family, then in the community, and then in the society since criminality and in morality are synonymous in some extent, a pose could be put as to why some persons before in morally and others do not like religion caste may also influence some aspect of the individual's behaviour.

During the course of the study, it was found that 37.23 per cent offenders belonged to Scheduled Castes while more than one-fourth respondents belonged to OBC's. Thus, only 18.52 per cent offenders were belonging to general castes. In a few cases, the proportion of women offenders were found predominantly belonging to Scheduled Castes. It may found more pronouncing in Ghazipur (75.0 per cent), Mahoba (66.67 per cent), Lucknow district jail (65.0 per cent), Barabanki (65.0 per cent), Naini (60.0 per cent), and Gorakhpur (60 per cent). Importantly, majority of the women offenders were found to be Hindus (85.86 per cent).

The proportion of Muslim offenders was reported highest in Bulandshahar (40.0 per cent) followed by Faizabad, Banda (33.3 per cent) while negligible proportions of Muslim offenders was reported in Naini and Gorakhpur. As far as religion is concerned, the social restrictions on women and also the people's notions about their domestic and outside roles in general are derived from the religious beliefs. Moreover, in Hindus religion, numerous regulation and restrictions are imposed on women.

These constrains continue to operate even in the contemporary era. Thus, religion as a system of belief as well as rituals continue to provide differential treatment to them.

Over the years these operational constraints on women may have an impact on their personality patterns. In view of these realities, such women may find it difficult to adjust with the changing social patterns in a culturally plural society like India. Differentials in regard to religion and casts may also develop strong or mild prejudices in the members of each sector due to which during emotionally charged circumstances atrocities of various types may be committed on the members of other community.

Obviously, therefore due to avoidance and discrimination, individuals belonging to other sectors may be alienated or even isolated. The sentiments of alienation and isolation may have their share in the occurrence of criminal acts even by women.

FAMILY OCCUPATION

There is no doubt the fact that a number of crimes are beings committed for economic reasons and economic condition of a person is dependent upon his/her occupational activity. In the present study, the influence of occupation on the offenders was significant. More than one third women offender was dependent on labour for their sustenance. Thus, the majority of the prison inmates were belonging to the rural economy i.e. agriculture and manual labour. These sectors contribute insignificant in the family income and most of the families dependent on it are economically poor.

BIRTH PLACE

Several studies demonstrate that women criminality is more pronounced in urban areas. The slums are hidden centres where criminals enjoy a decent life. The slum dwellers, belonging to poor economic class, generally are involved in economic crimes and also minor crimes related to drug abuse, sex and other crimes.

Even women criminality is higher in the slum pockets of urban centres. However, the present study reveals trial about 65.32 per cent women offenders belong to rural areas. The proportion of women offenders belonging to urban areas was recorded highest in Agra (75.00 per cent), followed by Varanasi

(60 per cent) and Ghaziabad (57.14 per cent). Thus, women criminality is not formed by geographical factors.

MARITAL STATUS

By and large, married women show a higher crime rate than those who are either unmarried or deserted or widowed. It was found during the study that married offenders accounted for 74.75 per cent of the total offenders. While widow offenders were reported to be just 15.49 per cent. This proportion was recorded highest in Varanasi (35.0 per cent) followed by Faizabad (25.0 per cent). Thus, it is clear from the survey that women criminality is predominantly in married class the greater preponderance of aggressive offences involving victims among the married offenders may be explained by the fact that most of the marriage were arranged by the parents without taking into consideration the couples wishes. As a result the girls were given in marriage when they might have lack of maturity, lack of responsibility and lack of scanty information regarding sex and sexual activities.

Most of these women offenders had an unhappy married life and had to content not only with an unsympathetic husband, but also with nagging and possessive in laws. This situation was further aggravated if the women failed to conceive within a short period of marriage. Barrenness is such a stigma in our society that it is by itself sufficient to put change and content upon the women, to which she adds her own ideas and notions and may start cursing herself. The stigma attached to separation of divorce still remains.

OCCUPATION PRIOR TO JAIL

Women offenders were enquired about their occupation prior to jail. The overwhelming majority reported that they were housewives (64.98 per cent), about 27.61 per cent women offenders were also labourers. This proportion was recorded highest in Ballia (60 per cent), Lucknow District Jail (45.0 per cent) and Bulandshahar (40.0 per cent). It is revealed from the field survey that women criminality is more pronounced in housewives.

EDUCATION

The distribution of offenders by their educational background highlighted the fact that an overwhelming majority of women offenders were illiterate (55.56 per cent) only a statistically insignificant fraction of the women offenders were educated above high school. The illiteracy was found more pronouncing in Ghazipur (95.0 per cent), Jaunpur (90.0 per cent), Meerut (83.33 per cent) and Bulandshahar (80.0 per cent). It shows that criminality in women is definitely linked with their illiteracy. It may be considered that as most of the women are illiteracy they cannot earn and there by supplement the family income.

Therefore, they are not able to solve the economic problems facing the family. These economic and social forces may affect the process of the social development of these women. Again, most of the women offenders were not professionally educated and thus, they fail to get rehabilitation. The educational levels of the husbands of women offenders were found to be low. More than one third respondents revealed that the educational level of their husbands in pathetic i.e. illiterate.

About 23.57 per cent husbands of women offenders were reported to be literate. The women offenders were asked regarding the importance of education for their children. About half of the respondents placed education as important both for girls and boys. However, education is more important for boys as per perception of women offenders. About half of the women offenders were of the view that coeducation may be implemented to some extent. However, only one fourth are in favour of co-education. Again, about half of the women prisoners were of the view that higher education to girls may be to some extent 103 (42.42 per cent). However, only 64 (21.55 per cent) are in favour of higher education.

FAMILY STRUCTURE AND ACCOMMODATION

The structure of the family in terms of its size, and living conditions play an important role in determining the behaviour of a person. Family accommodation affects the conditions of lodging, dwelling, amenities enjoyed, as also the sanitary conditions, which is turn, affects socialization, supervision and control of the members within the family. The situation in the family becomes more aggravated when the bigger sized families are housed in small, inadequate accommodation.

The problem of adjustment is very much associated with the structure of family and its size. It is revealed from the study that 69.70 per cent women offenders were belonging to nuclear family where family control prevails. About one fourth respondent reported that they belong to joint families. This was reported highest in Mahoba (66.67 per cent) followed by Meerut (33.33 per cent), Agra (33.33 per cent), Sultanpur (40 per cent) and Faizabad (30 per cent). Majority of the women offenders belong to large family size. The majority of the respondents were drawn from poor housing condition since large size of family cannot ensure proper housing conditions. Out of total family member, 51.47 per cent were males while 48.53 per cent were females. Again, more than half of the population has been reported to be unmarried (52.72 per cent) while percentage of married population has been reported to be small (36.29) per cent). Thus, it shows that the total family size is 7 members. During the course of the study, it was found that majority of the working population are housewives and labourers. Their income level is low.

Only a small proportion of the respondents belong to lower higher class of economy. Though, the majority of the respondents reported that they are living in their own house but houses not electrified and no toilet facility is available to them. They are dependent on indigenous hand pumps for drinking water. They are mainly living in Kachcha houses. The land holding size also reveals that most of the women offenders are belonging to small and marginal land size. Moreover, a high proportion of the respondents also revealed that they are landless.

RELATIONSHIP PATTERNS

As expenses accommodated through interaction during

the formative periods in familial setting play a dominating role in shaping the pattern of one's behaviour. Therefore, it thought important to delve into the relationships of the child with the family. The family behaviour towards women offenders was reported general (36.65 per cent) in most of the areas however; about 2.98 per cent respondents reported that their relations were tense and stressed.

It was reported highest in case of sister in law (10.10 per cent) mother in law (4.07 per cent) and husband (3.37 per cent). Similarly, respondents behaviour with their family members was reported to be normal in most of the cases (40.10 per cent) while 3.75 per cent respondents accepted that their behaviour is tense and stressed. It was recorded highest in case of sister law (13.47 per cent) and mother in laws (7.07 per cent). About two fifth respondents accepted that their relations with other relatives are not good.

Women's participation in decision-making process was enquired. Overall, the majority of the women offenders were of the view that their view in family matters is not taken seriously or encouraged. Only 2.22 per cent women accepted that their decision in family matters is being encouraged. Thus, women offenders are neglected in most of the decision being taken in families.

WOMEN CRIMINALITIES

The nature of criminal by women implied that the majority of women prisoners were imprisoned due to dowry deaths (42.42 per cent) and murder (23.57 per cent). The proportion of women offenders who were imprisoned due to dowry death was reported highest in Jaunpur (80.0 per cent) followed by Sultanpur (75.0 per cent), Azamgarh (70 per cent) and Mahoba (66.67 per cent).

Women criminality is more confined to murders and dowry cases. In case of murder, highest number of women offenders were found belonging to general castes and Scheduled Castes. However, majority of women offenders imprisoned for dowry cases were belonging to scheduled castes. The analysis of the causative factors in female criminality by and large sheds light on the nature of compulsions and strains that confront Indian women in the contemporary era. Crime is a chain of reaction to problems than apparently cannot be solved in any other way since it is a response, which a human being makes to inner emotional distress.

Looking at the incidence of crime in the perspective of the states of women in a society like India, cultural patterns, socio-economic conditions, disjunction between means and personal desires are all very significant and these act as inhibiting or encouraging factors in forcing women to take to different means for satisfying their desires.

FACILITIES AND PROGRAMMES FOR DEVELOPMENT OF CHILDREN OF WOMEN PRISONERS

The present stage involves the basic assumption that every inmate in prison will be influenced by the social and physical surroundings of the jail and that influence will be mediated through her expressed opinions, attitudes and perceptions. Importantly, contemporary society seems to have variety of modes in regard to the control of crime. Imprisonment is one of the most commonly used modes of handling the guilty.

The emphasis in recent years or reform is aimed at treatment and rehabilitation of offenders, with a view to modify the behaviour of the offenders. Imprisonment also provide protection from and to offenders as prisons isolate offenders from the general society so that they cannot commit crime for a specified period and other would not commit crime on them out of vengeance.

Since there are few women prisons, women who get sentenced or jailed are often found to be housed within the same institutions, and there are no separate maximum and minimum-security prisons for women. Women are visually put together into one cell in the jails and are unable to participate in rehabilitative programmes to which men have full access. The women prisoners are adequately separate from males and very often they are guarded by male guards and thus are the objects of sexual abuse. Although the physical surroundings of most of the institutions for female prisoners seems to be palatable, women inmates are usually put together into the cell and do not have access to the many types of rehabilitative programmes which are offered to men.

Of work programmes do exist, they mainly aim at preparing or keeping the offenders in her traditional female role, female offenders are usually offered programmes in sewing and other household skills and they are not motivated to study in spite of the fact that they are intelligent. Imprisonment imposes certain painful experiences on the convicted prisoners, which are often presumed to have to stress. Every man and women who enters prison undergoes prisonization to some extent although there may be variation in prisonization among the incoming inmates.

Prisonalization is a process of interlization of prison sub culture, which refers to the mores, customs, and general culture of the prison. The culture of prison pre supposes that there exists criminally diethetic values, attitudes and habits which govern the roles and influence the pattern, obviously the relationship dynamics and the life style of inmates is determined by these realities. A prisoner, therefore, has to assimilate the culture of prison.

LENGTH OF STAY OF WOMEN PRISONERS

Length of stay of mother prisoners in jail has got a great significance for the children living with them. Longer the stay of the children in jails entails greater possibilities of the children being affected by the jail environment. Length of stay of prisoners also depends upon their status in the prisons and on the type of crime they have committed. Majority of the women inmates were under trials. It was found that as good as 61.62 per cent women prisoners were living in jail for six months only. It was reported highest in Mahoba (100.0 per cent) followed by Gorakhpur (95.0 per cent), Agra (83.33 per cent) and Bulandshahar (80.0 per cent). The substantial numbers of women prisoners were living in jail for less than one year (19.19 per cent). Thus, a small proportion of women prisoners were reported to be living in jail for a long time.

Mother prisoners whose stay was more that one-year were mainly convicts. Almost all the women inmates were living in the same jail without any transfer. However, all the women prisoners in Adarsh Karagar, Lucknow were transfer cases.

DEPRIVATIONS

Criminal process beginning with arrest, passing through conviction and incarceration and evading in release and readjustment with society may involve a number of pains, losses and consequent deprivations. One of the methods generally used to prevent the offenders from repeating the crime in incapacitation by imprisonment in a prison. The prison tends to deprive the offenders of liberty for years.

These are usually regarded as deterrent measures. There has been attempt to fined out the way the prisoners feel the prison experience. Much depends on how inmates view the various experiences which they have undergone, or are currently undergoing once a prisoner has been put in a prison, it leads initially to physical isolation which may result in other kinds of deprivations, their keenness to face the readily of imprisonment and consequent deprivations may lead to evolution of habit patterns that attenuate the anxiety caused by pains and losses.

Deprivation refers strictly to dispossession or loss of privileges, opportunities, material goods and the like. Inmates were asked to express their problems regarding physical conditions of the prison in which they were imprisoned. According to inmates view it was pointed out that the problems related to physical conditions of the prison, such as lack of space and overcoming was not considered as critical by most of the prisoners. However, physical deprivations were caused due to improper, inefficient supply of essential facilities like water, electricity, sanitation etc. The individual may get conditioned to a particular level of physical amenities due to environmental reasons. Availability of these physical amenities at a particular level may not provide equal satisfaction to all the members of a given society; consequently, the failing of deprivation of satisfaction may be more affected by the background or expectations of an individual, rather than the availability of those amenities. It is surprising to note that the surveyed jails are over crowded and no separate women ward found in any jail. Even adequate clothing's is not available. Though light facility is available to inmates but fan facility is not available to them. To examine the nature of social deprivation of imprisonment, the data were collected regarding the opinions of the inmates of social atmosphere of the prison, they experienced after their incarceration. The major pain of imprisonment is the separation from children and the inevitable disruption of personal contacts with family members, apart from deprivation of liberty and deprivation of security.

The foremost thought, which constantly haunts the minds of these prisoners, is about their future. They are extremely worried about where to go after their release from prison. The do not think that the family members will welcome them on their return. Due to social stigma and different attitude of family members, they find it difficult to go back to their homes and, therefore, remain perturbed about their future. The next felt problem by the inmates was that of maintenance and care of children. They were anxious about the treatment of their children by the in laws and other family members in their absence.

CHILDREN IN JAILS

The women prisoners were asked about the deliveries in jail. Though majority of the respondents reported that they did not deliver any child in jail during their imprisonment however, 3.03 per cent inmates delivered the babies in jail. It may be noted here that pregnant women receive special treatment in jail particularly in central jails and qualified medical staff in government hospitals undertakes their deliveries.

It was reported that the poor women from slums of Delhi committed minor crimes and were jailed during the peak days of their pregnancies. These women got special treatment in jails and receive safe delivery of their pregnancies in government hospital. This has created serious concern for jail officials since it is basically misutilization of the facilities. Out of the surveyed women only 3 per cent women were pregnant while 20.19 per cent women were found to be lactating. Thus, most of the women inmates were general women. Again, only 135 women (45.45 per cent) accepted that their minor children are living with them. It is to be noted that most of the child population was reported to be in Adarsh Karagar, Lucknow (17.78 per cent) followed by Lucknow district jail (10.37 per cent) and Naini Jail (10.37 per cent).

Thus in Jaunpur and Ballia no child was reported living with their mothers in jail. Out of total children in jails, 38.52 per cent children were belonging to Scheduled Castes and Scheduled Tribes while 26.67 per cent were from backward castes. Thus, the majority of the children were belonging to lower castes and communities who are economically poor. Since the majority of the children were belonging to low age group, therefore, their educational levels were reported to be low.

About half of the children were found literate (42.96 per cent) while 36.30 per cent children were found to be illiterate. About half of the children were belonging to low-income families while 30.63 per cent children were from middle low-income families.

PROGRAMMES FOR CHILDREN AND WOMEN

A few programmes for rehabilitation of women prisoners have been implemented in jails of U.P. However, the coverage and effective implementation of such programmes is limited and mainly confined to central jails and special jails. The educational, training, and professional job oriented skills enhancing programmes are being run in jails for women prisoners.

However, the trades are traditional such as typing, data entry, sewing, knitting, preparing of furniture etc. All jails have arrangement through support of district government hospitals for medical and health check up, treatment, safe delivery of pregnancies etc. of women prisoners. In some jails, especially in central jails and special jails pregnant and lactating mothers get special diet. No training programme is being run in Azamgarh, and Ballia. In Jaunpur jail, a training centre was running earlier but due to very thin population of woman inmates, the centre is closed down. It is surprising to note that in Ballia district jail books were made available from NGO's for distribution among women prisoners so that literacy and education may be improved but these books were not distributed among inmates. In Varanasi jail the educated inmates initiated to educate illiterate inmates but due to low motivation among inmates the initiative failed. In Ghazipur jail authority arrange stationary and books for educational development of illiterate women inmates with the help of educated inmates.

In Barabanki district jail, Jan Shikshan Sansthan provided computer education to women inmates and also provided training in sewing and knitting trade. The jail officials accepted the fact that they are committed to ensure rehabilitation programmes but due to very nature of under trial of women inmates and also limited resources such programmes are not feasible to implement in every district jail. It has been attempted to ascertain as to how the children of women inmates are treated in prisons so what extent their basic needs in terms of food, clothes, health care, education, recreation etc. are taken care of by the jail authorities, what are the facilities, which are extended to them for their proper growth and redevelopment and above all, what kind of environment which has been provided to them to grow as a healthy and productive citizens of the country.

In order to obtain information in this respect, mother inmates of the children were mainly contacted with the assumption that they are the most reliable persons to provide correct information in this regard. Inmate mothers were asked about the status of meeting of requirements of children who were living with them. These requirements were relating to food, health care, education, crèche facility, availability of playground and recreation. In most of the jails there is no centre of Aganwadi, Balbadi, Nursery school, pre-primary school creche etc. It is because of the fact that the number of children is very low. Most of the children of women prisoners are living with their relatives. In Azamgarh, Jaunpur and Ballia district, no child of women prisoners goes to attend school for education. Though, there is no system or arrangement of schooling but health checkup, immunization, nurturing facilities are available for mother and child both in Azamgarh, Jaunpur and Ballia District. The children of Adarsh Karagar are enjoying facilities of education. About 24 children are presently getting education from a nearby public school.

The arrangement is being made by jail authority and expenses are being met by them. During the course of the study it is revealed that supplementary nutrition is being received by mothers to feed their children. However, they had to share their own food with their children. The children mainly get milk. The pregnant women get milk, and egg in Ballia district. But the children get ½ litre milk per day in each jail. The basic facilities, about which an enquiry was made, were of vital importance to the children of women prisoners.

General diet for women prisoners particularly women prisoners who had to give breastfeeding to children, needs to be properly supplemented. Some children who cannot consume the adult meal need to be given a special care for providing special type of food for them. Unfortunately, it was noticed that most of the jails did not have provision, except supply of ½ litre milk per day to supply such type of food to the children of women prisoners.

Children generally had to share their food with their mothers. Special health care facilities in form of regular health checkup and providing preventive measures becomes imperatives particularly when the children are required to live with their mothers prisoners in the same environment where other adult inmates also live.

In that situation, their vulnerability to diseases increases. Playgrounds, which are generally available in most of the jails, in some form of other, cannot cater to the needs of small children because they are not specially designed for them to suit their requirements. It was reported that jails have adequate facilities for health check up and immunization of children against major diseases. Out of 21 jails surveyed, recreation facilities for children were reported in 8 jails. In 12 jails very limited such facility is available. In 5 jails educational facility for children is available while in 4 jails, vocational training facility is available. Women are getting special diet during their pregnancies while health and medical facilities are available to them. However, the quality and access to such facilities may vary from jail to jail.

PROBLEMS FACED BY MOTHER PRISONERS

Jails are not the space where children should live with mothers. A jail can never provide a family environment in it, which a child very much deserves. In the jail, a women prisoner faces many problems in respect of her own daily requirements.

Her problems are found to increase manifold, in the event of their living with their children inside the jail. The jails are neither equipped with adequate infrastructure facilities to accommodate the children of women inmates in a befitting manner, nor the staff of the jails is properly trained to handle the problems arising out of living of children in jails. As a result all responsibilities of looking after the children fall on their Mothers.

Mother prisoners with their very limited resources naturally find lots of difficulties in meeting the requirements of their children in such a hostile situation as in jails. In order to understand the quantum and nature of problem mother prisoner face in jails in nurturing their children as well as their impression on the jail administration, women prisoners were enquired about. Women reported that proper care of their children is not ensured in most of the cases.

Though, in central jails the responses in favour of jail authorities. Most of the women inmates also not complaining to jail administration regarding their problems which they face. Though, most of the jail officials have sympathetic attitude to tackle the problem of children of women prisoners. However, majority of the inmates accepted that physical development of their children will hamper due to their imprisonments. The jail environment is also negative for the development of children of women prisoners. The quality of food, nutrition, education, health medical, education etc. is also found to be average, which is supposed to hamper the natural growth and development of children in jail. The accommodation facility in the jail is also not suitable for women prisoners. Particularly, for those women who have small kids along with themselves.

CONCLUDING OBSERVATIONS AND POLICY RECOMMENDATIONS

Female criminality is not a new phenomenon, however, the study of criminal behaviour has remained a relatively neglected area of research. The survey of literature also reveals that there is paucity of empirical data concerning crimes committed by women. Due to low incidence of female criminality, there is less emphasis on research in this field.

However, recently there has been increasing academic interest on female criminality since the industrialization, modernization, globalization, liberalization and marketization of economy and society has led to the growth of female crimes in India. The modernization process has brought certain fundamental changes in our socio-cultural life. Some of these changes have also affected the lives of women.

In the liberalized and globalized era of economy, there are more opportunities for women's empowerment however, these opportunities have also led emergence of new social conditions in which emancipation and liberation have become prominent. Indian women are also experiencing considerable stress and strain due to the impact of modernization which are being increasingly compelled to deviate from our traditional norms and report to anti social or criminal behaviour. The present study has been an attempt to understand the criminal behaviour among women. The empirical evidence has shown that both socio-cultural environment and economic factors have a vital role to play in the phenomenon of female crime. Thus, there is a considerable need for strengthening the loosening grip of the family and marriage over its members. These institutional control direct most of the behaviour of its member by internalizing in them certain values like loyalty, security, protection, love and affection and strict deference to its moral conduct.

Again, poverty, illiteracy, lack of education and ignorance combined with a social system dominated by tradition value system affect adversely to women leading to criminal behaviour. Since a large number of crimes committed by women are due to adjustment problems of interpersonal relations in family, there is need to adopt a flexible sentencing policy for female criminals. Many women are forced to bring their young children to prisons. These children suffered neglect which that to various problems. Such unfortunate children in jail spend the age at which children ought to be educated and socialized. There should be some arrangement for these children. These women can be given the benefit of probation and parole system. Also these may be suitable alternatives to imprisonment to deal with large number of simple offenders. Moreover, prisons should be well equipped with facilities of education earning, rehabilitation programmes etc.

Children grown up in a prison, which is devoid of normal environment familiar to proper growth and development. As an unhealthy environment and deprivation of homely facilities, children are likely to suffer from psychosocial problems which may manifest in some forms of juvenile delinquency in the later part of their life. Even, jail environment adversely affect their normal life and they develop habits of abnormal behaviour and get wrong orientation to life. Despite the provisions in jail manuals that jail authority will provide food, clothes, and necessary items for the survival of women prisoners and their young children but most of the jails are over crowded and lack most of basic amenities.

The medical and health facilities are also not available in jails. The children of women prisoners used to be taken care of by the some medical staff that is meant for adult prisoners. There is hardly any pediatrics available in any jail to provide special medical treatment to a child at the time of need. Mostly, the jail hospitals are not properly equipped for providing treatment to small kids. Even the physical infrastructure of jail is also not suitable for small kids since the jails are meant for adults only. Though, some form of educational programmes are reported to be prevalent for the children in some jails, but these programmes are fulfilling the requirements of the children of different age groups. This is also true in case of recreational facilities as well as educational facilities. Though, in some jails where creches are available to look after the children of women inmates, women inmates may participate in rehabilitation programmes but most of the jails lack such facilities. The role of jail staff in matter of caring and looking after the children of women inmates is found to be limited. They do not bother unless they receive any complaint from the women inmates regarding the problems of their children. Even the women coming from rural background hesitate to share their problems with jail staff.

It may also be noted that no specific staff or official is assigned to a specialized duty of looking after the children of women inmates. Secondly, jail staff is overstressed with assigned job and duties. Even jail staff is not trained in the specialized job of attending to the needs of small children. Thus, the attitudinal change among the staff to

POLICY RECOMMENDATIONS

- Before sending a women who is at her advance stage of pregnancy or lactating or is being accompanied with her young child to a jail, concerned authorities should ensure that whether jail has basic minimum facilities of health, recreation, accommodation and nutrition to care child and mother. In case, such facilities are not available in the jail, concrete efforts to avail such facilities should be made by jail authorities.
- The children must be separated from such a state of living, which is harmful for development of children.
- The women prisoners should be accommodated in a separate barrack and in case separate barrack is not existing in the jail, the primary consideration should be that the barrack is not overcrowded and children

of women prisoners get sufficient space for accommodation and their movement.

- The young children along with their mothers should be provided separate food, and nutrition. The food of kids may be supplemented by reasonable quantity of milk, fruits, sweets, baby food and other nutrition components as recommended by hospital doctors. During the illness of child, suitable food as prescribed by doctors should be made available to them.
- Children of women prisoners may be provided adequate clothes, bed sheets and other necessary materials for maintenance. Women prisoners should also be provided adequate quantity of clothes, bed sheets, bedding, sanitary napkins, soap, detergents, oil etc. for maintenance.
- In case of serious illness of the mother of young child, alternative arrangement for care of child is immediately made by jail authorities.
- Basic facilities like creche, Aganwadi centre, primary education centre, recreation etc. should be ensured in each jail. If not possible, at least proper arrangement for such facilities may be ensured through involvement of local reputed NGO's and government officials.
- Women prisoners should be provided adequate learning materials such as books, exercise books copies, pencils, slates, etc. so that they may be educationally empowered. Moreover, women prisoners should be imparted professional education, training and entrepreneurial skills for their proper rehabilitation. This type of arrangement may be ensured through strengthening encouraging and supporting local NGO's.
- Women prisoners may be exempted imprisonment. Moreover, women prisoners above the age of 65 years should be curtailed imprisonment and released them to live peacefully in the society.
- Women prisoners engaged in work programme should

be provided their due wages and honorarium so that their motivation for rehabilitation programmes may be sustained.

- Diversified recreational programmes should be made available to the children of different age groups. Play grounds, materials for indoor games and sports may be ensured by jail authorities. Again, jail authorities should arrange for site seeing in the organized festivals, fairs, and recreational events such as folk dances, songs theatre etc. Jail authorities may also organize programmes of recreation and spiritual theme.
- In order to encourage the work culture among women prisoners. It is necessary that every jail where children are living with their mothers should have a creche with proper staff.
- Prison administration has to be made more sensitive and responsive to the problems of the children of women prisoners. The jails should be provided sufficient resources to ensure that care, nourishment, protection, welfare and development of young children living with their mothers in jails.
- The jail staff should be provided training and orientation for coping up new changes and proper care and welfare of women prisoners along with their young children living with them in jails.
- Some fund should specifically be earmarked for the welfare of the children of women prisoners in the beginning of the year and utilized for the purpose, even if young children are not living in jail and funds are not utilized for that financial year such funds may be deposited as a emergency fund that may be utilized for the welfare of children of women prisoners at the need of hour.
- The Juvenile Justice Act also needs to be amended and young children of women prisoners may be included in the Act so that these neglected children can derive benefits of the Act for their care, protection, development and rehabilitation.

Bibliography

Aghatise, E.: *Violence Against Women*, Maharashtra: Pune Publication, 2004.

Anderson, B.: *Sex, Slaves and Citizens: The Politics of Antitrafficking*, Toronto: Thomson Nelson, 2008.

Bandyopadhyay, N.: *Streetwalkers Show the Way: Reframing the Global Debate on Trafficking of Women and Girls in Southeast Asia: Report* 309, Hyderabad: Economic and Political Weekly Press, 2005.

Bertozzi, S.: *Demography and Sex Work Characteristics of Female Sex Workers in India*, Maharashtra: Pune Publication, 2006.

Chattopadhyay, A.: *Social Development of Commercial Sex Workers in India: An Essential Step in HIV/AIDS Prevention*, Hyderabad: Economic and Political Weekly Press, 2005.

Cockburn, A.: *Combating Trafficking of Women and Children*, New Delhi: Long Life Publication, 2006.

D'Cunha, J.: *Trafficking in Persons: A Gender and Rights Perspective*, Toronto: Thomson Nelson, 2008.

Doezema, J.: *Who Gets to Choose? Coercion, Consent, and the UN Trafficking Protocol*, Maharashtra: Pune Publication, 2000.

Gajic-Veljanoski, O.: *Women Trafficked into Prostitution: Determinants, Human Rights and Health Needs. Transcultural Psychiatry*, Toronto: Thomson Nelson, 2007.

Jana, S.: *A Tale of Two Cities: Shifting the Paradigm of Anti-Trafficking Programmes*, New Delhi: Long Life Publication, 2003.

Jeffreys, S.: *The Traffic in Women: Human Rights Violation or Migration for Work*, Toronto: Thomson Nelson, 2006.

Kapur, Rajesh.: *Collateral Damage: Sacrificing Legitimacy in the Search for Justice*, Maharashtra: Pune Publication, 2001.

Kempadoo, K.: *Global Sex Workers: Rights, Resistance, Redefinition*, Hyderabad: Self Publication, 2000.

Madhusudana, B.: *Internal Trafficking of Women into Sex Work in India: Problems in Rehabilitation and Reintegration*, Hyderabad: Economic and Political Weekly Press, 2002.

Nag, M.: *Sex Workers of India: Diversity in Practice of Prostitution and Ways of Life*, Hyderabad: Economic and Political Weekly Press, 2006.

Nath, P.M.: *Human Trafficking: Dimensions, Challenges and Responses*, Toronto: Thomson Nelson, 2010.

Parker, Michael: *India's other Virus: Human Trafficking and the Spread of HIV*, New Delhi: Long Life Publication, 2003.

Index

A

Adequate 76, 94, 111, 120, 130
Affluent 45
Ancient India 1, 2

B

Bonded 103
Brothel 75, 76, 77, 78, 79, 80, 83, 86, 87, 89, 90, 98, 99, 104, 105, 115, 120, 124, 125, 129
Burglary 29, 34, 39, 40, 42, 43, 44, 45, 46, 47, 48, 51, 55

C

Cannabis 48, 49, 50, 51, 52, 53, 54, 55, 56, 57, 58, 59
Child Marriage 3, 11, 174, 177, 178, 179, 180, 181, 182, 183, 184, 185, 200, 219, 220, 225, 234, 238
Clientele 78, 84
Commodification 76, 165
Cosa Nostra 60
Criminal Organizations 69

D

Demographics 135, 137
Denial 77, 81, 109, 110
Deprivations 163, 245, 264, 290, 292
Deviance 15, 16, 17, 18, 20, 21, 22, 24, 25, 26, 27, 28, 47, 49, 159
Deviant Roles 24, 25
Doctrine 5, 86

E

Enforcement 77, 82, 83, 86, 88, 94, 96, 116, 120, 124, 128, 131
Ethnicity 37, 38, 57, 71
Eve Teasing 10, 216, 221, 222, 223
Eviction 89, 90, 92, 120, 124, 125, 211
Evidentiary 106, 112
Expediting 116
Externment 91, 92, 120, 125

F

Family Planning 184
Female Criminality 41, 43, 248, 249, 258, 259, 260, 261, 262, 263, 279, 288
Foeticide 163, 166, 168, 170

H

Historical Practices 3

I

Infanticide 6, 12, 38, 163, 164, 166, 167, 168, 169, 170, 171, 172, 173, 174, 175, 176, 177
Inherent 83, 92
International Crime 59, 67, 69

J

Jauhar 2, 3, 4
Jurisdiction 84, 85, 91, 92, 93, 94, 97, 102, 131, 178, 237, 238

L

Legislation 81, 82, 83, 92, 94, 103
Liability 80, 84, 87, 122
Litigation 94, 96, 97, 268

M

Mafia 60, 62, 160, 248
Medieval Period 2

P

Prison Visitors 231, 232, 234, 235, 237, 238, 242, 243
Prosecutor 90, 117, 119, 121, 123, 124
Psychosocial Care 114
Purdah 2, 3, 4, 5

R

Rational 151, 152, 153, 154, 155, 156, 157, 158, 159
Recruiting 74
Regime 82
Rehabilitation 94, 95, 96, 101, 126
Repatriation 105, 113

S

Salient Features 103
Sati 3, 4
Servitude 76
Sexual Exploitation 4, 74, 76, 80, 83, 85, 87, 90, 93, 124, 195, 198
Sexual Harassment 10, 163, 203, 215, 216, 217, 218, 219, 225
Shoplifting 35, 37, 38, 152, 153, 154, 155, 156, 157, 158, 159
Spectrum 85
Surveillance 91, 120, 125, 127, 128, 229

T

Terrorism 59, 60, 71, 72, 245, 247
Testimony 120, 122
Torture 80
Trafficked Adult 77

V

Victims 78, 80, 94, 98, 99, 101, 102, 103, 104, 106, 109, 110, 111, 112, 113, 118, 120, 124, 125, 126, 127, 131
Violations 38, 74, 77, 79, 80, 81, 84, 102, 118
Vulnerabilities 125, 128

W

Weapon 71, 85, 86, 91, 143, 146
Willful Women 158
Women Criminalities 279
Women Culture 7